Cultural Connector

Riley Dubois's Social Platforms

Nia Hernandez

ISBN: 9783100005550
Imprint: Telephasic Workshop
Copyright © 2024 Nia Hernandez.
All Rights Reserved.

Contents

Introduction	**1**
The Rise of Riley Dubois	1
Cultural Connector's Impact on Education	**27**
Revolutionizing Learning	27
Bibliography	**41**
Integrating Technology in the Classroom	54
Bibliography	**73**
Future Tech in Education	80
Bibliography	**103**
Bibliography	**109**
Cultural Connector's Impact on Social Connection	**111**
Bridging Cultural Divides	111
Revolutionizing Social Media	137
Bibliography	**145**
Bibliography	**157**
The Power of Online Movements	162
Bibliography	**169**
Bibliography	**183**
Cultural Connector's Impact on Arts and Entertainment	**191**

Transforming Creative Industries 191

Bibliography 203
Redefining Entertainment Experiences 217

Bibliography 227

Bibliography 231
The Impact of Cultural Connector on Media 244

Conclusion 269
The Legacy of Riley Dubois 269
Reflections on Cultural Connector's Future 279
Acknowledgments 285

Index 293

Introduction

The Rise of Riley Dubois

Early Life

Riley Dubois was born in a vibrant multicultural neighborhood in San Francisco, California, where the fusion of diverse cultures created a rich tapestry of experiences that would shape her worldview. From an early age, Riley exhibited a natural curiosity and an innate ability to connect with people from various backgrounds. This early exposure to diversity laid the foundation for her future endeavors as a cultural connector.

Riley's parents, both educators, instilled in her a love for learning and a passion for social justice. Her mother, a high school teacher, often brought home stories of her students' struggles and triumphs, while her father, a community college professor, emphasized the importance of education as a tool for empowerment. This nurturing environment fostered Riley's belief that education could bridge cultural divides and create opportunities for all.

As a child, Riley was fascinated by technology and its potential to connect people. At the age of ten, she received her first computer, a hand-me-down from her older brother. It was here that she began exploring the internet, discovering online communities that transcended geographical boundaries. This experience sparked her interest in digital communication and social media, which would later become instrumental in her career.

Throughout her formative years, Riley faced numerous challenges. She struggled with feelings of isolation as a biracial child in a predominantly homogeneous school. This experience of being an outsider fueled her desire to create inclusive spaces where everyone felt valued and heard. She often found solace in literature, devouring books that highlighted the importance of empathy and understanding across cultures.

Riley's high school years were marked by her involvement in various extracurricular activities, including the debate team and the student council. These platforms allowed her to hone her communication skills and advocate for her peers. During her junior year, she organized a multicultural fair that celebrated the diverse backgrounds of her classmates. This event not only showcased different cultures through food, music, and art but also fostered meaningful conversations about identity and belonging.

In her senior year, Riley received the prestigious National Honor Society scholarship, which recognized her academic achievements and commitment to community service. This accolade further motivated her to pursue higher education, where she could continue her mission of connecting cultures and empowering others.

Riley enrolled at the University of California, Berkeley, where she majored in Sociology and minored in Digital Media. Her time at Berkeley was transformative, as she immersed herself in courses that explored the intersections of culture, technology, and social change. One of her professors, Dr. Maria Gonzalez, introduced her to the concept of cultural capital, which refers to the non-financial social assets that promote social mobility. This theory resonated deeply with Riley, as she recognized the potential of digital platforms to democratize access to knowledge and resources.

Riley's academic journey was not without its obstacles. She faced imposter syndrome, questioning her place in a prestigious institution surrounded by peers from affluent backgrounds. However, she channeled these feelings into her activism, becoming a vocal advocate for underrepresented students on campus. She co-founded the Digital Equity Coalition, a student organization dedicated to addressing the digital divide and ensuring that all students had access to technology and internet resources.

Her college experience culminated in a groundbreaking thesis titled "The Role of Social Media in Fostering Cultural Understanding," where she analyzed the impact of online platforms on cross-cultural communication. This research not only solidified her passion for using technology as a means of connection but also provided her with the insights needed to launch her future venture, Cultural Connector.

In summary, Riley Dubois's early life was characterized by a blend of cultural richness, educational influence, and a deep-seated commitment to social justice. Her experiences as a biracial individual, coupled with her academic pursuits and community involvement, laid the groundwork for her future as an innovator in the realm of social connection and education. As she navigated the complexities of her identity and the challenges of her environment, Riley emerged with a clear vision:

to harness the power of technology to create a more inclusive and connected world.

A Natural Born Innovator

Riley Dubois exemplifies the concept of a natural born innovator, a term often associated with individuals who possess an innate ability to create, adapt, and implement new ideas that address societal needs. This section explores the characteristics that define Riley as an innovator, the theoretical frameworks surrounding innovation, and real-world examples that illustrate the impact of such natural talent.

Defining Natural Born Innovators

Natural born innovators are often characterized by several key traits:

- **Creativity:** The ability to think outside the box and generate novel ideas.
- **Resilience:** A willingness to face challenges and learn from failures.
- **Curiosity:** An insatiable desire to explore, learn, and understand the world.
- **Empathy:** The capacity to understand and share the feelings of others, which drives the motivation to solve problems.

Riley Dubois embodies these traits from an early age. As a child, Riley was known for crafting elaborate solutions to everyday problems, whether it was designing a makeshift water filter for a school project or developing a community garden to promote sustainability. This early exposure to problem-solving laid the groundwork for Riley's future endeavors.

Theoretical Frameworks of Innovation

To understand the essence of innovation, several theories provide insight into the processes and environments conducive to creative thinking. One prominent theory is the **Diffusion of Innovations** by Everett Rogers, which outlines how, why, and at what rate new ideas and technology spread. According to Rogers, innovators are crucial in the initial stages of the adoption process, often taking risks to implement new ideas.

The equation representing the rate of adoption can be expressed as:

$$R(t) = \frac{dN(t)}{dt} = p \cdot (N - N(t)) \tag{1}$$

where:

- $R(t)$ is the rate of adoption at time t,
- $N(t)$ is the number of adopters at time t,
- N is the total potential adopters,
- p is the coefficient of innovation.

Riley's ability to identify gaps in the market and respond with innovative solutions reflects the principles outlined in Rogers' theory, showcasing the role of natural innovators in driving societal change.

Real-World Examples of Innovation

Numerous examples illustrate how natural born innovators have transformed industries. One such figure is Steve Jobs, whose vision for user-friendly technology revolutionized the consumer electronics market. Jobs' emphasis on design and functionality led to products like the iPhone, which not only reshaped communication but also created an entirely new ecosystem of applications and services.

Similarly, Riley Dubois's journey can be likened to that of Jobs. After identifying a lack of platforms that effectively connected diverse cultural experiences, Riley launched Cultural Connector. This platform not only serves as a social media space but also as an educational tool that fosters cross-cultural understanding, reflecting the innovative spirit that defines Riley.

Challenges Faced by Innovators

Despite their innate abilities, natural born innovators often encounter significant challenges. The fear of failure can be a substantial barrier, as many innovators grapple with the societal pressures of success. Moreover, securing funding and support for new ideas can be daunting, particularly in traditional industries resistant to change.

Riley faced similar obstacles when launching Cultural Connector. Initial skepticism from potential investors about the viability of a culturally focused platform posed a challenge. However, Riley's resilience and commitment to the vision enabled the team to pivot and adapt their approach, ultimately leading to a successful launch.

Conclusion

In conclusion, Riley Dubois's journey as a natural born innovator is characterized by creativity, resilience, curiosity, and empathy. Through the lens of innovation theory and real-world examples, it is evident that individuals like Riley play a crucial role in shaping the future. Their ability to identify societal needs and craft innovative solutions not only drives progress but also inspires others to embrace their own creative potential. As we explore Riley's contributions further, it becomes clear that the essence of innovation lies in the intersection of passion, perseverance, and the desire to make a meaningful impact on the world.

Identifying a Need in Society

In the fast-paced world of the 21st century, societal needs have evolved, presenting both challenges and opportunities for innovators. Riley Dubois, with her keen insight and innate ability to connect with diverse communities, recognized a significant gap in the way people interacted, learned, and shared cultural experiences. This section delves into the critical process of identifying societal needs, the theoretical frameworks that underpin this endeavor, and the real-world problems that Riley aimed to address through her innovation, Cultural Connector.

Theoretical Frameworks for Identifying Needs

The identification of societal needs can be understood through various theoretical lenses. One prominent framework is the Maslow's Hierarchy of Needs, which posits that human motivations are structured in a hierarchy, ranging from basic physiological needs to self-actualization. As individuals progress through these levels, their needs become more complex and intertwined with social interactions and cultural exchanges.

$$\text{Maslow's Hierarchy:} \quad \begin{array}{c} \text{Self-Actualization} \\ \text{Esteem Needs} \\ \text{Love/Belonging} \\ \text{Safety Needs} \\ \text{Physiological Needs} \end{array} \quad (2)$$

Riley's approach to identifying societal needs aligns with the top tiers of this hierarchy, focusing on the need for belonging, esteem, and self-actualization through cultural connection. By fostering environments where individuals can share their stories and experiences, Riley aimed to address the innate human desire for connection and understanding.

Another relevant theory is the Social Change Theory, which emphasizes the role of social movements in addressing societal needs. This theory suggests that effective change occurs when individuals recognize shared problems and mobilize to create solutions. Riley's Cultural Connector emerged from this understanding, as she sought to create a platform that not only identified cultural divides but also provided a means to bridge them.

Recognizing Real-World Problems

In her quest to innovate, Riley Dubois observed several pressing issues within society that underscored the need for Cultural Connector. One significant problem was the increasing polarization within communities, exacerbated by socio-political divides and cultural misunderstandings. This polarization often led to a lack of empathy and communication between individuals from different backgrounds.

Moreover, the rise of digital communication, while facilitating connections, also gave birth to challenges such as cyberbullying, misinformation, and the erosion of meaningful dialogue. Riley recognized that while technology had the potential to connect people across the globe, it often fell short in fostering genuine understanding and cultural appreciation.

Another critical issue was the accessibility of educational resources. Many individuals, particularly those from marginalized communities, faced barriers to accessing quality education and cultural content. The traditional educational systems often failed to incorporate diverse perspectives, leading to a narrow understanding of global cultures.

Riley's identification of these problems was not merely observational; it was rooted in her own experiences and interactions within various communities. She engaged with individuals from diverse backgrounds, listening to their stories and understanding their struggles. This grassroots approach allowed her to pinpoint the specific needs of these communities, paving the way for her innovative solution.

Examples of Identified Needs

To illustrate the societal needs Riley aimed to address, consider the following examples:

- **Cultural Misunderstandings:** In a world where globalization is increasingly prevalent, misunderstandings between cultures can lead to conflict and division. Riley recognized the need for a platform that encouraged cultural exchange and dialogue, allowing individuals to share their traditions, values, and experiences.

- **Educational Inequities:** Access to quality education remains a significant barrier for many. Riley identified that students in underprivileged areas often lacked the resources and support necessary to thrive academically. Cultural Connector aimed to provide these students with access to diverse educational content and interactive learning experiences.

- **Mental Health Challenges:** The rise of social media has been linked to increased feelings of isolation and anxiety, particularly among young people. Riley understood that fostering genuine connections and providing safe online spaces could mitigate these challenges, promoting mental well-being through community support.

- **Digital Literacy Gaps:** As technology continues to evolve, the digital divide remains a pressing concern. Many individuals, especially older generations or those in low-income areas, struggle to navigate the digital landscape. Riley's vision included empowering these individuals with the skills and knowledge necessary to engage with technology confidently.

Through her comprehensive understanding of these societal needs, Riley Dubois laid the groundwork for Cultural Connector, a platform designed to address these issues head-on. By recognizing the importance of cultural connection, education, and social interaction, she sought to create a more inclusive and empathetic society.

In conclusion, identifying a need in society is a multifaceted process that requires a deep understanding of human motivations and the challenges faced by diverse communities. Riley Dubois's ability to recognize these needs, coupled with her innovative spirit, positioned her as a leader in the movement toward a more connected and culturally aware world. As we explore the subsequent chapters of this biography, we will see how these foundational insights guided the development of Cultural Connector and its profound impact on education, social connection, and the arts.

The Birth of Cultural Connector

The inception of Cultural Connector can be traced back to a pivotal moment in Riley Dubois's life, where the confluence of personal experiences and societal needs ignited a spark of innovation. Riley, a keen observer of the world around them, recognized a profound disconnect among diverse cultural groups, particularly in the digital landscape. This realization was not merely anecdotal; it was supported by emerging theories in social psychology and cultural studies, which emphasized the importance of intercultural communication in fostering understanding and collaboration.

One of the foundational theories that influenced Riley was the *Contact Hypothesis*, proposed by Gordon Allport in the 1950s. The hypothesis posits that under appropriate conditions, interpersonal contact is one of the most effective ways to reduce prejudice between majority and minority group members. Riley envisioned a platform that would facilitate such contact, allowing individuals from various backgrounds to engage in meaningful dialogue and cultural exchange. This was particularly relevant in an era where social media often amplified divisions rather than bridging them.

Riley's journey began with a series of community workshops aimed at exploring the barriers to cultural understanding. During these workshops, participants shared their experiences of isolation and misunderstanding, highlighting a common theme: the lack of accessible platforms for cross-cultural interaction. This feedback was crucial in shaping the vision for Cultural Connector. Riley noted, "If we can create a space where people feel safe to share their stories, we can begin to dismantle the walls that separate us."

The initial concept of Cultural Connector was to develop a digital platform that would serve as a *hub* for cultural exchange. This hub would not only allow users to share their stories but also engage in collaborative projects that celebrate diversity. The platform aimed to address several critical problems:

- **Language Barriers:** Many individuals felt excluded from discussions due to language differences. To combat this, Cultural Connector would incorporate real-time translation features, enabling users to communicate seamlessly across languages.

- **Cultural Misunderstandings:** Misconceptions often arise from a lack of knowledge about other cultures. The platform would feature educational resources, including articles, videos, and interactive content that promote cultural literacy.

- **Isolation in Digital Spaces:** Users frequently reported feelings of loneliness and disconnection online. Cultural Connector sought to create a sense of community through curated groups and events that fostered genuine connections.

To bring this vision to fruition, Riley assembled a diverse team of innovators, each bringing unique perspectives and expertise. This team included software developers, cultural anthropologists, and educators, all united by a shared goal: to create a platform that transcended geographical and cultural boundaries. The collaborative nature of the team was crucial, as it mirrored the very principles that Cultural Connector aimed to promote.

The development phase of Cultural Connector was marked by rigorous testing and feedback loops. Early prototypes were launched in select communities, allowing users to engage with the platform and provide insights into their experiences. This iterative process was guided by the principles of *User-Centered Design*, ensuring that the platform was tailored to the needs and preferences of its users. Feedback highlighted the importance of user experience; as one participant noted, "It's not just about sharing stories; it's about feeling heard and valued."

The birth of Cultural Connector also coincided with a broader societal shift towards digital interaction and globalization. As individuals increasingly turned to online platforms for socialization, the need for a space that prioritized cultural connection became evident. Riley's vision was not merely to create another social media platform, but to redefine how people interacted in the digital age.

By leveraging technology, Cultural Connector aimed to create a virtual environment where users could explore different cultures, participate in discussions, and collaborate on projects that celebrate diversity. The platform's architecture was designed to encourage exploration and interaction, with features such as:

- **Cultural Exchange Programs:** Users could participate in virtual exchanges, allowing them to experience different cultures firsthand through guided activities and interactions with peers from around the world.

- **Interactive Learning Modules:** These modules would educate users about various cultural practices, languages, and histories, promoting a deeper understanding of the world's diversity.

- **Community Events:** Regularly scheduled events, such as cultural festivals and discussion panels, would provide opportunities for users to engage with one another and learn from guest speakers.

The launch of Cultural Connector was met with enthusiasm, as users flocked to the platform, eager to share their stories and connect with others. The early success of the platform validated Riley's vision and underscored the importance of creating spaces that foster intercultural dialogue. As the platform grew, so did its impact, leading to a ripple effect in communities around the globe.

In conclusion, the birth of Cultural Connector was a response to the pressing need for cultural connection in an increasingly fragmented world. By harnessing the power of technology and prioritizing user experience, Riley Dubois and their team laid the groundwork for a platform that not only facilitated cultural exchange but also empowered individuals to share their narratives. This innovative approach would ultimately reshape the landscape of digital interaction, paving the way for a more inclusive and interconnected society.

Setting the Stage for Success

The journey of Riley Dubois towards establishing Cultural Connector was not merely a matter of innovative ideas and technological prowess; it required a carefully orchestrated strategy that involved meticulous planning, stakeholder engagement, and an acute awareness of the socio-cultural landscape. In this section, we will explore the foundational elements that set the stage for Riley's success, including the identification of key challenges, the establishment of strategic partnerships, and the implementation of a robust business model.

Identifying Key Challenges

Before launching Cultural Connector, Riley Dubois recognized that understanding the challenges in both the educational and social sectors was crucial. The landscape was riddled with issues such as unequal access to educational resources, cultural misunderstandings, and the pervasive influence of misinformation on social media. According to [?], these challenges could be quantified and categorized into three primary areas:

$$C = E + S + T \qquad (3)$$

where C represents the collective challenges, E is the educational barriers, S signifies social divides, and T encompasses technological limitations. By dissecting these challenges, Riley was able to tailor Cultural Connector's objectives to address these pressing issues directly.

Establishing Strategic Partnerships

Riley understood that to effectively tackle these challenges, collaboration with various stakeholders was essential. This included educators, technologists, cultural organizations, and community leaders. The importance of partnerships is highlighted in the theory of collaborative innovation, which posits that diverse perspectives can lead to more robust solutions [?].

Riley initiated dialogues with educational institutions, non-profits, and tech companies to create a coalition that would support the Cultural Connector initiative. For instance, a partnership with a leading educational technology firm allowed Cultural Connector to integrate cutting-edge tools into its platform, enhancing its functionality and appeal. The equation below illustrates the synergy created through partnerships:

$$S = P_1 + P_2 + P_3 \qquad (4)$$

where S is the synergy produced, and P_1, P_2, and P_3 represent the contributions of different partners. This collaborative approach not only pooled resources but also fostered a shared vision for a more connected world.

Implementing a Robust Business Model

To ensure sustainability and scalability, Riley devised a business model that would support the long-term vision of Cultural Connector. This model was based on a hybrid approach that combined elements of both for-profit and non-profit structures, allowing for flexibility in funding and operations. The model can be represented as follows:

$$BM = F + R + C \qquad (5)$$

where BM is the business model, F represents funding sources (grants, donations, and revenue), R is revenue generation through premium services, and C signifies community engagement initiatives.

This diverse revenue strategy not only ensured financial viability but also aligned with Riley's mission of accessibility and inclusivity. By offering free basic services while providing premium features for a fee, Cultural Connector could cater to a broad audience, ensuring that those who needed it most could access the platform without financial barriers.

Creating a Visionary Framework

At the heart of Riley's strategy was a visionary framework that encompassed the core values of Cultural Connector: inclusivity, creativity, and empowerment. This framework guided decision-making processes and served as a compass for the organization's growth. Riley articulated a clear vision statement, which resonated with potential users and partners alike:

"To create a world where cultural connections transcend boundaries, fostering understanding and collaboration through innovative technology."

This vision was not just a statement; it was a call to action that inspired stakeholders to rally around the mission of Cultural Connector. It also provided a basis for evaluating the impact of the initiative, as success would be measured not only by growth metrics but by the meaningful connections fostered through the platform.

Navigating the Regulatory Landscape

In addition to the strategic elements outlined above, Riley also had to navigate the complex regulatory landscape surrounding technology and education. This included understanding data privacy laws, intellectual property rights, and the ethical implications of using technology in educational contexts.

The General Data Protection Regulation (GDPR) and the Children's Online Privacy Protection Act (COPPA) were particularly significant, as they set stringent guidelines for how user data could be collected and utilized. Riley ensured that Cultural Connector was compliant with these regulations from the outset, implementing robust data protection measures and transparent user agreements. This proactive approach mitigated potential legal risks and built trust among users.

Conclusion

Setting the stage for success involved a multifaceted approach that combined a deep understanding of challenges, strategic partnerships, a robust business model, a visionary framework, and compliance with regulatory requirements. Riley Dubois's foresight and strategic planning were instrumental in laying the groundwork for Cultural Connector, ultimately positioning it as a leader in the realm of social platforms aimed at fostering cultural connections. This foundation not only facilitated the launch of Cultural Connector but also ensured its sustainability and relevance in an ever-evolving technological landscape.

Riley's Vision for the Future

Riley Dubois envisions a future where technology acts as a bridge to connect diverse cultures, enhance educational opportunities, and foster social cohesion. This vision is grounded in the belief that the digital landscape can be harnessed to create inclusive environments where everyone, regardless of their background, can thrive. By leveraging advancements in technology, Riley aims to address the pressing challenges faced by society today, while simultaneously preparing for the uncertainties of tomorrow.

Theoretical Framework

Riley's vision is informed by several key theories, including **Constructivist Learning Theory**, which posits that learners construct knowledge through experiences and interactions. This theory emphasizes the importance of active engagement and collaboration in the learning process. Additionally, **Social Learning Theory** underlines the significance of observing and modeling behaviors, attitudes, and emotional reactions of others. Together, these theories form the foundation of Riley's approach to revolutionizing education and social connection through the Cultural Connector platform.

Addressing Problems in Education

In the current educational landscape, disparities in access to quality education persist, particularly in underserved communities. Riley identifies the following problems:

- **Digital Divide:** Many students lack access to the internet and technology, hindering their ability to participate in modern learning environments.

- **Engagement Deficit:** Traditional educational methods often fail to engage students, leading to decreased motivation and poor academic outcomes.

- **Cultural Insensitivity:** Educational materials frequently overlook diverse perspectives, resulting in a lack of representation for various cultural backgrounds.

Riley's vision seeks to address these issues by creating an educational ecosystem that is both accessible and engaging. The Cultural Connector platform will utilize adaptive learning technologies to personalize educational experiences, ensuring that each student's unique needs and learning styles are met.

Innovative Solutions

To realize this vision, Riley proposes several innovative solutions:

1. **Adaptive Learning Technologies:** By employing artificial intelligence (AI), Cultural Connector will analyze student performance data to tailor

educational content and delivery methods to individual learning styles. This approach not only enhances engagement but also improves educational outcomes.

2. **Virtual Reality (VR) and Augmented Reality (AR):** Integrating immersive technologies will allow students to experience learning in a way that transcends traditional classroom boundaries. For example, history lessons could involve virtual field trips to ancient civilizations, fostering a deeper understanding of cultural contexts.

3. **Collaborative Learning Environments:** Riley envisions creating online spaces where students from diverse backgrounds can collaborate on projects, share experiences, and learn from one another. This will not only enhance cultural awareness but also promote empathy and understanding.

4. **Global Partnerships:** Cultural Connector will establish partnerships with educational institutions worldwide to facilitate cross-cultural exchanges. This initiative will enable students to engage with peers from different countries, broadening their perspectives and enhancing their global citizenship.

Fostering Social Connection

Riley's vision extends beyond education to encompass the broader social landscape. Recognizing the increasing polarization in society, Riley aims to leverage technology to foster social cohesion. Key components of this vision include:

- **Safe Online Spaces:** Cultural Connector will prioritize creating online environments where individuals can engage in meaningful dialogue without fear of harassment or discrimination. This includes implementing robust moderation tools and promoting positive interactions.

- **Empowering Marginalized Voices:** The platform will amplify the voices of underrepresented communities, providing them with a platform to share their stories and experiences. This initiative aims to challenge stereotypes and foster a culture of understanding.

- **Promoting Digital Literacy:** Recognizing the importance of informed online engagement, Riley's vision includes initiatives to enhance digital literacy skills among users. This will empower individuals to navigate the complexities of the digital landscape responsibly and ethically.

Examples of Implementation

To illustrate the potential of Riley's vision, several pilot programs will be launched:

1. **Cultural Exchange Programs:** Partnering with schools in different countries, students will participate in virtual exchanges, sharing their cultural practices, languages, and traditions. This initiative will be supported by interactive online platforms that facilitate discussions and collaborative projects.

2. **Community Storytelling Initiatives:** Local communities will be encouraged to share their stories through multimedia platforms, allowing individuals to document their experiences and connect with others. This initiative aims to foster empathy and understanding across diverse groups.

3. **Gamified Learning Experiences:** By integrating game-based learning into educational content, students will be motivated to engage with the material in a fun and interactive way. For example, a history lesson could involve a role-playing game where students assume the roles of historical figures and make decisions based on real events.

Conclusion

Riley Dubois's vision for the future is a bold and transformative approach to education and social connection. By harnessing the power of technology, Riley aims to create a world where learning is accessible, engaging, and inclusive. Through the Cultural Connector platform, Riley seeks to empower individuals to connect with one another, embrace diversity, and cultivate a sense of global citizenship. As we move forward, it is essential to embrace the challenges and opportunities that lie ahead, ensuring that technology serves as a force for good in shaping our society.

Overcoming Obstacles

Riley Dubois's journey to establishing Cultural Connector was not without its challenges. As a natural-born innovator, Riley faced numerous obstacles that tested her resilience, creativity, and determination. This section explores the significant hurdles she encountered and the strategies she employed to overcome them, ultimately shaping her vision and the mission of Cultural Connector.

Identifying Resistance to Change

One of the first obstacles Riley encountered was resistance to change from traditional educational institutions. Many educators and administrators were hesitant to embrace innovative technologies and methodologies, fearing they would disrupt the established curriculum. To address this, Riley conducted extensive research to demonstrate the effectiveness of her ideas.

She utilized the **Diffusion of Innovations Theory** proposed by Rogers (1962), which emphasizes the process by which new ideas and technologies spread within a culture. This theory outlines several key factors influencing adoption, including perceived advantages, compatibility with existing values, complexity, trialability, and observability.

Riley organized workshops and seminars where educators could experience Cultural Connector's tools firsthand, showcasing their benefits in real-time. By creating a safe environment for exploration, she gradually transformed skepticism into enthusiasm, enabling educators to see the potential of her innovations.

Navigating Financial Constraints

Another significant challenge was securing funding for her ambitious project. Many investors were reluctant to invest in an unproven concept, particularly one that sought to revolutionize education. To navigate this financial constraint, Riley adopted a multifaceted approach:

- **Crowdfunding:** Riley launched a crowdfunding campaign on platforms like Kickstarter and Indiegogo, effectively communicating her vision and the potential impact of Cultural Connector. By sharing compelling stories and testimonials from early users, she was able to garner support from individuals passionate about educational reform.

- **Partnerships:** She sought partnerships with non-profit organizations and educational institutions that shared her vision. These collaborations not only provided financial support but also added credibility to her initiative. For example, a partnership with a prominent educational foundation allowed her to secure a grant that funded the initial development of the platform.

- **Bootstrapping:** Riley also employed bootstrapping strategies, using her savings and revenue generated from early adopters to reinvest in the business. This approach allowed her to maintain control over her vision while demonstrating to potential investors that there was a market demand for Cultural Connector.

Addressing Technological Challenges

The technological landscape posed its own set of challenges. Developing a robust and user-friendly platform required significant technical expertise, which Riley initially lacked. To overcome this obstacle, she:

- **Assembled a Diverse Team:** Recognizing her limitations, Riley focused on building a diverse team of innovators, each with unique skills and backgrounds. This included software developers, educators, and designers who shared her passion for transforming education. By fostering a collaborative environment, the team was able to leverage their collective expertise to create a platform that was both innovative and accessible.

- **Emphasized User-Centered Design:** The team adopted a user-centered design approach, conducting user testing and gathering feedback from educators and students throughout the development process. This iterative process allowed them to identify and address usability issues early, ensuring the final product met the needs of its users.

- **Invested in Training:** To ensure the team remained at the forefront of technological advancements, Riley prioritized ongoing training and professional development. This investment not only enhanced the team's skills but also fostered a culture of continuous learning and adaptation.

Building a Supportive Community

Finally, building a supportive community around Cultural Connector was essential for its success. Riley recognized that fostering a sense of belonging among users would encourage engagement and collaboration. To achieve this, she implemented several strategies:

- **Online Forums and Workshops:** Riley created online forums where educators could share experiences, resources, and best practices. Additionally, she organized regular workshops that encouraged collaboration and networking among users, fostering a sense of community and shared purpose.

- **Highlighting Success Stories:** By showcasing success stories from users who had benefited from Cultural Connector, Riley inspired others to engage with the platform. These narratives not only validated the platform's effectiveness but also built a sense of pride among users, reinforcing their commitment to the community.
- **Feedback Loops:** Riley established feedback loops where users could contribute suggestions for improvements and new features. This approach empowered users, making them feel valued and invested in the platform's evolution.

In conclusion, Riley Dubois's journey to establish Cultural Connector was fraught with challenges. Through strategic planning, collaboration, and a commitment to community building, she overcame these obstacles, paving the way for a transformative platform that continues to impact education, social connection, and the arts. Her story serves as a testament to the power of resilience and innovation in the face of adversity.

Building a Team of Innovators

In the journey of creating Cultural Connector, Riley Dubois understood that innovation is rarely a solitary endeavor. The complexities of modern societal challenges require diverse perspectives and collaborative problem-solving. Thus, building a team of innovators was not just a strategic choice; it was essential for the success of Cultural Connector. This section delves into the principles, challenges, and strategies involved in assembling a dynamic team capable of driving innovation.

The Importance of Diversity in Innovation

Research has consistently shown that diverse teams outperform homogeneous ones in problem-solving and creativity. According to a study by [?], diverse groups bring a wider range of experiences and viewpoints, leading to more innovative solutions. Riley recognized that to tackle the multifaceted issues of education and social connection, her team needed to reflect the diversity of the communities they aimed to serve.

$$\text{Innovation} = f(Diversity, Collaboration, Resources) \tag{6}$$

Where: - $Diversity$ represents the varied backgrounds and perspectives of team members. - $Collaboration$ denotes the interactions and teamwork dynamics. - $Resources$ includes the tools and support available for innovation.

Riley actively sought individuals from different cultural, educational, and professional backgrounds, ensuring that the team could approach challenges from multiple angles. This diversity not only fostered creativity but also helped in understanding the needs of a global audience.

Identifying Core Values and Vision

To build a cohesive team, Riley emphasized the importance of shared values and a common vision. During the initial stages of team formation, she conducted workshops that focused on defining the mission of Cultural Connector. This process allowed team members to align their personal goals with the overarching objectives of the organization.

Riley articulated a vision that revolved around inclusivity, empowerment, and innovation. The team adopted the following core values:

- **Empathy:** Understanding and valuing the perspectives of others.
- **Collaboration:** Working together to achieve common goals.
- **Innovation:** Encouraging creativity and experimentation.
- **Inclusivity:** Ensuring that all voices are heard and respected.

These values became the foundation for decision-making and team dynamics, fostering an environment where every member felt valued and motivated to contribute.

Recruitment Strategies for Innovators

Riley employed innovative recruitment strategies to attract top talent. Traditional hiring methods often fail to uncover the unique qualities of potential innovators. Instead, she focused on creating an engaging recruitment process that highlighted the mission of Cultural Connector.

1. **Hackathons and Innovation Challenges:** Riley organized events that allowed candidates to showcase their problem-solving skills in real-world scenarios. This approach not only identified skilled individuals but also assessed their ability to work collaboratively under pressure.

2. **Social Media Outreach:** Leveraging social media platforms, Riley promoted the values and mission of Cultural Connector, attracting like-minded individuals who were passionate about making a difference.

3. **Networking and Partnerships:** Collaborating with educational institutions and innovation hubs provided access to a pool of emerging talent. Riley established partnerships with universities to create internship programs that would serve as a talent pipeline.

These strategies ensured that the team was composed of individuals who were not only skilled but also aligned with the mission of Cultural Connector.

Fostering a Culture of Innovation

Once the team was assembled, Riley focused on fostering a culture of innovation. This involved creating an environment where experimentation was encouraged, and failure was viewed as a learning opportunity.

- **Continuous Learning:** The team engaged in regular training sessions and workshops to stay updated on the latest trends in technology and education. This commitment to learning ensured that the team remained adaptable and innovative.

- **Open Communication:** Riley implemented an open-door policy, encouraging team members to share ideas and feedback freely. This transparency fostered trust and collaboration, essential components of an innovative culture.

- **Recognition and Rewards:** Celebrating successes, both big and small, motivated the team to continue pushing boundaries. Riley introduced a recognition program that highlighted innovative contributions, reinforcing the value of creativity within the team.

Navigating Challenges in Team Dynamics

Building a team of innovators is not without challenges. Conflicts may arise due to differing opinions, communication styles, or work ethics. Riley recognized the importance of addressing these challenges proactively.

- **Conflict Resolution Strategies:** Riley implemented conflict resolution training, equipping team members with the skills to address disagreements constructively. This training emphasized the importance of empathy and understanding in resolving conflicts.

- **Team-Building Activities:** Regular team-building exercises helped strengthen relationships among team members. These activities fostered camaraderie and improved collaboration, making it easier to navigate challenges together.

- **Feedback Loops:** Establishing regular feedback sessions allowed team members to express concerns and suggestions. This practice not only improved team dynamics but also contributed to the overall growth of Cultural Connector.

The Role of Leadership in Team Development

Riley's leadership style played a crucial role in the success of Cultural Connector. She adopted a transformational leadership approach, inspiring her team to achieve their full potential.

$$\text{Team Success} = \alpha \cdot (\text{Leadership Style}) + \beta \cdot (\text{Team Dynamics}) \qquad (7)$$

Where: - α represents the impact of leadership style on team success. - β signifies the influence of team dynamics on overall performance.

Riley led by example, demonstrating commitment, resilience, and a passion for innovation. Her ability to inspire and motivate her team was instrumental in overcoming challenges and achieving their goals.

Conclusion

In summary, building a team of innovators was a foundational aspect of Riley Dubois's journey with Cultural Connector. By prioritizing diversity, shared values, innovative recruitment, a culture of innovation, and effective leadership, Riley created a dynamic team capable of addressing the complex challenges of education and social connection. The collaborative spirit fostered within the team not only propelled Cultural Connector forward but also set the stage for continued innovation in the future.

Launching Cultural Connector

The launch of Cultural Connector was not merely a business endeavor; it was a movement aimed at reshaping the landscape of social interaction and education through technology. Riley Dubois, with her innovative spirit and tenacity, orchestrated this launch to address the growing need for a platform that could bridge cultural divides and foster global connections.

The Vision and the Mission

Riley's vision for Cultural Connector was clear: to create a digital space where individuals from diverse backgrounds could come together, share their stories, and learn from one another. This vision was grounded in the belief that technology could be a powerful tool for cultural exchange, fostering empathy and understanding in an increasingly polarized world. The mission was articulated through the following objectives:

- To provide a platform for users to share their cultural experiences and narratives.
- To facilitate educational resources that promote cultural awareness and appreciation.
- To leverage technology to connect individuals across geographical and cultural boundaries.

Identifying the Challenges

However, launching Cultural Connector was not without its challenges. The initial phase was marked by several obstacles that required strategic planning and innovative solutions:

- **Technological Barriers:** Ensuring that the platform was accessible and user-friendly for individuals with varying levels of digital literacy was paramount. Riley and her team conducted extensive user testing to gather feedback and refine the interface.
- **Cultural Sensitivity:** Given the platform's focus on cultural exchange, it was essential to develop guidelines that promoted respectful interactions. The team collaborated with cultural experts to create a framework that acknowledged and celebrated diversity while mitigating the risk of cultural appropriation.
- **Monetization and Sustainability:** Developing a sustainable business model was crucial for the longevity of Cultural Connector. The team explored various revenue streams, including partnerships with educational

institutions, sponsorships, and premium membership options for enhanced features.

- **Security and Privacy:** Protecting user data and ensuring a safe online environment were non-negotiable priorities. The team implemented robust security measures, including encryption protocols and strict privacy policies, to build trust within the user community.

The Launch Strategy

To successfully launch Cultural Connector, Riley devised a multi-faceted strategy that included:

- **Community Engagement:** Prior to the official launch, Riley hosted a series of focus groups and community events to engage potential users and gather insights. This grassroots approach not only built excitement but also created a sense of ownership among early adopters.

- **Partnerships:** Collaborating with schools, cultural organizations, and influencers played a pivotal role in the launch. These partnerships helped amplify the message and reach a broader audience.

- **Social Media Campaigns:** Leveraging social media was essential for generating buzz around the launch. The team created engaging content that highlighted user stories and showcased the platform's unique features, driving traffic to the Cultural Connector website.

- **Pilot Programs:** Before the official launch, Riley initiated pilot programs in select schools and communities to test the platform's functionality and gather feedback. This iterative approach allowed for real-time adjustments and demonstrated the platform's potential impact.

The Launch Day

On launch day, the excitement was palpable. A virtual event was organized, featuring guest speakers from various cultural backgrounds who shared their experiences and the importance of cultural connection. The event was streamed live, attracting thousands of viewers and creating a sense of global community.

The official launch of Cultural Connector was marked by the introduction of key features, including:

- **Story Sharing:** Users could post personal narratives, fostering empathy and understanding among different cultures.

- **Cultural Exchange Programs:** The platform facilitated virtual exchange programs where users could engage in discussions and activities centered around their cultural practices.

- **Educational Resources:** A library of resources was made available, including articles, videos, and interactive content that promoted cultural awareness and education.

Initial Reception and Feedback

The initial reception of Cultural Connector exceeded expectations. Users praised the platform for its intuitive design and meaningful content. Feedback highlighted the following:

- **Empowerment of Voices:** Users appreciated the opportunity to share their stories and connect with others, fostering a sense of belonging and community.

- **Educational Value:** Educators noted the platform's potential as a teaching tool, enhancing students' understanding of global cultures.

- **Safe Environment:** The emphasis on creating a respectful and safe space resonated with users, encouraging them to engage openly.

Measuring Success

To assess the success of the launch, Riley and her team established key performance indicators (KPIs), including user engagement metrics, community growth, and feedback ratings. The early data indicated a positive trajectory, with a steady increase in user registrations and active participation.

$$\text{Engagement Rate} = \frac{\text{Total Interactions}}{\text{Total Users}} \times 100 \qquad (8)$$

This formula allowed the team to quantify user engagement and identify areas for improvement.

Looking Ahead

With the successful launch of Cultural Connector, Riley Dubois and her team turned their attention to future developments. The focus shifted to enhancing the platform's features, expanding partnerships, and continuously fostering a vibrant community. The journey of Cultural Connector was just beginning, and the potential for growth and impact was limitless.

In conclusion, the launch of Cultural Connector exemplified Riley Dubois's innovative spirit and commitment to cultural connection. By addressing societal needs through technology, Cultural Connector set the stage for a new era of global interaction and understanding, paving the way for future innovations in social platforms.

Cultural Connector's Impact on Education

Revolutionizing Learning

Creating Interactive Learning Experiences

The landscape of education is undergoing a profound transformation, with interactive learning experiences emerging as a cornerstone of modern pedagogy. Riley Dubois, through Cultural Connector, has championed the integration of interactivity in educational settings, recognizing its potential to enhance engagement, retention, and comprehension among learners.

Theoretical Foundations

The concept of interactive learning is grounded in several educational theories, notably Constructivism and Experiential Learning. Constructivist theorists, such as Piaget and Vygotsky, argue that learners construct knowledge through experiences and social interactions. Vygotsky's Social Development Theory emphasizes the importance of social interaction in learning, positing that cognitive development is largely driven by collaborative dialogue and shared experiences.

Experiential Learning, as proposed by Kolb, further supports the need for interactive experiences in education. Kolb's Learning Cycle consists of four stages: Concrete Experience, Reflective Observation, Abstract Conceptualization, and Active Experimentation. This cycle illustrates how learners engage with material through direct experience, reflect on their learning, conceptualize the lessons, and apply them in new contexts.

Challenges of Traditional Learning Environments

Traditional educational models often rely on passive learning methods, such as lectures and rote memorization, which can lead to disengagement and a lack of critical thinking skills. According to a study by the National Training Laboratories, retention rates for passive learning methods hover around 5% to 10%, while interactive learning methods can increase retention rates to as high as 75% to 90%. This stark contrast highlights the urgent need for educators to adopt more engaging pedagogical strategies.

Implementing Interactive Learning Experiences

Riley Dubois's Cultural Connector platform exemplifies how technology can facilitate interactive learning experiences. The platform employs various tools and methodologies to create engaging educational environments, including:

- **Gamification:** Incorporating game-like elements in educational content, such as points, badges, and leaderboards, motivates students and fosters a competitive yet collaborative atmosphere. Research indicates that gamification can lead to higher engagement levels and improved academic performance.

- **Virtual Reality (VR):** VR technology immerses students in simulated environments, allowing for experiential learning that is both engaging and impactful. For instance, students can explore historical sites, conduct virtual science experiments, or interact with complex systems in a controlled setting.

- **Collaborative Projects:** By facilitating group projects that require teamwork and communication, Cultural Connector encourages students to engage with peers from diverse backgrounds. These collaborations not only enhance learning but also foster essential social skills.

- **Interactive Multimedia:** Integrating videos, animations, and interactive simulations into lessons caters to various learning styles and keeps students engaged. For example, a biology lesson on cellular processes can be transformed into an interactive simulation where students manipulate variables to see real-time effects on cell behavior.

Case Studies and Examples

Several educational institutions have successfully implemented interactive learning experiences, showcasing the effectiveness of this approach:

1. **Khan Academy:** This online learning platform uses interactive exercises and instructional videos to create a personalized learning environment. Students can progress at their own pace, receiving immediate feedback on their performance, which significantly enhances their understanding of complex subjects.

2. **MIT Media Lab:** The Media Lab has pioneered the use of interactive technologies in education, developing tools such as Scratch, a programming language designed for children. Scratch allows students to create interactive stories, games, and animations, fostering creativity and problem-solving skills.

3. **PBL (Project-Based Learning):** Schools that adopt PBL methodologies encourage students to engage in real-world projects that require critical thinking and collaboration. For instance, students may work together to design a sustainable garden, integrating concepts from biology, environmental science, and mathematics.

Conclusion

Creating interactive learning experiences is not merely a trend; it is an essential evolution in educational practice. As demonstrated by Riley Dubois and the Cultural Connector platform, interactivity fosters deeper engagement, enhances retention, and prepares students for the complexities of the modern world. By embracing interactive methodologies, educators can cultivate a generation of learners who are not only knowledgeable but also equipped with the skills necessary to navigate an increasingly interconnected and dynamic society.

$$\text{Retention Rate} = \frac{\text{Active Engagement}}{\text{Passive Learning}} \times 100\% \qquad (9)$$

Engaging Students Across the Globe

In today's interconnected world, the ability to engage students across geographical boundaries has become a necessity for educational innovation. Riley Dubois's Cultural Connector platform exemplifies this by leveraging technology to create global classrooms that transcend traditional barriers. This subsection explores the importance of engaging students worldwide, the challenges faced, and the innovative solutions implemented through Cultural Connector.

The Importance of Global Engagement

Engaging students from diverse backgrounds enriches the learning experience, fostering a sense of global citizenship and cultural appreciation. Theoretical frameworks such as Vygotsky's Social Development Theory emphasize the role of social interaction in learning. Vygotsky posited that cognitive development is largely driven by social interactions, particularly in a cultural context. This theory supports the notion that when students engage with peers from different cultures, they not only enhance their understanding of the subject matter but also develop critical thinking skills and empathy.

Furthermore, the Global Competence Framework developed by the Organisation for Economic Co-operation and Development (OECD) highlights the need for students to acquire skills that prepare them for a globalized world. Engaging students globally enables them to:

- Develop cross-cultural communication skills
- Appreciate diverse perspectives
- Collaborate on international projects
- Address global issues collectively

Challenges in Global Engagement

Despite the benefits, there are significant challenges in engaging students across the globe:

- **Time Zone Differences:** Coordinating schedules for live interactions can be problematic due to varying time zones, often leading to disengagement.
- **Language Barriers:** Differences in language can hinder communication and understanding among students, creating a divide that may discourage participation.
- **Access to Technology:** Not all students have equal access to the necessary technology, such as high-speed internet and devices, which can create inequities in participation.

- **Cultural Sensitivity:** Navigating cultural differences requires careful consideration to avoid misunderstandings and ensure respectful interactions.

Innovative Solutions through Cultural Connector

To address these challenges, Cultural Connector employs several innovative strategies:

Time Zone Management The platform uses asynchronous learning methods, allowing students to engage with content and peers at their convenience. This flexibility accommodates different time zones, enabling students to participate without the pressure of real-time interactions.

Language Support Cultural Connector incorporates translation tools and multilingual resources that facilitate communication among students. By providing content in multiple languages and offering real-time translation during discussions, the platform helps bridge language gaps.

Technology Accessibility Cultural Connector partners with educational institutions and non-profits to provide devices and internet access to underserved communities. This initiative ensures that all students, regardless of their socio-economic background, can participate fully in global learning experiences.

Cultural Training The platform offers training modules for students and educators that focus on cultural sensitivity and awareness. By educating users about different cultural norms and practices, Cultural Connector fosters an environment of respect and understanding.

Examples of Global Engagement Initiatives

Cultural Connector has successfully implemented various initiatives that exemplify its commitment to global engagement:

Global Classroom Projects One notable project involved students from five different countries collaborating on a climate change initiative. Using Cultural Connector, students shared their local environmental challenges and proposed solutions, fostering a sense of shared responsibility and teamwork. The project culminated in a virtual summit where students presented their findings to a global audience, demonstrating the power of collaborative learning.

Cultural Exchange Programs Cultural Connector also facilitates virtual exchange programs where students can engage in discussions about their cultures, traditions, and values. For instance, a recent exchange between students in Japan and Brazil focused on traditional festivals, allowing participants to share videos and presentations about their respective celebrations, thus enriching their cultural understanding.

Global Competitions The platform hosts international competitions that encourage students to work together on creative projects, such as digital storytelling and art. These competitions not only promote engagement but also celebrate diversity, as students showcase their unique perspectives and talents.

Conclusion

Engaging students across the globe is crucial for fostering a rich, inclusive educational environment. Through innovative solutions and strategic initiatives, Cultural Connector addresses the challenges of global engagement, ensuring that all students can benefit from a diverse learning experience. By harnessing the power of technology and collaboration, Riley Dubois's vision for a connected world becomes a reality, paving the way for future generations to thrive in an increasingly interconnected society.

$$\text{Global Engagement} = \text{Cultural Awareness} + \text{Collaborative Learning} + \text{Technology Acces} \tag{10}$$

Breaking Down Barriers to Education Access

Access to education remains a significant challenge across the globe, with barriers that are often systemic, economic, and cultural. Riley Dubois's Cultural Connector aims to dismantle these barriers through innovative approaches that leverage technology and community engagement. This section explores the theoretical foundations, existing problems, and practical examples of how Cultural Connector addresses these challenges.

Theoretical Framework

The theoretical framework for breaking down barriers to education access can be informed by several educational theories, including:

- **Social Constructivism:** This theory posits that knowledge is constructed through social interactions and cultural contexts. By fostering collaborative learning environments, Cultural Connector enhances educational access for diverse populations.

- **Universal Design for Learning (UDL):** UDL emphasizes the importance of creating flexible learning environments that accommodate individual learning differences. This approach is integral to Cultural Connector's mission, as it seeks to tailor educational experiences to meet the needs of all learners.

- **Critical Pedagogy:** This approach focuses on empowering marginalized voices and challenging traditional power dynamics in education. Cultural Connector embodies this philosophy by promoting inclusivity and representation in educational content.

Identifying Barriers to Access

The barriers to education access can be categorized into several key areas:

- **Economic Barriers:** Many students face financial constraints that limit their ability to pursue education. This includes tuition fees, cost of materials, and transportation expenses.

- **Geographical Barriers:** Students in remote or rural areas often lack access to quality educational institutions and resources. This geographical isolation can hinder their educational opportunities.

- **Technological Barriers:** The digital divide remains a significant issue, with many students lacking access to the necessary technology and internet connectivity to engage in online learning.

- **Cultural and Linguistic Barriers:** Language differences and cultural misunderstandings can impede effective communication in educational settings, making it difficult for some students to thrive.

- **Policy Barriers:** Inequitable education policies can create systemic obstacles that disproportionately affect marginalized groups, including racial minorities and low-income families.

Innovative Solutions by Cultural Connector

Cultural Connector employs a multifaceted approach to break down these barriers:

- **Affordable Learning Platforms:** By offering low-cost or free educational resources and courses, Cultural Connector addresses economic barriers. For example, the platform provides a range of open educational resources (OER) that allow learners to access high-quality materials without financial strain.

- **Mobile Learning Initiatives:** Recognizing the geographical barriers faced by students in remote areas, Cultural Connector has developed mobile learning applications that enable users to access educational content from their smartphones. This approach not only increases accessibility but also empowers learners to engage with materials on their own terms.

- **Community Partnerships:** Cultural Connector collaborates with local organizations to create community learning hubs. These hubs provide resources, mentorship, and support for students, particularly in underserved areas. By fostering a sense of community, these initiatives help to bridge the gap between formal education and local knowledge.

- **Language and Cultural Support:** To address linguistic barriers, Cultural Connector offers multilingual resources and translation services. This ensures that non-native speakers can access educational materials in their preferred language, promoting inclusivity and understanding.

- **Advocacy for Policy Change:** Cultural Connector actively engages in advocacy efforts aimed at reforming education policies that perpetuate inequity. By collaborating with policymakers and stakeholders, the organization seeks to create a more equitable educational landscape for all learners.

Case Studies and Examples

Several case studies illustrate the impact of Cultural Connector's initiatives in breaking down barriers to education access:

- **The Remote Learning Project:** In partnership with local governments, Cultural Connector launched a project in rural areas of a developing country, providing tablets loaded with educational content to students. This initiative not only improved access to learning materials but also enhanced digital literacy among students and teachers alike.

- **The Language Exchange Program:** Cultural Connector implemented a language exchange program that pairs native speakers with learners seeking to improve their language skills. This initiative not only facilitates language acquisition but also fosters cultural exchange and understanding among participants.

- **Community Learning Hubs in Urban Areas:** In urban settings, Cultural Connector established learning hubs that offer after-school programs for students from low-income families. These hubs provide tutoring, access to technology, and a safe space for students to collaborate and learn together.

Conclusion

Breaking down barriers to education access is a complex but essential endeavor. Through innovative solutions, Cultural Connector is making strides towards creating an inclusive educational environment where all learners can thrive. By addressing economic, geographical, technological, cultural, and policy barriers, Riley Dubois's vision for education is not just a dream; it is becoming a reality for countless individuals around the world. As we look to the future, the continued efforts of Cultural Connector will be crucial in ensuring that education is a right, not a privilege.

Bridging the Gap Between Traditional and Digital Education

The educational landscape is undergoing a seismic shift, driven by the rapid integration of digital technologies into traditional educational frameworks. This transition is not merely a technological upgrade; it represents a fundamental change in how knowledge is disseminated, acquired, and understood. The challenge lies in effectively bridging the gap between traditional education, characterized by face-to-face interactions and standardized curricula, and digital education, which offers personalized learning experiences and global connectivity.

Theoretical Framework

To understand this transition, we can draw on the *Community of Inquiry* framework proposed by Garrison, Anderson, and Archer (2000), which emphasizes three essential elements of a meaningful educational experience: cognitive presence, social presence, and teaching presence. This framework can be applied to both traditional and digital learning environments, revealing the need for a balanced integration of these elements to foster deep learning.

$$\text{Cognitive Presence} = \text{Critical Thinking} + \text{Knowledge Construction} \quad (11)$$

In traditional settings, cognitive presence is often facilitated through direct instructor engagement and structured discussions. In contrast, digital education relies on asynchronous communication tools and collaborative platforms, which can enhance cognitive presence through peer interaction and self-directed learning.

Identifying the Problems

Despite the potential benefits of digital education, significant barriers hinder the successful integration of these two paradigms. Key issues include:

- **Resistance to Change:** Educators and institutions often exhibit reluctance to adopt new technologies, rooted in a fear of the unknown and a desire to maintain established pedagogical practices.

- **Digital Divide:** Disparities in access to technology and the internet create inequities in educational opportunities, particularly for marginalized communities.

- **Quality of Content:** The vast amount of digital resources can lead to confusion regarding the quality and reliability of educational materials, making it difficult for educators to curate effective learning experiences.

- **Training and Support:** Many educators lack the necessary training to effectively integrate technology into their teaching practices, resulting in underutilization of digital tools.

Bridging Strategies

To effectively bridge the gap between traditional and digital education, several strategies can be implemented:

1. **Hybrid Learning Models:** Institutions can adopt blended learning approaches that combine face-to-face instruction with online resources. This model allows for flexibility and caters to diverse learning styles. For example, a flipped classroom model encourages students to engage with content online before participating in interactive, in-person discussions.

2. **Professional Development:** Ongoing training programs for educators are essential to equip them with the skills needed to navigate digital tools effectively. Workshops, webinars, and peer mentoring can foster a culture of continuous learning and adaptation.
3. **Collaborative Platforms:** Utilizing platforms like Google Classroom or Microsoft Teams can facilitate communication and collaboration between students and teachers, regardless of location. These tools promote engagement and provide a space for sharing resources and feedback.
4. **Inclusive Content Creation:** Encouraging students and educators to contribute to digital content creation can enhance the relevance and diversity of educational materials. Projects that involve students in the development of digital resources can also foster a sense of ownership and agency in their learning.
5. **Data-Driven Decision Making:** Leveraging data analytics can help educators assess student performance and engagement levels, allowing for tailored interventions and support. By analyzing patterns in learning behaviors, educators can adapt their teaching strategies to meet the needs of individual students.

Examples of Successful Integration

Several institutions have successfully bridged the gap between traditional and digital education, serving as models for others to follow:

- **The University of Southern California (USC):** USC has implemented a hybrid model that combines traditional lectures with online discussions and assignments. This approach has increased student engagement and improved learning outcomes.
- **Khan Academy:** This online platform provides free educational resources that complement traditional curricula. By offering video lessons and practice exercises, Khan Academy enables students to learn at their own pace, reinforcing concepts taught in the classroom.
- **EdX and Coursera:** These platforms offer massive open online courses (MOOCs) that allow learners from around the world to access high-quality education. By partnering with universities, they provide opportunities for students to engage with content that may not be available in their local institutions.

Conclusion

Bridging the gap between traditional and digital education is not merely an option; it is a necessity in the modern educational landscape. By embracing hybrid learning models, providing professional development, and fostering collaboration, educators can create inclusive environments that cater to the needs of all learners. As we move forward, the integration of technology in education must be guided by a commitment to equity, quality, and innovation. Only then can we ensure that all students are equipped with the skills and knowledge necessary to thrive in an increasingly digital world.

Empowering Educators with New Tools

The advent of digital technology has fundamentally transformed the educational landscape, providing educators with innovative tools that enhance teaching effectiveness and student engagement. In this section, we explore how Cultural Connector empowers educators by equipping them with various resources, methodologies, and technologies designed to facilitate a more dynamic and inclusive learning environment.

The Importance of Empowerment

Empowering educators is crucial for several reasons. First, teachers are the frontline agents of change in education. According to the *National Education Association*, effective teaching is one of the most significant factors influencing student achievement. Thus, when educators are provided with the right tools, they can positively impact student outcomes. Furthermore, empowered educators are more likely to embrace innovation, adapt to changing educational demands, and foster a culture of continuous improvement within their institutions.

Innovative Tools for Educators

Cultural Connector offers a suite of innovative tools designed to meet the diverse needs of educators. These tools include:

- **Interactive Lesson Planning Software:** This tool allows educators to create engaging, interactive lesson plans that incorporate multimedia resources, collaborative activities, and real-time feedback mechanisms. Research indicates that interactive learning experiences can improve retention rates by up to 30% [1].

- **Professional Development Platforms:** Cultural Connector provides access to online professional development courses, webinars, and peer-to-peer learning communities. These resources enable educators to stay updated on the latest pedagogical trends and instructional strategies. A study by the *American Educational Research Association* found that ongoing professional development can lead to a 21% increase in teacher effectiveness [2].

- **Data Analytics Tools:** Educators can utilize data analytics tools to track student progress and identify learning gaps. By analyzing data, teachers can tailor their instruction to meet the specific needs of each student. For instance, the implementation of data-driven decision-making has been shown to improve student performance by 15% [3].

- **Collaborative Platforms:** Cultural Connector fosters collaboration among educators through platforms that facilitate resource sharing, lesson co-creation, and peer feedback. Collaborative teaching strategies have been linked to increased student engagement and motivation [4].

- **Gamification Tools:** By integrating gamification into the classroom, Cultural Connector enables educators to create motivating learning environments. Gamification has been shown to enhance student engagement and retention rates, with studies indicating a 34% increase in student participation [5].

Addressing Challenges in Education

Despite the availability of innovative tools, educators face several challenges in integrating these resources into their teaching practices. Common obstacles include:

- **Resistance to Change:** Many educators may be hesitant to adopt new technologies due to a lack of familiarity or fear of the unknown. To mitigate this, Cultural Connector emphasizes the importance of providing comprehensive training and support to help educators feel confident in using new tools.

- **Time Constraints:** Educators often face demanding schedules, leaving little time for professional development or technology integration. Cultural Connector addresses this issue by offering flexible, on-demand training resources that educators can access at their convenience.

- **Equity in Access:** Not all educators have equal access to technology and resources, which can create disparities in the classroom. Cultural Connector prioritizes equitable access by partnering with schools in underserved communities to provide necessary tools and training.

Case Studies and Examples

Several case studies illustrate the positive impact of Cultural Connector's tools on educators and their students:

- **Case Study 1: Interactive Lesson Planning** - A middle school in Chicago implemented Cultural Connector's interactive lesson planning software. Teachers reported a 40% increase in student engagement and a significant improvement in test scores over the semester.

- **Case Study 2: Professional Development** - A district in California integrated Cultural Connector's professional development platform into their teacher training program. As a result, teachers felt more prepared and confident in their instructional practices, leading to a 25% increase in student achievement.

- **Case Study 3: Data Analytics** - An elementary school in New York utilized data analytics tools to identify struggling students. Targeted interventions resulted in a 30% improvement in reading proficiency among at-risk students within one academic year.

Conclusion

Empowering educators with new tools through Cultural Connector not only enhances teaching practices but also leads to improved student outcomes. By addressing the challenges educators face and providing innovative resources, Cultural Connector is paving the way for a more effective and inclusive educational landscape. As we continue to embrace the potential of technology in education, it is essential to ensure that educators are equipped with the tools they need to thrive in this ever-evolving environment.

Bibliography

[1] Smith, J. (2022). *The Impact of Interactive Learning on Student Retention*. Journal of Educational Research.

[2] Jones, A. (2021). *Professional Development and Teacher Effectiveness*. American Educational Research Journal.

[3] Brown, L. (2023). *Data-Driven Decision Making in Education*. Educational Leadership.

[4] Davis, K. (2020). *The Benefits of Collaborative Teaching Strategies*. Teaching and Teacher Education.

[5] Taylor, R. (2022). *Gamification in the Classroom: Enhancing Student Engagement*. Journal of Educational Psychology.

Improving Educational Outcomes for All

In the quest to enhance educational outcomes universally, the Cultural Connector platform embodies a transformative approach that integrates technology, pedagogy, and inclusivity. This section delves into the multifaceted strategies employed by Riley Dubois and her team to ensure that educational improvements are not just a privilege for a select few but a right accessible to all learners, regardless of their background or circumstances.

Theoretical Framework

The foundation of improving educational outcomes for all lies in the principles of Universal Design for Learning (UDL). UDL emphasizes the need for flexible learning environments that accommodate individual learning differences. According to CAST (Center for Applied Special Technology), UDL is built on three primary principles:

1. **Multiple Means of Engagement:** Providing learners with various ways to engage with content, fostering motivation and interest.

2. **Multiple Means of Representation:** Presenting information in multiple formats to cater to diverse learning styles and preferences.

3. **Multiple Means of Action and Expression:** Allowing students to demonstrate their knowledge in various ways, accommodating different strengths and capabilities.

By applying these principles, Cultural Connector aims to create an educational ecosystem that supports all learners effectively.

Identifying Barriers to Learning

To improve educational outcomes, it is crucial to identify the barriers that inhibit learning. These barriers can be categorized into several domains:

- **Socioeconomic Factors:** Students from low-income families often lack access to resources, technology, and support systems that facilitate learning.

- **Cultural and Linguistic Diversity:** Students from diverse backgrounds may struggle with language barriers and cultural differences that affect their learning experience.

- **Learning Disabilities:** Students with learning disabilities require tailored approaches to overcome challenges in traditional educational settings.

- **Geographic Disparities:** Rural or underserved urban areas may have limited access to quality educational resources and trained educators.

Recognizing these barriers allows Cultural Connector to tailor its strategies effectively, ensuring that no learner is left behind.

Innovative Solutions and Examples

Cultural Connector employs a range of innovative solutions designed to address the identified barriers and improve educational outcomes:

1. **Personalized Learning Paths** By leveraging data analytics and artificial intelligence, Cultural Connector creates personalized learning experiences that adapt to each student's unique needs. For instance, the platform analyzes student performance data to recommend customized learning materials, ensuring that students progress at their own pace. This approach has shown promise in improving engagement and retention rates among students.

2. **Language Support Tools** To bridge language barriers, Cultural Connector incorporates real-time translation tools and multilingual resources. For example, a student learning English as a second language can access content in their native language alongside English, facilitating comprehension and encouraging participation. This dual-language approach has been particularly effective in classrooms with diverse linguistic backgrounds.

3. **Accessibility Features** Cultural Connector prioritizes accessibility by integrating features such as text-to-speech, speech-to-text, and customizable font sizes. These tools cater to students with visual impairments or learning disabilities, ensuring that all learners can access and engage with content effectively. A case study involving a visually impaired student demonstrated significant improvements in reading comprehension and engagement after utilizing these features.

4. **Community and Parental Engagement** Recognizing the role of community and family in education, Cultural Connector fosters partnerships with local organizations and encourages parental involvement through workshops and resources. For instance, a pilot program in a low-income neighborhood provided parents with training on how to support their children's learning at home, resulting in improved student performance and family engagement.

Measuring Success

To assess the effectiveness of these initiatives, Cultural Connector employs a robust evaluation framework that includes both qualitative and quantitative metrics. Key performance indicators (KPIs) such as student engagement rates, academic achievement, and feedback from educators and families are analyzed to gauge success. For example, a longitudinal study conducted over three years revealed a 25% increase in overall student achievement scores in schools that implemented Cultural Connector's strategies.

Conclusion

Improving educational outcomes for all is a complex yet achievable goal. Through the application of UDL principles, the identification of barriers, and the implementation of innovative solutions, Cultural Connector exemplifies how technology can be harnessed to create equitable educational opportunities. As Riley Dubois continues to refine and expand her vision, the impact of Cultural Connector on education will resonate across generations, paving the way for a more inclusive and effective learning landscape.

Making Learning Fun and Interactive

In the rapidly evolving landscape of education, making learning fun and interactive has become a crucial objective for educators and innovators alike. The integration of engaging methodologies not only enhances student motivation but also fosters a deeper understanding of the material. This section explores various strategies and theories that support the notion of interactive and enjoyable learning experiences.

Theoretical Foundations

One of the foundational theories supporting interactive learning is **Constructivism**, which posits that learners construct knowledge through experiences and reflections. According to Piaget (1952), learning is an active process where students build new ideas based on their current and past knowledge. This theory encourages educators to create environments where students can explore, ask questions, and share ideas, thereby making the learning process more engaging.

Another relevant theory is **Experiential Learning**, proposed by Kolb (1984). This model emphasizes the role of experience in the learning process and consists of four stages: concrete experience, reflective observation, abstract conceptualization, and active experimentation. By incorporating these stages into educational practices, educators can create interactive learning environments that resonate with students' personal experiences.

Challenges in Traditional Learning Environments

Traditional education often relies on passive learning methods, where students are expected to absorb information through lectures and rote memorization. This approach can lead to disengagement and a lack of enthusiasm for learning. Research indicates that passive learning environments can diminish student retention rates, with studies showing that students retain only about 10% of what they hear in lectures (Fletcher, 2019).

Moreover, the one-size-fits-all approach in traditional classrooms fails to address the diverse learning styles present among students. According to Gardner's Theory of Multiple Intelligences (1983), students possess different types of intelligences, such as linguistic, logical-mathematical, spatial, and interpersonal. Recognizing these differences is essential for creating inclusive and engaging learning experiences.

Strategies for Making Learning Fun and Interactive

To combat the challenges of traditional learning, educators can implement various strategies that promote interactivity and enjoyment. Some effective methods include:

- **Gamification:** Incorporating game elements into the learning process can significantly enhance engagement. For example, platforms like Kahoot! allow educators to create quizzes that students can participate in using their devices, turning assessments into competitive and enjoyable activities.

- **Project-Based Learning (PBL):** PBL encourages students to work on real-world projects that require critical thinking, collaboration, and creativity. For instance, students might design a sustainable garden for their school, integrating science, math, and environmental studies into a single project.

- **Interactive Technology:** Utilizing tools such as virtual reality (VR) and augmented reality (AR) can transform the learning experience. For example, using VR to explore historical sites can immerse students in the subject matter, making learning both fun and memorable.

- **Collaborative Learning:** Group work and peer-to-peer learning foster social interaction and allow students to learn from one another. This method encourages dialogue, teamwork, and the sharing of diverse perspectives, making the learning process more dynamic.

Examples of Successful Implementation

Several educational institutions have successfully implemented interactive learning strategies. For instance, *High Tech High* in San Diego utilizes project-based learning to engage students in interdisciplinary projects. Students work collaboratively on projects that address real-world problems, allowing them to apply their knowledge in meaningful ways.

Additionally, *The Khan Academy* has revolutionized learning by offering interactive video lessons and practice exercises. Students can learn at their own pace, receive instant feedback, and engage with the material in a way that suits their learning style.

Conclusion

Making learning fun and interactive is not just a trend; it is a necessity in modern education. By leveraging theories such as Constructivism and Experiential Learning, educators can create environments that foster engagement, motivation, and deeper understanding. The challenges of traditional learning methods can be overcome through innovative strategies such as gamification, project-based learning, and collaborative approaches. As we continue to explore the potential of interactive learning, the future of education looks promising, with students at the center of the learning experience.

References

1. Fletcher, J. (2019). *The Impact of Passive Learning on Student Retention*. Educational Research Journal.

2. Gardner, H. (1983). *Frames of Mind: The Theory of Multiple Intelligences*. Basic Books.

3. Kolb, D. A. (1984). *Experiential Learning: Experience as the Source of Learning and Development*. Prentice Hall.

4. Piaget, J. (1952). *The Origins of Intelligence in Children*. International Universities Press.

Fostering Collaboration and Critical Thinking

In the rapidly evolving landscape of education, fostering collaboration and critical thinking has become paramount. Riley Dubois's Cultural Connector platform exemplifies how technology can be harnessed to create environments conducive to these essential skills. This subsection explores the theoretical foundations, challenges, and practical examples associated with promoting collaboration and critical thinking in educational contexts.

Theoretical Foundations

Collaboration and critical thinking are deeply intertwined skills that are essential for success in the 21st century. Theories such as Vygotsky's Social Development Theory highlight the importance of social interaction in cognitive development. Vygotsky posits that learning is inherently a social process, where knowledge is constructed through collaboration with others. This theory underlines the necessity of collaborative learning environments where students can engage in dialogue, share perspectives, and co-construct knowledge.

Critical thinking, defined by Facione (2011) as "the intellectually disciplined process of actively and skillfully conceptualizing, applying, analyzing, synthesizing, and evaluating information," is crucial for students to navigate the complexities of modern life. The integration of collaborative learning strategies not only promotes critical thinking but also enhances students' abilities to work effectively in teams, a skill increasingly sought after by employers.

Challenges to Collaboration and Critical Thinking

Despite the evident benefits, several challenges hinder the effective fostering of collaboration and critical thinking in educational settings. One significant challenge is the traditional education model, which often emphasizes rote memorization over inquiry-based learning. This model can stifle creativity and discourage students from engaging in collaborative problem-solving.

Moreover, varying levels of digital literacy among students can impede collaborative efforts. As students engage with technology, disparities in their ability to navigate digital tools can lead to unequal participation, undermining the collaborative process. Additionally, the fear of failure or judgment can inhibit students from expressing their ideas, further stifling critical thinking.

Practical Examples

Cultural Connector addresses these challenges through innovative features designed to foster collaboration and critical thinking. For instance, the platform incorporates project-based learning modules that require students to work in teams to solve real-world problems. In these modules, students are encouraged to engage in discussions, brainstorm solutions, and critically evaluate their approaches.

An example of this in action is the "Global Solutions Challenge," where students from diverse backgrounds collaborate on issues such as climate change or social justice. By working together, they not only develop critical thinking skills but also gain insights into different cultural perspectives, enhancing their understanding and empathy.

Furthermore, the platform employs tools like discussion forums and collaborative document editing, allowing students to engage in asynchronous discussions. This flexibility enables students to reflect on their ideas and contribute thoughtfully, fostering a culture of critical inquiry.

The use of digital storytelling tools also exemplifies how Cultural Connector promotes collaboration. Students can create multimedia presentations that require them to synthesize information, evaluate sources, and present their findings creatively. This process encourages critical thinking as students must assess the credibility of their sources and articulate their viewpoints effectively.

Assessment of Collaborative and Critical Thinking Skills

To measure the effectiveness of fostering collaboration and critical thinking, Cultural Connector employs a variety of assessment strategies. One approach is the use of peer evaluations, where students assess each other's contributions to group projects. This not only holds students accountable but also encourages them to reflect on their own collaborative skills.

Rubrics that emphasize critical thinking skills, such as analysis, synthesis, and evaluation, are integrated into project assessments. For instance, a rubric may include criteria such as:

$$\text{Critical Thinking Score} = \frac{\text{Analysis} + \text{Synthesis} + \text{Evaluation}}{3} \qquad (12)$$

This formula allows educators to quantify students' critical thinking abilities based on their performance in collaborative projects.

Conclusion

In conclusion, fostering collaboration and critical thinking through the Cultural Connector platform represents a significant advancement in educational practices. By leveraging technology to create interactive and engaging learning experiences, Riley Dubois's initiative empowers students to develop essential skills that are vital for their future success. As educators embrace these innovative approaches, they can cultivate a new generation of learners who are not only knowledgeable but also capable of critical thought and collaborative problem-solving in an increasingly complex world.

BIBLIOGRAPHY 49

Adapting to Different Learning Styles

In the realm of education, recognizing and adapting to different learning styles is crucial for fostering an inclusive environment that promotes effective learning. The concept of learning styles, which posits that individuals have preferred ways of absorbing, processing, and retaining information, has gained significant traction in educational theory. Prominent models, such as Howard Gardner's Theory of Multiple Intelligences and Neil Fleming's VARK model, provide frameworks for understanding the diversity of learning preferences.

Theoretical Frameworks

Gardner's Theory of Multiple Intelligences suggests that intelligence is not a single entity but a combination of various types of intelligences. Gardner identifies at least eight distinct intelligences, including:

- **Linguistic** (word smart)
- **Logical-Mathematical** (number smart)
- **Spatial** (picture smart)
- **Musical** (music smart)
- **Bodily-Kinesthetic** (body smart)
- **Interpersonal** (people smart)
- **Intrapersonal** (self smart)
- **Naturalistic** (nature smart)

This theory underscores the importance of tailoring educational experiences to cater to the varied strengths of learners. For example, a student with strong spatial intelligence may benefit from visual aids and hands-on activities, while a student with interpersonal intelligence may thrive in collaborative group settings.

Fleming's VARK model categorizes learners into four primary styles:

- **Visual** (prefer diagrams, charts, and graphs)
- **Aural** (prefer listening and discussion)
- **Read/Write** (prefer text-based input)

- **Kinesthetic** (prefer hands-on experiences)

Understanding these styles allows educators to create differentiated instruction that meets the needs of all students.

Challenges in Adapting to Learning Styles

Despite the theoretical support for learning styles, several challenges arise in their practical application. One significant issue is the lack of empirical evidence validating the effectiveness of tailoring instruction to learning styles. Studies, such as those conducted by Pashler et al. (2008), suggest that there is insufficient scientific support for the idea that matching instruction to learning styles significantly enhances learning outcomes.

Furthermore, educators may face logistical challenges when attempting to accommodate various learning preferences within a single classroom. Limited resources, time constraints, and standardized curricula can hinder the implementation of differentiated instructional strategies. Teachers may also struggle with their biases, inadvertently favoring certain styles over others based on their own preferences.

Practical Strategies for Adaptation

To effectively adapt to different learning styles, educators can employ a variety of strategies that promote inclusivity and engagement:

1. **Varied Instructional Methods:** Incorporate a mix of teaching methods, such as lectures, discussions, hands-on activities, and multimedia presentations. This approach caters to diverse learning preferences and keeps students engaged.

2. **Flexible Grouping:** Utilize heterogeneous grouping strategies that allow students to collaborate with peers who have different strengths. This fosters a richer learning environment and encourages peer-to-peer learning.

3. **Choice in Assignments:** Provide students with options for how they demonstrate their understanding of a topic. For instance, they might choose to create a visual presentation, write a report, or perform a skit. This empowers students to leverage their strengths.

4. **Assessment Variety:** Use diverse assessment methods, such as quizzes, projects, presentations, and portfolios, to gauge student learning. This not

only accommodates different learning styles but also provides a more comprehensive view of student progress.

5. **Technology Integration:** Leverage educational technology tools that allow for personalized learning experiences. For example, platforms like Google Classroom and Kahoot! enable students to engage with content in ways that align with their preferences.

Examples in Practice

One notable example of adapting to different learning styles is the implementation of **flipped classrooms**. In this model, students engage with instructional content at home (often through video lectures) and use classroom time for interactive activities that reinforce learning. This approach caters to a range of learning styles, allowing visual learners to benefit from video content while kinesthetic learners engage in hands-on activities during class.

Another example is the use of **project-based learning** (PBL). In PBL, students work on real-world projects that require collaboration, critical thinking, and creativity. This method allows for the integration of various learning styles, as students can approach projects in ways that align with their strengths, whether through research, artistic expression, or technical skills.

Conclusion

Adapting to different learning styles is essential for creating an inclusive educational environment that supports the diverse needs of students. While challenges exist in implementing these adaptations, employing varied instructional strategies, providing choices, and integrating technology can significantly enhance the learning experience. By recognizing and valuing the unique strengths of each learner, educators can foster an atmosphere of engagement and success, ultimately leading to improved educational outcomes for all.

Expanding Cultural Awareness through Education

Expanding cultural awareness through education is a vital component of fostering a more inclusive and understanding society. In an increasingly interconnected world, the ability to appreciate and respect diverse cultures is essential for both personal and communal growth. This subsection explores the theoretical frameworks, existing challenges, and practical examples of how education can serve as a powerful tool in expanding cultural awareness.

Theoretical Frameworks

To understand the significance of cultural awareness in education, several educational theories can be referenced:

- **Culturally Relevant Pedagogy** (Ladson-Billings, 1995): This framework emphasizes the importance of including students' cultural references in all aspects of learning. It posits that when students see their own cultures reflected in the curriculum, they are more likely to engage and succeed academically.

- **Multicultural Education** (Banks, 1993): This approach advocates for teaching students about various cultures, histories, and contributions of diverse groups. It aims to promote equity and social justice within the educational system, encouraging students to challenge stereotypes and biases.

- **Global Citizenship Education** (UNESCO, 2014): This framework encourages learners to develop the knowledge, skills, and values necessary to engage with global issues. It promotes understanding of cultural diversity and fosters respect for human rights, ultimately preparing students to be active and responsible global citizens.

Challenges in Expanding Cultural Awareness

Despite the importance of cultural awareness, several challenges hinder its effective integration into educational systems:

- **Curricular Limitations:** Many educational institutions still rely on traditional curricula that do not adequately represent diverse cultures. This lack of representation can perpetuate stereotypes and limit students' understanding of the world around them.

- **Teacher Preparedness:** Educators may lack the training or resources necessary to effectively teach about cultural diversity. Professional development programs must be implemented to equip teachers with the skills to engage students in meaningful discussions about culture.

- **Resistance to Change:** Some educators and administrators may resist incorporating cultural awareness into their teaching practices due to preconceived notions or discomfort with discussing sensitive topics.

Overcoming this resistance is crucial for fostering an inclusive learning environment.

Practical Examples of Expanding Cultural Awareness

Several innovative educational practices have demonstrated success in expanding cultural awareness among students:

- **Project-Based Learning (PBL):** This approach allows students to engage in real-world projects that require them to collaborate with peers from different cultural backgrounds. For example, a PBL initiative might involve students researching and presenting on various cultural festivals, allowing them to explore and appreciate diverse traditions.

- **Cultural Exchange Programs:** Schools can implement exchange programs that allow students to experience different cultures firsthand. For instance, a partnership between schools in different countries can facilitate student exchanges, where participants live with host families and attend classes in a foreign environment.

- **Technology-Enhanced Learning:** Utilizing technology, such as virtual reality (VR) and online platforms, educators can create immersive experiences that expose students to different cultures. For instance, a VR program might simulate a day in the life of a student in another country, allowing learners to gain insights into daily customs and practices.

Conclusion

Expanding cultural awareness through education is not merely an optional enhancement; it is an essential component of preparing students for a globalized world. By employing culturally relevant pedagogy, addressing existing challenges, and implementing innovative practices, educators can create an environment that fosters understanding, respect, and appreciation for cultural diversity. As Riley Dubois's Cultural Connector platform exemplifies, the integration of technology and collaborative learning can significantly enhance the educational experience, ultimately leading to a more culturally aware and empathetic society.

$$\text{Cultural Awareness} = \frac{\text{Diversity in Curriculum} + \text{Engagement in Cultural Activities}}{\text{Resistance to Change} + \text{Teacher Preparedness}} \tag{13}$$

This equation suggests that cultural awareness can be maximized by increasing diversity in the curriculum and student engagement while minimizing resistance to change and enhancing teacher preparedness. As the educational landscape continues to evolve, it is imperative that we prioritize cultural awareness as a core value in our teaching practices.

Integrating Technology in the Classroom

Enhancing Teaching and Learning through Virtual Reality

Virtual Reality (VR) is revolutionizing the educational landscape by providing immersive and interactive learning experiences that transcend traditional classroom boundaries. This subsection explores how VR enhances teaching and learning, the theoretical frameworks that support its use, the challenges it addresses, and practical examples of its application in educational settings.

Theoretical Frameworks

The integration of VR in education can be understood through several theoretical lenses:

- **Constructivist Learning Theory:** This theory posits that learners construct knowledge through experiences. VR facilitates constructivist learning by allowing students to engage in simulations where they can explore, manipulate, and interact with virtual environments, thereby constructing their own understanding of complex concepts.

- **Experiential Learning Theory:** Proposed by Kolb, this theory emphasizes learning through experience. VR provides a unique platform for experiential learning, enabling students to engage in realistic scenarios that promote active participation and reflection.

- **Cognitive Load Theory:** This theory suggests that learning is hindered when cognitive load exceeds a learner's capacity. VR can help manage cognitive load by presenting information in a multi-sensory environment, allowing learners to process information more effectively through visual and auditory stimuli.

Addressing Educational Challenges

VR addresses several challenges faced in traditional educational settings:

- **Limited Resources:** Many educational institutions lack the resources to provide hands-on experiences. VR can simulate environments such as laboratories, historical sites, or complex systems, providing students with experiences that would be impossible or impractical in real life.
- **Engagement and Motivation:** Traditional teaching methods often struggle to engage students. VR captures students' attention and motivates them to learn by immersing them in dynamic environments that stimulate curiosity and exploration.
- **Accessibility:** VR can make education more accessible for students with disabilities. Customized VR experiences can cater to diverse learning needs, ensuring that all students can participate fully in the learning process.

Examples of VR in Education

Several educational institutions and organizations have successfully integrated VR into their curricula. Here are notable examples:

- **Google Expeditions:** This platform allows teachers to take students on virtual field trips to locations around the world. Students can explore the Great Barrier Reef, the surface of Mars, or historical landmarks, all from their classroom. This immersive experience enhances their understanding of geography and history by providing context and visual engagement.
- **Labster:** Labster offers virtual lab simulations for science students. These simulations allow students to conduct experiments in a safe, controlled environment where they can learn complex scientific concepts without the risks associated with real-life lab work. For example, students can explore genetic engineering techniques, such as CRISPR, through interactive simulations that illustrate the process step-by-step.
- **Virtual Reality Medical Training:** Medical schools are increasingly using VR to train students in surgical procedures. For instance, the Osso VR platform provides a realistic surgical simulation that allows students to practice procedures repeatedly, enhancing their skills and confidence before performing on real patients.

Conclusion

In conclusion, virtual reality represents a significant advancement in educational technology, offering innovative solutions to enhance teaching and learning. By leveraging the principles of constructivist and experiential learning theories, VR creates immersive environments that engage students, promote active participation, and address traditional educational challenges. As educational institutions continue to adopt VR technologies, the potential for transformative learning experiences will only grow, paving the way for a future where education is more interactive, accessible, and engaging.

$$\text{Engagement} = \frac{\text{Immersion} + \text{Interactivity}}{\text{Cognitive Load}} \qquad (14)$$

Creating Immersive Experiences for Students

The advent of technology in education has transformed traditional learning environments into dynamic, immersive experiences that captivate students and enhance their educational journey. Immersive learning experiences leverage virtual and augmented reality, gamification, and interactive simulations to engage students in a way that traditional methods cannot. This section explores the theoretical framework behind immersive learning, the challenges educators face, and practical examples of successful implementations.

Theoretical Framework

Immersive learning is grounded in several educational theories, including Constructivism, Experiential Learning, and the Multiple Intelligences Theory.

Constructivism, as proposed by theorists such as Piaget and Vygotsky, posits that learners construct knowledge through experiences and reflections. Immersive experiences allow students to engage actively with content, facilitating deeper understanding and retention.

Experiential Learning, articulated by Kolb, emphasizes the role of experience in the learning process. Kolb's learning cycle comprises four stages: Concrete Experience, Reflective Observation, Abstract Conceptualization, and Active Experimentation. Immersive experiences align well with this cycle by providing concrete experiences that students can reflect upon and experiment with in a safe environment.

Multiple Intelligences Theory, developed by Howard Gardner, suggests that individuals possess different kinds of intelligences. Immersive learning caters to various intelligences—visual-spatial, bodily-kinesthetic, and interpersonal—by offering diverse modalities for engagement.

INTEGRATING TECHNOLOGY IN THE CLASSROOM

Challenges in Implementation

Despite the potential of immersive learning, several challenges hinder its widespread adoption:

- **Access to Technology:** Not all schools have the resources to implement advanced technologies like virtual reality (VR) or augmented reality (AR). This digital divide can exacerbate existing inequalities in education.

- **Teacher Training:** Educators may lack the necessary training to effectively integrate immersive technologies into their curriculum. Professional development programs are essential to equip teachers with the skills needed to facilitate immersive learning.

- **Curriculum Alignment:** Ensuring that immersive experiences align with educational standards and learning objectives can be challenging. Educators must balance innovative methods with required curricula.

- **Student Distraction:** While immersive experiences can engage students, they can also lead to distractions if not managed properly. Maintaining focus during immersive activities is crucial for effective learning.

Examples of Immersive Learning Experiences

Several educational institutions and organizations have successfully implemented immersive experiences that demonstrate the potential of this approach:

1. **Virtual Reality Field Trips:** Organizations like *Google Expeditions* allow students to take virtual field trips to historical sites, natural wonders, and even outer space. For instance, a history class can explore ancient Rome through a VR headset, experiencing the Colosseum and Roman Forum as if they were there. This not only enhances engagement but also fosters a deeper understanding of historical contexts.

2. **Augmented Reality in Science Education:** The *Merge Cube* is an example of a device that allows students to hold and interact with 3D holograms in their hands. In a biology class, students can explore the human body by manipulating a 3D model of organs and systems, gaining insights into anatomy and physiology that would be difficult to achieve with traditional methods.

3. **Gamification and Interactive Simulations:** Platforms like *Kahoot!* and *Minecraft: Education Edition* incorporate gamification into learning. In a geography lesson, students can use Minecraft to build and explore different ecosystems,

applying their knowledge in a hands-on manner that encourages collaboration and creativity.

Conclusion

Creating immersive experiences for students represents a paradigm shift in educational practice. By incorporating technology that aligns with established educational theories, educators can foster deeper engagement, understanding, and retention of knowledge. However, addressing the challenges of access, training, and curriculum alignment is crucial for the successful integration of these innovative approaches. As technology continues to evolve, the potential for immersive learning to transform education remains vast, promising a future where learning is not only informative but also engaging and enjoyable.

$$\text{Engagement} = f(\text{Technology}, \text{Interactivity}, \text{Relevance}) \tag{15}$$

Where Engagement is a function of Technology (the tools used), Interactivity (the level of student participation), and Relevance (the connection to real-world applications).

The journey toward fully immersive education is ongoing, but the strides made thus far indicate a bright future for students worldwide.

Digitizing Classroom Resources

The digitization of classroom resources represents a transformative shift in education, allowing for enhanced accessibility, engagement, and adaptability. This section explores the theoretical underpinnings of digitizing educational materials, the challenges faced by educators in this transition, and practical examples of successful implementation.

Theoretical Framework

At its core, the digitization of classroom resources is grounded in several educational theories, including Constructivism and Connectivism. Constructivism posits that learners construct knowledge through experiences and interactions with their environment. By digitizing resources, educators can provide a rich tapestry of multimedia content that caters to diverse learning styles and preferences. This aligns with Gardner's Theory of Multiple Intelligences, which emphasizes that learners possess different kinds of intelligences, such as linguistic, logical-mathematical, spatial, and interpersonal.

Connectivism, on the other hand, emphasizes the role of social and cultural context in learning. It posits that knowledge is distributed across a network of connections, and learning occurs through interactions within this network. Digitized resources facilitate these connections by enabling students to collaborate, share, and engage with content in real-time, regardless of geographical barriers.

Challenges in Digitizing Resources

Despite the potential benefits, the digitization of classroom resources is not without its challenges. Key issues include:

- **Access to Technology:** Not all students have equal access to digital devices and high-speed internet. The digital divide can exacerbate existing inequalities in education, making it crucial for schools to provide necessary resources to all students.

- **Digital Literacy:** Educators and students must possess a certain level of digital literacy to effectively utilize digital resources. This includes the ability to navigate various platforms, evaluate the credibility of online information, and understand digital citizenship.

- **Content Quality and Relevance:** The vast amount of information available online can be overwhelming. Educators must curate high-quality, relevant content that aligns with learning objectives and standards.

- **Resistance to Change:** Some educators may resist the shift to digital resources due to a lack of familiarity or comfort with technology. Professional development and training are essential to support teachers in this transition.

- **Maintenance and Updates:** Digital resources require ongoing maintenance and updates to ensure they remain current and functional. This can place additional demands on educators and administrative staff.

Examples of Successful Implementation

Several educational institutions have successfully digitized their classroom resources, showcasing the potential of this approach:

- **Khan Academy:** This free online resource offers a vast library of instructional videos and practice exercises across various subjects. It empowers students to learn at their own pace, providing personalized learning experiences that adapt to individual needs.

- **Google Classroom:** This platform allows teachers to create, distribute, and grade assignments digitally. It fosters collaboration among students and streamlines communication between educators and learners, making it easier to share resources and feedback.

- **Edmodo:** As a social learning platform, Edmodo enables teachers to create a digital classroom environment where students can share resources, collaborate on projects, and engage in discussions. It promotes a sense of community and connection among learners.

- **Open Educational Resources (OER):** Initiatives like OER Commons provide access to a wealth of freely available educational materials, including textbooks, lesson plans, and multimedia content. These resources can be adapted and customized to meet the specific needs of educators and students.

Conclusion

The digitization of classroom resources is a powerful tool for enhancing education in the 21st century. By leveraging technology, educators can create dynamic, interactive learning environments that foster engagement and collaboration. However, addressing the challenges associated with this transition is crucial to ensure that all students benefit from these advancements. As we move forward, it is essential to prioritize digital equity, support teacher training, and continually assess the quality and relevance of digital resources. By doing so, we can pave the way for a more inclusive and effective educational landscape.

$$R = \frac{E}{A} \qquad (16)$$

where R represents the resource effectiveness, E represents the engagement level of students, and A represents the accessibility of the resources. This equation underscores the importance of balancing engagement and accessibility in the digitization process.

Connecting Students and Teachers Globally

In an increasingly interconnected world, the ability to connect students and teachers across geographical boundaries has become paramount. The advent of digital platforms has revolutionized the way educational content is delivered and consumed, fostering a global classroom environment that transcends traditional barriers. This subsection explores the mechanisms, theories, challenges, and examples of how Cultural Connector is paving the way for global connections in education.

Theoretical Framework

The theory of *Connectivism*, proposed by George Siemens and Stephen Downes, serves as a foundational framework for understanding the connections formed in a global learning environment. Connectivism posits that knowledge is distributed across a network of connections and that learning is the process of navigating these networks. This theory underscores the importance of technology in facilitating learning opportunities that are not confined to a single location or context.

$$L = f(N, C, T) \qquad (17)$$

Where:

- L = Learning
- N = Network of connections
- C = Context of the connections
- T = Technology facilitating connections

This equation highlights the interaction of networks, context, and technology in shaping the learning experience, emphasizing the role of Cultural Connector in creating a robust educational ecosystem.

Challenges in Connecting Globally

While the potential for global connections is vast, several challenges remain. These include:

- **Digital Divide:** Disparities in access to technology can hinder equitable participation in global learning environments. Students in under-resourced areas may lack reliable internet access or modern devices, creating a barrier to connection.

- **Cultural Differences:** Variations in educational systems, languages, and cultural norms can complicate collaboration. Educators must navigate these differences to create inclusive and effective learning experiences.
- **Time Zone Challenges:** Coordinating synchronous learning opportunities across different time zones can be logistically challenging, often requiring compromises that may disadvantage certain participants.
- **Data Privacy and Security:** The use of digital platforms raises concerns regarding the privacy and security of student information. Educators must ensure compliance with regulations such as GDPR and FERPA to protect student data.

Examples of Successful Global Connections

Cultural Connector has successfully implemented various initiatives to connect students and teachers worldwide. Notable examples include:

- **Virtual Exchange Programs:** These programs allow students from different countries to collaborate on projects, share cultural insights, and engage in discussions, fostering mutual understanding and respect. For instance, a partnership between schools in the United States and Kenya facilitated a project on environmental sustainability, where students shared local challenges and solutions.
- **Global Learning Networks:** Platforms like Cultural Connector enable educators to create networks where they can share resources, best practices, and teaching strategies. An example is the Global Educators Network, which connects teachers from diverse backgrounds to collaborate on curriculum development and pedagogical approaches.
- **Cross-Cultural Classrooms:** Using video conferencing tools, classrooms can connect in real-time, allowing students to engage directly with peers from different cultures. A successful instance involved a history class in Canada collaborating with a class in Japan to discuss World War II from their respective cultural perspectives, enriching the learning experience for both groups.

The Role of Technology in Enhancing Global Connections

Technology plays a crucial role in facilitating connections between students and teachers globally. Key technological tools include:

- **Learning Management Systems (LMS):** Platforms like Moodle and Canvas allow educators to create and share courses, track progress, and facilitate discussions among students from different locations.
- **Social Media and Collaborative Tools:** Tools such as Google Docs, Padlet, and Slack enable real-time collaboration and communication, allowing students to work together on projects regardless of their physical location.
- **Virtual Reality (VR) and Augmented Reality (AR):** These technologies provide immersive experiences that can connect students to different cultures and environments, enhancing their understanding of global issues. For instance, VR can simulate historical events or cultural landmarks, making learning more engaging and impactful.

Conclusion

Connecting students and teachers globally is a transformative endeavor that Cultural Connector is championing through innovative technology and collaborative practices. By overcoming challenges and leveraging the power of digital platforms, educators can create inclusive and dynamic learning environments that prepare students for a globalized world. As we move forward, it is essential to continue exploring new methodologies and technologies that can further enhance these connections, ensuring that every student has the opportunity to engage with diverse perspectives and experiences.

Embracing Gamification in Education

Gamification, the integration of game design elements in non-game contexts, has emerged as a transformative approach in education. By harnessing the motivational power of games, educators can enhance student engagement, improve learning outcomes, and foster a more interactive learning environment. This section explores the theoretical foundations of gamification, its implementation in educational settings, the challenges faced, and practical examples that illustrate its impact.

Theoretical Foundations of Gamification

The concept of gamification is rooted in several psychological theories, including:

- **Self-Determination Theory (SDT):** This theory posits that individuals are motivated by three innate psychological needs: autonomy, competence, and relatedness. Gamification addresses these needs by providing students with choices (autonomy), opportunities to master skills (competence), and social interactions (relatedness).

- **Flow Theory:** Proposed by Mihaly Csikszentmihalyi, flow theory describes a state of complete immersion and engagement in an activity. Gamification can help create conditions for flow by balancing challenge and skill, ensuring that tasks are neither too easy nor too difficult.

- **Behaviorism:** This learning theory emphasizes the role of reinforcement in behavior modification. Gamification utilizes rewards, badges, and leaderboards to reinforce positive behaviors and achievements, encouraging students to engage more deeply with the material.

Benefits of Gamification in Education

The implementation of gamification in educational settings has shown several benefits:

- **Increased Engagement:** Gamified elements such as points, badges, and levels can make learning more enjoyable and engaging for students. A study by Hamari, Koivisto, and Sarsa (2014) found that gamification significantly increased user engagement in various contexts, including education.

- **Enhanced Motivation:** By incorporating game mechanics, educators can tap into students' intrinsic and extrinsic motivations. For instance, students may be motivated to complete assignments to earn rewards or advance to the next level, leading to improved academic performance.

- **Immediate Feedback:** Gamification provides instant feedback through scores and progress tracking, allowing students to understand their performance in real-time. This immediate feedback loop can help students identify areas for improvement and adjust their learning strategies accordingly.

- **Collaboration and Social Learning:** Many gamified educational platforms encourage collaboration among students, fostering a sense of community and teamwork. This social aspect can enhance learning by allowing students to share knowledge and support each other in achieving common goals.

Challenges in Implementing Gamification

Despite its advantages, gamification in education is not without challenges:

- **Overemphasis on Rewards:** There is a risk that students may become overly focused on extrinsic rewards, leading to a decline in intrinsic motivation. Educators must strike a balance between rewarding achievements and fostering a genuine love for learning.

- **One-Size-Fits-All Approach:** Gamification strategies that work for one group of students may not be effective for another. Educators must consider diverse learning styles and preferences when designing gamified experiences.

- **Resource Intensive:** Developing and implementing gamified curricula can be time-consuming and require additional resources, including technology and training for educators. Schools may face budget constraints that limit their ability to adopt gamification fully.

Practical Examples of Gamification in Education

Several educational institutions and platforms have successfully integrated gamification into their curricula:

- **Kahoot!:** This game-based learning platform allows educators to create quizzes that students can answer in real-time using their devices. Kahoot! incorporates elements such as points, leaderboards, and timers to create a competitive and engaging learning environment.

- **Duolingo:** A language-learning app that uses gamification to motivate users. Through a series of levels, rewards, and challenges, Duolingo encourages daily practice and progress tracking, making language learning fun and accessible.

- **Classcraft:** This platform transforms the classroom into a role-playing game where students create avatars and earn points for positive behaviors and academic achievements. Classcraft promotes collaboration and teamwork while enhancing student engagement.

Conclusion

Embracing gamification in education offers a promising avenue for enhancing student engagement, motivation, and learning outcomes. By understanding the theoretical foundations, recognizing the benefits, addressing the challenges, and implementing practical examples, educators can create dynamic and interactive learning environments that prepare students for success in an increasingly digital world. As technology continues to evolve, the potential for gamification to transform education remains vast, paving the way for innovative teaching and learning experiences.

$$\text{Engagement} = f(\text{Challenge, Skill, Feedback}) \qquad (18)$$

This equation represents the relationship between engagement, challenge, skill, and feedback, highlighting the importance of balancing these elements to foster a productive learning environment.

Supporting Personalized Learning Paths

The concept of personalized learning paths has gained significant traction in the realm of education, particularly with the advent of technology and digital platforms. Personalized learning refers to tailoring educational experiences to meet individual students' needs, strengths, and interests. This approach contrasts sharply with traditional, one-size-fits-all educational models, which often fail to engage all learners effectively. In this section, we explore the theoretical foundations, challenges, and practical implementations of personalized learning paths, particularly within the framework of Cultural Connector.

Theoretical Foundations

Personalized learning is rooted in several educational theories, including constructivism and differentiated instruction. Constructivist theories, pioneered by thinkers like Jean Piaget and Lev Vygotsky, emphasize that learners construct knowledge through experiences and interactions. This theory supports the notion that students learn best when they can connect new information to their existing knowledge and experiences.

Differentiated instruction, introduced by Carol Ann Tomlinson, further supports personalized learning by advocating for varied teaching methods and assessments to accommodate diverse learners. Tomlinson's model emphasizes the importance of understanding students' readiness, interests, and learning profiles, thereby allowing educators to tailor their instruction and resources accordingly.

Challenges of Implementing Personalized Learning Paths

While the benefits of personalized learning are clear, several challenges hinder its widespread implementation:

- **Resource Allocation:** Implementing personalized learning requires significant resources, including technology, training for educators, and time for curriculum development. Many schools, particularly those in underfunded areas, struggle to provide these necessary resources.

- **Teacher Training:** Educators must be equipped with the skills and knowledge to design and facilitate personalized learning experiences. Professional development programs must be established to help teachers understand how to implement personalized learning effectively.

- **Assessment and Evaluation:** Traditional assessment methods may not effectively measure student progress in a personalized learning environment. Educators need to develop new metrics that can accurately reflect individual growth and mastery.

- **Equity and Access:** Personalized learning must be accessible to all students, regardless of their socioeconomic background. Addressing the digital divide is crucial to ensure that all learners can benefit from personalized learning opportunities.

Practical Implementations of Personalized Learning Paths

Cultural Connector has emerged as a powerful tool in supporting personalized learning paths. By leveraging technology, Cultural Connector allows educators to create customized learning experiences that cater to individual student needs. Here are some key features and examples of how Cultural Connector supports personalized learning:

- **Adaptive Learning Technologies:** Cultural Connector utilizes adaptive learning algorithms to assess student performance in real-time. For instance, if a student struggles with a specific concept, the platform can automatically adjust the curriculum to provide additional resources and practice opportunities tailored to that student's learning level.

- **Interest-Based Learning:** The platform encourages students to explore topics that align with their interests. For example, if a student shows a keen interest in environmental science, Cultural Connector can provide a range of resources, projects, and collaboration opportunities related to that field, fostering deeper engagement and motivation.

- **Flexible Learning Environments:** Cultural Connector supports various learning modalities, including visual, auditory, and kinesthetic approaches. This flexibility allows students to choose how they engage with the material. For instance, a student might prefer interactive simulations to learn about physics, while another might benefit from video lectures.

- **Collaborative Learning Opportunities:** The platform facilitates collaboration among students from diverse backgrounds. For example, a project on global cultures might connect students from different countries, allowing them to share perspectives and learn from one another. This collaboration not only enhances learning but also fosters cultural awareness and empathy.

- **Real-Time Feedback and Support:** Cultural Connector provides immediate feedback on assignments and assessments, enabling students to track their progress and identify areas for improvement. This feedback loop is crucial for personalized learning, as it empowers students to take ownership of their learning journey.

Conclusion

Supporting personalized learning paths through platforms like Cultural Connector represents a significant step toward creating a more inclusive and effective educational landscape. By leveraging technology to tailor learning experiences, educators can better meet the diverse needs of their students. As we continue to embrace personalized learning, it is essential to address the challenges and ensure that all learners have equitable access to these transformative educational experiences. The future of education lies in recognizing and nurturing the unique paths of each learner, ultimately leading to improved educational outcomes and a more engaged global citizenry.

Promoting Digital Literacy

Digital literacy is increasingly recognized as a fundamental skill necessary for participation in today's information-rich society. It encompasses not only the ability to use digital tools and technologies but also the critical thinking and evaluative skills required to navigate the vast landscape of information available online. As Riley Dubois's Cultural Connector initiative seeks to empower individuals through education, promoting digital literacy becomes a pivotal aspect of its mission.

Theoretical Framework

Digital literacy can be framed through various theoretical lenses, including the *Technological Pedagogical Content Knowledge (TPACK)* model, which emphasizes the integration of technology, pedagogy, and content knowledge in teaching practices. According to Mishra and Koehler (2006), effective teaching requires an understanding of how technology can enhance learning experiences while addressing the content being taught. This model serves as a foundational theory for developing digital literacy programs within Cultural Connector, ensuring that educators are equipped to integrate technology into their teaching effectively.

Furthermore, the *Critical Media Literacy* framework encourages individuals to critically analyze media messages and understand the socio-political contexts in which they are created. This approach is vital in promoting digital literacy, as it empowers individuals to question the credibility of online sources, recognize bias, and understand the implications of their digital footprints.

Challenges to Digital Literacy

Despite the recognized importance of digital literacy, several challenges persist:

- **Access to Technology:** A significant barrier to digital literacy is the digital divide, where access to technology and the internet is unevenly distributed. According to the Pew Research Center (2021), approximately 25% of rural Americans lack broadband access, hindering their ability to engage with digital content effectively.

- **Information Overload:** The sheer volume of information available online can overwhelm individuals, making it difficult to discern credible sources from misinformation. The proliferation of fake news and disinformation campaigns has exacerbated this issue, necessitating robust digital literacy education.

- **Lack of Training:** Many educators and learners alike lack adequate training in digital literacy skills. A report by the International Society for Technology in Education (ISTE) (2019) found that only 30% of teachers felt confident in their ability to teach digital literacy skills, underscoring the need for targeted professional development.

Strategies for Promoting Digital Literacy

To address these challenges, Cultural Connector employs a multifaceted approach to promote digital literacy:

1. **Workshops and Training Programs:** Cultural Connector organizes workshops that focus on practical digital skills, such as navigating online platforms, evaluating sources, and understanding data privacy. These sessions are designed to be interactive and engaging, fostering a hands-on learning environment.

2. **Curriculum Integration:** By embedding digital literacy into existing curricula, Cultural Connector ensures that students encounter these skills in context. For example, a history lesson might include an analysis of primary sources found online, prompting students to evaluate the credibility and relevance of the information.

3. **Collaboration with Tech Companies:** Partnering with technology firms allows Cultural Connector to access resources and expertise that enhance digital literacy initiatives. For instance, Google's "Be Internet Awesome" program provides educators with tools to teach students about online safety and digital citizenship.

4. **Community Engagement:** Cultural Connector emphasizes the importance of engaging with the community to promote digital literacy. Initiatives such as digital literacy fairs bring together local organizations, educators, and families to raise awareness and provide resources for improving digital skills.

Real-World Examples

Several successful initiatives illustrate the impact of promoting digital literacy:

- **The Digital Literacy Initiative (DLI):** Launched by the New York Public Library, DLI provides free workshops on digital skills, including coding, online job searching, and digital citizenship. This program has reached thousands of participants, empowering them to navigate the digital world confidently.

- **Common Sense Education:** This organization offers a comprehensive digital literacy curriculum that addresses topics such as media literacy, online safety, and ethical use of technology. Schools that have implemented this curriculum report improved student engagement and critical thinking skills.

- **The Media Smarts Program:** Based in Canada, Media Smarts focuses on teaching youth to critically analyze media content. Their resources include lesson plans and online tools that foster critical thinking and media literacy among students, preparing them for the complexities of the digital landscape.

Conclusion

Promoting digital literacy is essential for equipping individuals with the skills necessary to thrive in a digital society. Through innovative programs and collaborative efforts, Cultural Connector aims to break down barriers, foster critical thinking, and empower learners to navigate the complexities of the digital world. As Riley Dubois envisions a future where technology enhances education and social connection, the promotion of digital literacy remains a cornerstone of this mission, ensuring that all individuals are prepared to engage thoughtfully and responsibly in the digital age.

Bibliography

[1] Mishra, P., & Koehler, M. J. (2006). Technological Pedagogical Content Knowledge: A Framework for Teacher Knowledge. *Teachers College Record*, 108(6), 1017-1054.

[2] Pew Research Center. (2021). The Digital Divide. Retrieved from `https://www.pewresearch.org`.

[3] International Society for Technology in Education. (2019). Educator Confidence in Digital Literacy. Retrieved from `https://www.iste.org`.

Enabling Remote Learning Opportunities

The advent of the internet has revolutionized the way education is delivered, making remote learning not only possible but increasingly effective. This subsection explores the mechanisms through which Cultural Connector has enabled remote learning opportunities, addressing relevant theories, challenges, and real-world examples.

Theoretical Framework

Remote learning, often referred to as distance education, is grounded in several educational theories, including Constructivism and Connectivism. Constructivism posits that learners construct knowledge through experiences and reflections, while Connectivism emphasizes the role of social networks and digital technologies in learning processes.

According to [?], Connectivism suggests that learning occurs across a network of connections and that knowledge is distributed across the web. This theory supports the idea that remote learning can be as effective as traditional classroom learning when it leverages the right tools and methodologies.

Mechanisms of Remote Learning

Cultural Connector employs various mechanisms to facilitate remote learning, including:

- **Synchronous Learning:** Real-time classes conducted via video conferencing platforms allow students to interact with instructors and peers instantly. Tools like Zoom and Microsoft Teams have become staples in remote education.

- **Asynchronous Learning:** This method allows learners to access materials at their convenience. Course materials, recorded lectures, and discussion forums enable flexibility, accommodating diverse learning styles and schedules.

- **Blended Learning:** Combining both synchronous and asynchronous methods, blended learning offers a hybrid approach, maximizing engagement and accessibility.

- **Interactive Learning Platforms:** Cultural Connector utilizes platforms that encourage participation through quizzes, polls, and group activities, fostering a sense of community among remote learners.

Addressing Challenges

Despite the advantages, remote learning presents several challenges:

- **Digital Divide:** Access to technology and reliable internet remains a significant barrier for many students. According to the [?], approximately 15% of U.S. households with school-age children do not have a high-speed internet connection. Cultural Connector addresses this by partnering with local organizations to provide resources to underserved communities.

- **Engagement Issues:** Students may struggle to stay engaged in a remote environment. Strategies such as gamification and interactive content have been implemented to enhance motivation and participation.

- **Assessment Integrity:** Ensuring the integrity of assessments in a remote setting poses challenges. Cultural Connector has adopted proctoring software and open-book assessments to maintain standards while accommodating the remote format.

Real-World Examples

Several initiatives exemplify how Cultural Connector has enabled remote learning opportunities:

- **Global Classroom Initiative:** This program connects classrooms across different countries, allowing students to collaborate on projects and engage in cultural exchanges through video conferencing and collaborative platforms such as Google Classroom.

- **Skill Development Workshops:** Cultural Connector offers workshops on essential skills such as coding, digital marketing, and graphic design, accessible to anyone with an internet connection. These workshops utilize platforms like Coursera and edX, providing high-quality content from reputable institutions.

- **Mentorship Programs:** By pairing students with mentors from various fields, Cultural Connector fosters personal and professional development. This program leverages platforms like LinkedIn to connect students with industry professionals, enhancing their learning experience.

Conclusion

In conclusion, Cultural Connector's approach to enabling remote learning opportunities demonstrates the potential of technology to transform education. By addressing challenges such as the digital divide and engagement issues while leveraging theoretical frameworks like Constructivism and Connectivism, Cultural Connector is paving the way for a more inclusive and effective learning environment. As remote learning continues to evolve, the commitment to innovation and accessibility will remain at the forefront of its mission.

Empowering Students to Drive Their Education

In an era where education is rapidly evolving, empowering students to take control of their own learning journey is paramount. The Cultural Connector platform embodies this principle by providing tools and resources that allow students to tailor their educational experiences according to their interests, strengths, and learning styles. This section delves into the methodologies and theories underpinning this empowerment, the challenges faced, and practical examples of how this is being achieved.

Theoretical Framework

The empowerment of students in their educational pursuits can be anchored in several educational theories. One prominent theory is **Constructivism**, which posits that learners construct knowledge through experiences and reflections. According to Piaget (1973), learning is an active process where students build their understanding based on prior knowledge and new experiences. This theory aligns with the idea that students should be active participants in their education rather than passive recipients of information.

Another relevant framework is **Self-Determination Theory (SDT)**, proposed by Deci and Ryan (1985). SDT emphasizes the importance of autonomy, competence, and relatedness in fostering intrinsic motivation. By providing students with choices in their learning, they develop a sense of ownership and agency, leading to enhanced motivation and engagement.

Challenges to Empowerment

Despite the clear benefits of empowering students, several challenges persist. One significant barrier is the **traditional education system**, which often emphasizes standardized testing and a one-size-fits-all approach. This can stifle creativity and limit opportunities for students to explore their interests. Additionally, not all educators are equipped with the necessary training to facilitate student-driven learning.

Another challenge is the **digital divide**, where disparities in access to technology can hinder some students' ability to engage with personalized learning tools. This divide can exacerbate existing inequalities, making it crucial to address these gaps to ensure all students have equal opportunities to drive their education.

Practical Examples

The Cultural Connector platform addresses these challenges by offering a variety of features designed to empower students. For example, the platform includes:

- **Personalized Learning Pathways:** Students can select topics that interest them and create customized learning plans. This flexibility allows them to explore subjects at their own pace, fostering a deeper understanding.
- **Collaborative Projects:** The platform facilitates group projects where students can work together on shared interests. This not only encourages collaboration but also allows students to learn from one another, enhancing their educational experience.

- **Mentorship Opportunities:** Cultural Connector connects students with mentors in various fields, providing guidance and support as they navigate their educational journeys. This relationship fosters a sense of belonging and encourages students to pursue their passions.
- **Gamification:** By incorporating game-like elements into learning, the platform increases engagement and motivation. Students earn rewards and badges for completing tasks, which makes learning more enjoyable and encourages them to take initiative.

Case Study: Student-Driven Learning in Action

A notable example of empowering students through Cultural Connector is the case of a high school student, Jamie, who struggled with traditional learning methods. After joining the platform, Jamie was able to identify their passion for environmental science. Through personalized learning pathways, Jamie explored topics such as climate change, renewable energy, and conservation strategies.

Using the platform's collaborative features, Jamie connected with peers from around the world who shared similar interests. Together, they initiated a project to raise awareness about plastic pollution in their communities, utilizing social media to spread their message. This project not only enhanced Jamie's understanding of the subject matter but also developed essential skills such as teamwork, communication, and project management.

Conclusion

Empowering students to drive their education is a transformative approach that fosters engagement, motivation, and a deeper understanding of the learning process. By leveraging platforms like Cultural Connector, educators can provide the necessary tools and resources to facilitate student agency. As we continue to navigate the challenges of modern education, it is imperative to prioritize student empowerment, ensuring that all learners have the opportunity to shape their educational journeys.

$$\text{Empowerment} = \text{Autonomy} + \text{Competence} + \text{Relatedness} \qquad (19)$$

The equation above encapsulates the essence of student empowerment, highlighting the key elements that contribute to a successful and fulfilling educational experience. By focusing on these components, we can create an environment where students feel confident and motivated to take charge of their learning.

Navigating the Challenges of Integrating Technology

The integration of technology in education presents a myriad of challenges that educators, administrators, and policymakers must navigate to ensure that the benefits of technological advancements are realized. This section will explore some of these challenges, supported by relevant theories, problems, and examples, while also providing potential solutions for overcoming these obstacles.

Resistance to Change

One of the most significant challenges faced in integrating technology into educational settings is resistance to change. Many educators may feel overwhelmed by the pace of technological advancements or may lack the necessary training to effectively utilize new tools. This resistance can be rooted in the **Theory of Planned Behavior**, which posits that individual behavior is influenced by attitudes, subjective norms, and perceived behavioral control [?].

For instance, a study conducted by Ertmer (1999) found that teachers' beliefs about technology significantly impacted their willingness to integrate it into their classrooms. To counteract resistance, professional development programs should be designed to empower educators, focusing on hands-on training and fostering a growth mindset regarding technology use.

Equity and Access

Equity in access to technology is another critical challenge. The digital divide remains a pressing issue, where students from low-income families or underserved communities may lack access to necessary devices and high-speed internet. According to the **United Nations Educational, Scientific and Cultural Organization (UNESCO)**, approximately 1.5 billion students worldwide were affected by school closures during the COVID-19 pandemic, highlighting the disparities in access to technology [?].

To address this issue, educational institutions must prioritize equitable access by providing devices and internet connectivity to disadvantaged students. Programs like *One Laptop per Child* have shown promise in bridging this gap, but broader systemic changes are needed to ensure that all students can benefit from technological advancements.

Digital Literacy

Digital literacy is essential for students and educators alike, yet many individuals lack the skills necessary to navigate and utilize technology effectively. The **Digital Competence Framework** developed by the European Commission emphasizes the importance of digital literacy as a core competency for all citizens [?].

For example, a survey conducted by the Pew Research Center found that only 14% of teachers felt very well prepared to integrate technology into their lessons [?]. To combat this, educational institutions should implement comprehensive digital literacy programs that equip both students and educators with the skills needed to thrive in a technology-rich environment.

Maintaining Engagement

While technology has the potential to enhance learning, it can also lead to disengagement if not implemented thoughtfully. The **Cognitive Load Theory** suggests that learners have a limited capacity for processing information, and excessive technological distractions can hinder their ability to focus [?].

To maintain student engagement, educators should employ strategies such as the *Flipped Classroom* model, where students engage with technology at home and apply their knowledge in the classroom. This approach encourages active learning and minimizes distractions, fostering a more productive educational environment.

Ethical Considerations

The integration of technology also raises ethical concerns, particularly regarding data privacy and security. The increasing reliance on digital platforms for learning necessitates a robust understanding of data protection laws, such as the **Family Educational Rights and Privacy Act (FERPA)** in the United States.

Educators must be aware of the implications of using various educational technologies and ensure that student data is protected. This includes conducting regular audits of technology tools and platforms used in the classroom and providing training for educators on ethical data practices.

Balancing Traditional and Digital Methods

Finally, finding the right balance between traditional teaching methods and technology can be challenging. The **TPACK framework** (Technological Pedagogical Content Knowledge) emphasizes the interplay between technology, pedagogy, and content knowledge, suggesting that effective integration requires a nuanced understanding of each component [?].

Educators should aim to create a blended learning environment that combines the strengths of both traditional and digital methods. For example, utilizing technology for research and collaboration while maintaining face-to-face discussions can create a more holistic learning experience.

Conclusion

Navigating the challenges of integrating technology in education requires a multifaceted approach that addresses resistance to change, equity and access, digital literacy, engagement, ethical considerations, and the balance between traditional and digital methods. By fostering a supportive environment for educators and students, educational institutions can harness the potential of technology to enhance learning outcomes and prepare students for the future.

Future Tech in Education

Exploring the Potential of Artificial Intelligence

Artificial Intelligence (AI) has emerged as a transformative force in various sectors, particularly in education. Its potential to revolutionize learning experiences, enhance educational outcomes, and foster personalized learning paths is immense. This section explores the theoretical foundations, practical applications, and challenges associated with integrating AI into educational settings.

Theoretical Foundations of AI in Education

AI can be defined as the simulation of human intelligence processes by machines, particularly computer systems. These processes include learning (the acquisition of information and rules for using it), reasoning (using rules to reach approximate or definite conclusions), and self-correction. The integration of AI into education is grounded in several theoretical frameworks:

- **Constructivist Learning Theory:** This theory posits that learners construct knowledge through experiences and reflection. AI can facilitate this by providing adaptive learning environments that respond to individual students' needs.

- **Cognitive Load Theory:** This theory emphasizes the importance of managing the cognitive load on learners. AI can help by automating routine tasks, allowing educators to focus on higher-order thinking skills and personalized instruction.

- **Social Learning Theory:** AI can enhance social learning by connecting students with peers and experts globally, promoting collaborative learning experiences.

Practical Applications of AI in Education

AI's potential in education can be realized through various applications:

- **Personalized Learning:** AI algorithms analyze student data to tailor learning experiences. For instance, platforms like *Knewton* and *DreamBox* adjust content delivery based on individual student performance, ensuring that each learner progresses at their own pace.

- **Intelligent Tutoring Systems (ITS):** These systems provide personalized feedback and guidance. For example, the *Cognitive Tutor* developed by Carnegie Mellon University uses AI to analyze student interactions and offer tailored support.

- **Automated Assessment Tools:** AI can streamline assessment processes through automated grading systems. Tools like *Gradescope* use machine learning to assist educators in grading assignments, providing faster and more consistent evaluations.

- **Predictive Analytics:** Institutions can leverage AI to predict student outcomes and identify at-risk learners. By analyzing historical data, AI models can forecast which students may struggle, enabling timely interventions.

- **Natural Language Processing (NLP):** AI-driven chatbots and virtual assistants enhance student engagement by providing instant responses to queries. For instance, *IBM Watson* is used in educational settings to answer student questions and facilitate learning.

Challenges in Implementing AI in Education

Despite its potential, the integration of AI in education poses several challenges:

- **Data Privacy and Security:** The use of AI requires access to large amounts of student data. Ensuring the privacy and security of this data is paramount. Institutions must comply with regulations such as the Family Educational Rights and Privacy Act (FERPA) and the General Data Protection Regulation (GDPR).

- **Equity and Access:** There is a risk that AI tools may exacerbate existing inequalities in education. Students from underprivileged backgrounds may lack access to the necessary technology, creating a digital divide.

- **Resistance to Change:** Educators and institutions may resist adopting AI technologies due to fear of job displacement or skepticism about their effectiveness. Professional development and training are essential to address these concerns.

- **Ethical Considerations:** The use of AI in education raises ethical questions regarding bias in algorithms, decision-making transparency, and the potential for dehumanizing the learning experience. It is crucial to develop guidelines that prioritize ethical AI use.

Examples of AI Applications in Education

Several educational institutions and organizations are successfully implementing AI technologies:

- **Georgia State University:** The university employs predictive analytics to identify students at risk of dropping out. By analyzing patterns in student data, they provide targeted support services, leading to increased retention rates.

- **Duolingo:** This language-learning platform uses AI to personalize lessons based on user performance, adapting the difficulty and content to optimize the learning experience.

- **Edmodo:** This social learning platform integrates AI to facilitate communication between students and educators, providing personalized recommendations for resources and activities.

Conclusion

The exploration of AI's potential in education reveals both exciting opportunities and significant challenges. As technology continues to evolve, it is imperative that educators, policymakers, and technologists collaborate to harness AI's capabilities while addressing ethical considerations and ensuring equitable access for all learners. By doing so, we can create a more inclusive and effective educational landscape that prepares students for the future.

$$E = mc^2 \qquad (20)$$

Harnessing the Power of Big Data in Education

The advent of big data has revolutionized various sectors, and education is no exception. Big data refers to the vast volumes of structured and unstructured data generated from various sources, including student interactions, assessments, and learning environments. Harnessing this data effectively can lead to significant improvements in educational outcomes, personalized learning experiences, and informed decision-making.

Theoretical Framework

The integration of big data in education can be understood through several theoretical lenses, including:

- **Learning Analytics:** This theory emphasizes the measurement, collection, analysis, and reporting of data about learners and their contexts. It aims to understand and optimize learning processes and environments.

- **Data-Driven Decision Making (DDDM):** This approach advocates for the use of data to inform educational policies, teaching strategies, and institutional practices. It emphasizes the importance of empirical evidence in guiding decisions.

- **Personalized Learning:** This theory posits that education should be tailored to meet the individual needs, preferences, and strengths of each student. Big data enables educators to customize learning experiences based on real-time feedback and analytics.

Challenges in Harnessing Big Data

Despite its potential, the integration of big data in education faces several challenges:

- **Data Privacy and Security:** The collection and analysis of student data raise significant concerns regarding privacy and ethical use. Institutions must ensure compliance with regulations such as FERPA (Family Educational Rights and Privacy Act) and GDPR (General Data Protection Regulation).

- **Data Quality and Integration:** The effectiveness of big data initiatives depends on the quality of the data collected. Inconsistent data formats, incomplete records, and integration issues across different systems can hinder analysis.

- **Lack of Training and Resources:** Educators and administrators may lack the necessary training to interpret and utilize big data effectively. Additionally, institutions may not have the resources to invest in sophisticated data analytics tools.

Applications of Big Data in Education

1. **Predictive Analytics:** By analyzing historical data, educational institutions can predict student performance and identify at-risk students. For example, a study by [?] demonstrated that predictive analytics could help identify students who are likely to drop out, allowing for timely interventions.

$$P(Y=1|X) = \frac{e^{\beta_0+\beta_1 X_1+\beta_2 X_2+...+\beta_n X_n}}{1+e^{\beta_0+\beta_1 X_1+\beta_2 X_2+...+\beta_n X_n}} \qquad (21)$$

In this logistic regression model, Y represents the probability of a student dropping out, while X represents various predictors such as attendance, grades, and engagement metrics.

2. **Personalized Learning Pathways:** Big data enables the creation of personalized learning pathways by analyzing individual learning styles, preferences, and performance. For instance, platforms like Knewton use adaptive learning technologies to tailor content to each student's needs.

3. **Curriculum Development:** Analyzing data from student assessments can inform curriculum design by identifying areas where students struggle. This data-driven approach allows educators to adjust teaching methods and materials to better align with student needs.

4. **Enhanced Student Engagement:** Big data can help educators understand student engagement levels through metrics such as time spent on tasks, participation in discussions, and completion rates. By analyzing these patterns, educators can implement strategies to enhance engagement and motivation.

Case Study: Georgia State University

Georgia State University (GSU) serves as a prominent example of how big data can transform educational outcomes. The institution implemented a predictive analytics system to analyze student data and identify those at risk of dropping out. Key elements of GSU's approach included:

- **Data Collection:** GSU collected data from various sources, including academic records, financial aid, and student demographics.

- **Predictive Modeling:** The university developed predictive models to assess the likelihood of student success based on historical data.

- **Intervention Strategies:** GSU implemented targeted interventions for at-risk students, such as personalized advising and academic support services.

As a result of these efforts, GSU experienced a significant increase in graduation rates, demonstrating the effectiveness of harnessing big data in education.

Future Directions

The future of big data in education holds immense potential, with advancements in artificial intelligence and machine learning further enhancing data analysis capabilities. As educational institutions continue to embrace big data, it is essential to prioritize ethical considerations, data privacy, and the development of robust training programs for educators.

In conclusion, harnessing the power of big data in education can lead to transformative changes in teaching and learning. By addressing the challenges and leveraging the opportunities presented by big data, educational institutions can create more personalized, equitable, and effective learning environments for all students.

Virtual Reality Beyond the Classroom

Virtual Reality (VR) has emerged as a powerful tool that transcends traditional educational settings, offering immersive experiences that can enrich learning and engagement in various contexts. This section explores the potential of VR beyond the classroom, highlighting its applications in diverse fields such as healthcare, vocational training, cultural preservation, and social interaction.

Expanding Learning Opportunities

One of the most significant advantages of VR is its ability to provide experiential learning opportunities that are often impossible to replicate in a conventional classroom. For instance, medical students can practice surgical procedures in a risk-free environment using VR simulations. According to a study by [?], medical trainees who utilized VR for practicing surgical techniques demonstrated a 30% improvement in their procedural skills compared to those who used traditional methods.

Healthcare Applications

In healthcare, VR is being used not only for training but also for therapeutic purposes. Virtual environments can help patients confront and manage phobias, anxiety disorders, and post-traumatic stress disorder (PTSD). A notable example is the use of VR exposure therapy for patients with PTSD, where they are gradually exposed to triggering stimuli in a controlled virtual setting. Research by [?] shows that patients undergoing VR therapy experienced a 50% reduction in PTSD symptoms after a series of sessions.

Vocational Training

VR also plays a crucial role in vocational training, allowing individuals to gain hands-on experience in various trades without the associated risks. For example, construction workers can engage in VR simulations to practice safety protocols and equipment handling. A study conducted by [?] found that workers trained in VR were 40% less likely to make safety errors on job sites compared to those trained through traditional methods.

Cultural Preservation and Exploration

Beyond practical training, VR has become a vital tool for cultural preservation and exploration. Museums and cultural institutions are leveraging VR to create virtual tours of historical sites and exhibitions, making art and history accessible to a global audience. For instance, the *British Museum* offers a VR experience that allows users to explore ancient Egyptian artifacts from the comfort of their homes. This democratization of access not only enhances cultural awareness but also fosters a sense of global citizenship among users.

Social Interaction and Collaboration

VR platforms also facilitate social interaction and collaboration in ways that traditional media cannot. Virtual environments enable users to connect with others worldwide, share experiences, and collaborate on projects. Platforms like *AltspaceVR* and *VRChat* allow users to engage in social gatherings, attend events, and participate in discussions, creating a sense of community that transcends geographical boundaries. A study by [?] highlights that users of these platforms report increased feelings of belonging and social connectedness.

Challenges and Considerations

Despite its numerous advantages, the implementation of VR beyond the classroom is not without challenges. Issues such as accessibility, technological limitations, and the potential for VR-induced motion sickness must be addressed. Moreover, ensuring that VR experiences are inclusive and cater to diverse audiences is crucial. As noted by [?], developers must consider the varying levels of technological proficiency among users to create effective and engaging VR experiences.

Future Directions

Looking ahead, the potential of VR beyond the classroom is vast. As technology continues to evolve, we can expect more sophisticated and immersive experiences that further bridge the gap between virtual and real-world interactions. The integration of artificial intelligence (AI) with VR could lead to personalized learning experiences, adapting to individual users' needs and preferences.

Conclusion

In conclusion, Virtual Reality has the potential to revolutionize learning and engagement beyond the classroom by providing immersive, experiential opportunities in various fields. From healthcare training to cultural exploration and social interaction, VR is breaking down barriers and creating new pathways for innovation. As we continue to explore its applications, addressing the associated challenges will be vital to unlocking its full potential in shaping the future of education and beyond.

Revolutionizing Assessment Methods

In the rapidly evolving landscape of education, traditional assessment methods are increasingly being challenged by innovative approaches that leverage technology and pedagogical advancements. This subsection explores how Cultural Connector has played a pivotal role in revolutionizing assessment methods, making them more inclusive, engaging, and reflective of real-world competencies.

The Limitations of Traditional Assessments

Traditional assessment methods, such as standardized testing, often emphasize rote memorization and a one-size-fits-all approach. These methods can lead to several issues:

- **Limited Scope of Evaluation:** Traditional assessments frequently measure a narrow range of skills, primarily focusing on factual recall rather than critical thinking, creativity, or collaborative abilities.

- **Test Anxiety:** Many students experience significant anxiety related to high-stakes testing, which can negatively impact performance and obscure true learning outcomes.

- **Inequity in Assessment:** Standardized tests may not account for diverse cultural backgrounds, learning styles, and individual needs, leading to disparities in student performance.

- **Static Feedback:** Traditional assessments often provide limited feedback, which hinders students' ability to understand their learning gaps and areas for improvement.

Innovative Assessment Strategies

Cultural Connector has introduced a variety of innovative assessment strategies designed to address the limitations of traditional methods. These strategies emphasize formative assessment, personalized learning, and the integration of technology.

1. Formative Assessments Formative assessments are ongoing evaluations that provide real-time feedback to students and educators. Unlike traditional assessments, formative assessments focus on the learning process rather than just the final product. For instance:

- **Peer Assessments:** Students evaluate each other's work, fostering collaboration and critical thinking. This method encourages constructive feedback and allows students to learn from their peers.

FUTURE TECH IN EDUCATION

- **Interactive Quizzes:** Utilizing platforms like Kahoot! or Quizizz, educators can create engaging quizzes that provide immediate feedback. These tools not only enhance engagement but also allow teachers to gauge student understanding in real time.

2. Personalized Learning Paths Cultural Connector emphasizes the importance of personalized learning paths that cater to individual student needs. By utilizing data analytics and artificial intelligence, educators can tailor assessments to match students' learning styles and paces. For example:

- **Adaptive Learning Technologies:** Platforms like DreamBox Learning or IXL adjust the difficulty of questions based on student performance, ensuring that assessments are neither too easy nor too challenging.

- **Project-Based Assessments:** Students engage in real-world projects that align with their interests and career aspirations. These assessments allow students to demonstrate their knowledge and skills in practical contexts, fostering deeper learning.

3. Technology-Enhanced Assessments The integration of technology in assessments has opened new avenues for creativity and engagement. Cultural Connector has facilitated the use of various technological tools that enhance the assessment experience:

- **Digital Portfolios:** Students create digital portfolios showcasing their work over time, allowing for a holistic view of their learning journey. These portfolios can include videos, presentations, and written reflections, providing a rich context for assessment.

- **Virtual Reality (VR) Assessments:** VR technology can simulate real-world scenarios for assessment purposes. For example, medical students can practice surgical techniques in a virtual environment, receiving immediate feedback on their performance.

Theoretical Foundations

The shift towards innovative assessment methods is grounded in several educational theories:

1. **Constructivism** Constructivist theory posits that learners construct knowledge through experiences and interactions. Innovative assessments align with this theory by promoting active learning and allowing students to demonstrate their understanding in diverse ways.

2. **Multiple Intelligences Theory** Howard Gardner's theory of multiple intelligences recognizes that students possess different types of intelligences, such as linguistic, logical-mathematical, and interpersonal. By diversifying assessment methods, educators can cater to various intelligences, ensuring a more equitable evaluation of student capabilities.

3. **Formative Assessment Theory** Formative assessment theory emphasizes the importance of feedback in the learning process. Research shows that timely and constructive feedback significantly enhances student learning outcomes, making formative assessments a crucial component of effective education.

Challenges and Considerations

While the revolution in assessment methods presents numerous benefits, it also poses challenges that must be addressed:

- **Technology Access:** Not all students have equal access to technology, which can create disparities in assessment opportunities. Educators must ensure that all students have the necessary tools to participate in innovative assessments.
- **Training for Educators:** Teachers require training to effectively implement new assessment methods. Professional development programs must be established to equip educators with the skills and knowledge needed to navigate these changes.
- **Balancing Assessment Types:** A shift towards innovative assessments should not entirely replace traditional methods. A balanced approach that incorporates both types of assessments can provide a comprehensive evaluation of student learning.

Conclusion

Cultural Connector's efforts in revolutionizing assessment methods are paving the way for a more inclusive, engaging, and effective educational landscape. By

FUTURE TECH IN EDUCATION

embracing innovative strategies, educators can foster a deeper understanding of student learning, ultimately preparing them for success in an increasingly complex world. As we look to the future, it is essential to continue exploring and refining these assessment methods to ensure that all students have the opportunity to thrive.

$$\text{Learning Outcome} = f(\text{Engagement, Feedback, Personalization}) \qquad (22)$$

Adapting to the Rapid Pace of Technological Advancements

The rapid pace of technological advancements presents both opportunities and challenges for educators, students, and educational institutions. In this section, we explore how Cultural Connector has adapted to these changes, ensuring that learning environments remain relevant and effective in the face of continuous innovation.

Understanding the Landscape of Technological Change

The landscape of technology is characterized by exponential growth, often described by Moore's Law, which posits that the number of transistors on a microchip doubles approximately every two years, leading to increased computational power and decreasing costs. This rapid advancement necessitates a flexible and dynamic approach to education.

$$\text{Performance} \propto (\text{Transistor Count})^2 \qquad (23)$$

This equation highlights the relationship between the growth of transistor count and overall performance, which in turn influences the capabilities of educational technologies. As new tools and platforms emerge, educators must be equipped to integrate them into their curricula effectively.

The Challenges of Keeping Pace

Adapting to technological advancements is not without its challenges. Educators often face difficulties in:

- **Professional Development:** Continuous training is essential for educators to remain proficient in new technologies. However, many institutions struggle to provide adequate resources and time for professional development.

- **Curriculum Relevance:** As technology evolves, curricula can quickly become outdated. This necessitates a regular review and update of educational content to ensure it aligns with current technological capabilities and societal needs.
- **Resource Allocation:** Many schools and educational institutions face budget constraints that limit their ability to invest in the latest technologies, creating disparities in access to educational resources.

Strategies for Adaptation

Cultural Connector has implemented several strategies to help educators and students adapt to the rapid pace of technological advancements:

- **Agile Curriculum Development:** By adopting an agile approach to curriculum development, Cultural Connector enables educators to make iterative changes based on the latest technological trends and student feedback. This flexibility ensures that educational content remains relevant and engaging.
- **Collaborative Learning Environments:** Utilizing online platforms for collaborative learning allows students to engage with peers globally, enhancing their learning experience and exposing them to diverse perspectives. For example, Cultural Connector's virtual classrooms facilitate real-time collaboration on projects, allowing students to leverage technology to enhance their learning outcomes.
- **Partnerships with Tech Companies:** Collaborating with technology companies enables educational institutions to gain early access to new tools and resources. These partnerships can also provide training and support for educators, ensuring they are well-equipped to integrate new technologies into their teaching practices.

Case Studies

Several case studies illustrate how Cultural Connector has successfully adapted to technological advancements:

- **Case Study 1: Virtual Reality in History Education**
  In a pilot program, Cultural Connector introduced virtual reality (VR) experiences in history classes. Students explored ancient civilizations

through immersive VR simulations, enhancing their understanding and engagement. Feedback indicated a 40% increase in student interest in historical topics, demonstrating the effectiveness of adapting to new technologies.

- **Case Study 2: Gamification in Mathematics**
  By integrating gamification into mathematics lessons, Cultural Connector transformed traditional learning methods. Students participated in interactive math challenges that adapted to their skill levels, resulting in a 30% improvement in overall math scores among participants.

The Role of Artificial Intelligence

Artificial intelligence (AI) plays a crucial role in adapting to technological advancements. AI can personalize learning experiences, analyze student performance data, and provide real-time feedback. For instance, Cultural Connector employs AI-driven analytics to identify students' strengths and weaknesses, allowing educators to tailor their instruction accordingly.

Preparing for Future Changes

To remain effective in the face of ongoing technological advancements, Cultural Connector emphasizes the importance of fostering a growth mindset among educators and students. This mindset encourages continuous learning, adaptability, and resilience in navigating the ever-changing technological landscape.

In conclusion, adapting to the rapid pace of technological advancements is essential for the future of education. Through innovative strategies, collaborative efforts, and the integration of cutting-edge technologies, Cultural Connector empowers educators and students to thrive in an increasingly digital world. The journey of adaptation is ongoing, and with a commitment to embracing change, the future of education can be bright and transformative.

Creating Equitable Opportunities for All Students

In the context of modern education, creating equitable opportunities for all students is a critical imperative that addresses systemic disparities and promotes inclusivity. This subsection explores the theoretical frameworks, challenges, and practical examples of how the Cultural Connector platform aims to bridge the equity gap in education.

Theoretical Frameworks

Equity in education is grounded in several key theoretical frameworks, including:

- **Social Justice Theory:** This framework emphasizes fairness and equality, advocating for the redistribution of resources to ensure that marginalized groups receive the support they need to succeed. This theory aligns with the principles of the Cultural Connector, which seeks to provide all students, regardless of their background, with access to high-quality educational resources.

- **Universal Design for Learning (UDL):** UDL promotes the idea that education should be accessible to all learners by providing multiple means of engagement, representation, and action. The Cultural Connector incorporates UDL principles to create content that is adaptable to diverse learning needs.

- **Critical Pedagogy:** This approach encourages educators to question the status quo and empower students to become active participants in their learning. By fostering a culture of inquiry and dialogue, Cultural Connector encourages students to engage with content that reflects their identities and experiences.

Challenges to Equity in Education

Despite the theoretical frameworks advocating for equitable education, several challenges persist:

- **Socioeconomic Disparities:** Students from low-income families often face barriers such as limited access to technology, inadequate learning environments, and fewer educational opportunities. According to the National Center for Education Statistics, students from low-income households are less likely to have access to advanced coursework or extracurricular activities that enhance their educational experience.

- **Cultural and Linguistic Barriers:** English Language Learners (ELLs) and students from diverse cultural backgrounds may struggle to engage with curricula that do not reflect their experiences. This disconnect can hinder their academic performance and sense of belonging in school.

- **Implicit Bias in Education:** Research has shown that implicit biases among educators can lead to lower expectations for students from marginalized backgrounds, affecting their academic outcomes. A study by the American Psychological Association found that teachers may unconsciously favor students who share their racial or socioeconomic backgrounds, perpetuating inequities.

Practical Examples of Creating Equitable Opportunities

The Cultural Connector platform employs various strategies to address these challenges and create equitable opportunities for all students:

- **Access to Resources:** Cultural Connector provides free access to a wealth of educational materials, including interactive lessons, videos, and assessments. By removing financial barriers, the platform ensures that all students can engage with high-quality content, regardless of their socioeconomic status.

- **Multilingual Support:** To accommodate ELLs and culturally diverse students, Cultural Connector offers resources in multiple languages and culturally relevant content. This approach not only enhances comprehension but also fosters a sense of belonging for students from various backgrounds.

- **Professional Development for Educators:** Cultural Connector invests in training programs for educators to raise awareness of implicit bias and equip them with strategies to create inclusive classrooms. By fostering a culturally responsive teaching environment, educators can better support the diverse needs of their students.

- **Community Partnerships:** Collaborating with local organizations and community leaders allows Cultural Connector to reach underserved populations. By leveraging community resources, the platform can provide additional support, mentorship, and enrichment opportunities to students who need them most.

- **Data-Driven Decision Making:** Cultural Connector utilizes data analytics to identify gaps in student performance and engagement. By analyzing usage patterns and outcomes, the platform can adapt its offerings to better meet the needs of all learners, ensuring that interventions are targeted and effective.

Conclusion

Creating equitable opportunities for all students is not merely an educational goal; it is a societal imperative. The Cultural Connector platform exemplifies how technology can be harnessed to dismantle barriers and foster inclusivity in education. By addressing the challenges of socioeconomic disparities, cultural barriers, and implicit bias, Cultural Connector is paving the way for a future where every student, regardless of their background, has the opportunity to succeed.

Through ongoing commitment to equity, innovation, and community engagement, we can envision a world where education is a powerful equalizer, empowering all students to thrive in an increasingly complex and interconnected society.

Addressing the Digital Divide

The digital divide refers to the gap between individuals who have access to modern information and communication technology (ICT) and those who do not. This divide can manifest in various forms, including differences in access to the internet, digital literacy skills, and the ability to use technology effectively. Addressing the digital divide is crucial for ensuring equitable educational opportunities, fostering social inclusion, and promoting economic growth.

Theoretical Framework

The concept of the digital divide can be analyzed through several theoretical lenses, including the Social Capital Theory and the Capability Approach.

Social Capital Theory posits that social networks, relationships, and norms facilitate cooperation and access to resources. In the context of the digital divide, individuals with higher social capital are more likely to have access to technology and the internet, as they can leverage their networks to gain information and resources. Conversely, those with limited social capital may struggle to access these technologies, further entrenching their disadvantage.

Capability Approach, developed by Amartya Sen, emphasizes the importance of individuals' capabilities to achieve desired outcomes. In this context, access to digital technology is not merely about having physical devices or internet connectivity; it is also about the ability to utilize these tools effectively to enhance one's quality of life, including education, employment, and social participation.

Challenges of the Digital Divide

Several challenges contribute to the persistence of the digital divide:

- **Economic Barriers:** The cost of devices and internet services remains a significant barrier for many individuals and families. According to a report by the Pew Research Center, approximately 30% of low-income households lack a reliable internet connection, which directly impacts their ability to engage in online learning and access educational resources.

- **Geographical Disparities:** Rural and remote areas often suffer from inadequate infrastructure, resulting in limited access to high-speed internet. The Federal Communications Commission (FCC) reported that as of 2020, 14 million Americans lack access to broadband, with a disproportionate number residing in rural areas.

- **Digital Literacy:** Even when access to technology is available, a lack of digital literacy can hinder effective utilization. Research from the International Telecommunication Union (ITU) indicates that 57% of people in developing countries do not possess the necessary skills to navigate the digital landscape, which limits their ability to benefit from online educational resources.

- **Cultural Factors:** Cultural attitudes towards technology can also contribute to the digital divide. In some communities, skepticism towards digital tools and platforms may prevent individuals from fully engaging with technology, thereby limiting their opportunities for learning and social connection.

Examples of Addressing the Digital Divide

Several initiatives have been implemented globally to address the digital divide, with varying degrees of success:

- **Community Internet Programs:** In many urban and rural areas, community organizations have launched initiatives to provide free or low-cost internet access. For example, the *EveryoneOn* initiative in the United States aims to connect low-income families to affordable internet service and digital literacy training.

- **Government Policies:** Governments worldwide are recognizing the importance of bridging the digital divide. In 2021, the Biden administration announced the *Emergency Broadband Benefit*, a program designed to help low-income households pay for internet service during the COVID-19 pandemic.

- **Public-Private Partnerships:** Collaborations between technology companies and educational institutions have emerged to provide resources and training. For instance, Google has partnered with various organizations to offer free online courses aimed at improving digital skills among underserved populations.

- **Mobile Technology:** The proliferation of smartphones has provided new opportunities for bridging the digital divide. In many developing countries, mobile devices serve as the primary means of internet access. Programs like *M-Pesa* in Kenya have demonstrated how mobile technology can enhance access to financial services and educational resources, empowering individuals in underserved communities.

Conclusion

Addressing the digital divide is a multifaceted challenge that requires a comprehensive approach involving various stakeholders, including governments, non-profit organizations, and the private sector. By recognizing the theoretical underpinnings of the digital divide and implementing targeted interventions, we can work towards creating a more equitable society where all individuals have the opportunity to thrive in the digital age. As Riley Dubois envisions a future where technology serves as a bridge rather than a barrier, it is imperative that we prioritize efforts to close the digital divide and empower individuals with the tools they need to succeed.

$$\text{Digital Inclusion} = \frac{\text{Access} + \text{Skills} + \text{Usage}}{\text{Barriers}} \qquad (24)$$

This equation emphasizes that digital inclusion is a function of access, skills, and usage, all divided by the barriers that individuals face. By systematically addressing these components, we can foster a more inclusive digital landscape that benefits everyone.

Ethical Considerations for Tech in Education

The integration of technology in education has revolutionized the learning landscape, offering unprecedented opportunities for enhancing educational outcomes. However, this rapid advancement also raises significant ethical considerations that educators, policymakers, and technologists must address to ensure that technology serves the best interests of all students.

Data Privacy and Security

One of the foremost ethical concerns in educational technology is the protection of student data. As schools increasingly adopt digital platforms, they collect vast amounts of personal information, including academic performance, behavioral data, and even biometric information. According to the Family Educational Rights and Privacy Act (FERPA), educational institutions must safeguard students' privacy and ensure that data is not misused.

$$\text{Privacy Risk} = \frac{\text{Number of Data Breaches}}{\text{Total Data Collected}} \qquad (25)$$

This equation highlights the importance of minimizing data breaches relative to the amount of data collected. A high privacy risk indicates a need for more stringent data protection measures.

Equity and Access

The digital divide remains a pressing ethical issue in education. While technology has the potential to enhance learning, it can also exacerbate existing inequalities. Students from low-income families may lack access to necessary devices or reliable internet, creating a disparity in educational opportunities.

Research by the Pew Research Center indicates that approximately 15% of U.S. households with school-age children do not have internet access. This gap can lead to significant differences in academic performance and engagement, as students without access are unable to participate fully in digital learning environments.

Bias in Educational Algorithms

As educational institutions increasingly rely on algorithms to personalize learning, there is a risk of perpetuating biases present in the data used to train these systems. For example, if an algorithm is trained on historical data that reflects systemic inequalities, it may inadvertently disadvantage certain groups of students.

$$\text{Bias} = \frac{\text{Number of Biased Outcomes}}{\text{Total Outcomes}} \qquad (26)$$

This equation illustrates how bias can be quantified, emphasizing the need for transparency and fairness in the development of educational technologies.

Ethical Use of Artificial Intelligence

The use of artificial intelligence (AI) in education presents both opportunities and challenges. While AI can provide personalized learning experiences, it also raises ethical questions regarding autonomy and agency. For instance, if students become overly reliant on AI-driven tools, they may lose critical thinking and problem-solving skills.

Furthermore, the use of AI in assessment can lead to ethical dilemmas. Automated grading systems may not accurately reflect a student's understanding or creativity, leading to potential misinterpretations of their abilities.

Informed Consent and Student Autonomy

Informed consent is a fundamental ethical principle that must be upheld in educational technology. Students and their guardians should be fully aware of how their data will be used and the implications of using specific technologies.

Educational institutions must ensure that consent forms are clear and accessible, avoiding technical jargon that may confuse parents and students. Moreover, students should be empowered to make choices about their learning experiences, fostering a sense of agency in their educational journey.

The Role of Educators in Ethical Technology Integration

Educators play a crucial role in navigating the ethical landscape of technology in education. They must be equipped with the knowledge and skills to critically assess the tools they use and advocate for practices that prioritize student well-being.

Professional development programs should include training on ethical considerations in technology use, enabling educators to make informed decisions that align with their values and the best interests of their students.

Conclusion

In conclusion, while technology holds the potential to transform education positively, it is imperative to address the ethical considerations that accompany its integration. By prioritizing data privacy, equity, bias mitigation, informed consent, and the role of educators, we can create a more inclusive and ethical educational environment that benefits all students.

The future of educational technology depends not only on innovation but also on our commitment to ethical principles that safeguard the rights and dignity of every learner.

Bibliography

[1] U.S. Department of Education. (n.d.). Family Educational Rights and Privacy Act (FERPA). Retrieved from https://www2.ed.gov/policy/gen/guid/fpco/ferpa/index.html

[2] Pew Research Center. (2021). Digital Divide Persists Even as Lower-Income Americans Make Gains in Tech Adoption. Retrieved from https://www.pewresearch.org/fact-tank/2021/06/04/digital-divide-persists-even-as-lower-income-americans-make-ga

Preparing Students for Future Careers

In an ever-evolving job market, it is crucial to equip students with the skills and knowledge necessary to thrive in their future careers. The integration of technology in education, particularly through platforms like Cultural Connector, plays a pivotal role in this preparation. This section will explore the methodologies, theories, and practical examples that illustrate how educational innovations are aligning with the demands of the future workforce.

Theoretical Frameworks

To understand how to prepare students for future careers, we can draw upon several educational theories:

- **Constructivist Theory:** This theory posits that learners construct their own understanding and knowledge of the world through experiences and reflecting on those experiences. By engaging students in real-world problem-solving and project-based learning, we can foster critical thinking and adaptability, which are essential skills in the modern workplace.

- **Connectivism:** Proposed by George Siemens and Stephen Downes, connectivism emphasizes the role of social and cultural context in learning. In a digitally connected world, students must learn how to navigate networks, access information, and collaborate with others. Cultural Connector embodies this principle by connecting students from diverse backgrounds, allowing them to share knowledge and perspectives.

- **Experiential Learning:** David Kolb's experiential learning theory suggests that knowledge is created through the transformation of experience. This approach is vital for career preparation, as it encourages students to engage in internships, simulations, and hands-on projects that mimic real-world scenarios.

Key Skills for Future Careers

The future workforce will demand a variety of skills, including:

- **Digital Literacy:** As technology continues to advance, digital literacy becomes increasingly important. Students must be proficient in using digital tools, understanding data privacy, and navigating online platforms. Cultural Connector offers resources and training to enhance students' digital skills, preparing them for tech-centric careers.

- **Critical Thinking and Problem-Solving:** Employers seek individuals who can analyze complex problems and develop innovative solutions. By incorporating project-based learning into the curriculum, students can practice these skills in a collaborative environment, reflecting real workplace dynamics.

- **Collaboration and Communication:** In the global economy, teamwork and effective communication across cultures are essential. Cultural Connector fosters collaboration by connecting students internationally, allowing them to work on projects and engage in dialogue that enhances their interpersonal skills.

- **Adaptability and Lifelong Learning:** The rapid pace of change in technology and job requirements necessitates a mindset of continuous learning. Educators must instill a love for learning and the ability to adapt to new challenges. Platforms that offer ongoing education and training opportunities will be crucial in this regard.

Practical Examples

Several initiatives exemplify how educational innovations are preparing students for future careers:

- **Virtual Internships:** Companies are increasingly offering virtual internships, allowing students to gain experience from anywhere in the world. For instance, Cultural Connector partners with organizations to provide students with remote internship opportunities that align with their career interests, enabling them to build professional networks and gain practical skills.

- **Industry Collaboration:** Educational institutions are collaborating with industries to create curricula that reflect current job market needs. For example, a partnership between a university and a tech company might lead to the development of a course on artificial intelligence, where students work on real projects that address industry challenges.

- **Hackathons and Innovation Challenges:** Events like hackathons encourage students to work in teams to solve real-world problems within a limited timeframe. These events not only foster creativity and teamwork but also provide students with exposure to potential employers who value practical skills and innovative thinking.

Addressing Challenges

While preparing students for future careers, several challenges must be addressed:

- **The Skills Gap:** There is often a disconnect between what students learn and the skills employers require. Continuous feedback from industry partners can help bridge this gap by informing curriculum development.

- **Equity in Access:** Not all students have equal access to technological resources and opportunities. Initiatives aimed at providing underrepresented students with access to technology and mentorship programs are essential to ensure equitable career preparation.

- **Mental Health and Well-Being:** The pressure to succeed in an increasingly competitive job market can impact students' mental health. Educational platforms must prioritize students' well-being by promoting a balanced approach to career preparation that includes support systems and resources for mental health.

Conclusion

Preparing students for future careers requires a multifaceted approach that integrates technology, fosters essential skills, and addresses the challenges of the modern workforce. By leveraging platforms like Cultural Connector, educators can create an environment that not only equips students with the necessary tools for success but also nurtures their growth as adaptable, collaborative, and innovative individuals. As we move forward, it is imperative to embrace the evolving landscape of education and continuously adapt our strategies to meet the demands of the future workforce.

$$\text{Future Career Success} = \text{Skills} + \text{Experience} + \text{Networking} \qquad (27)$$

In summary, the future of work is bright for those who embrace learning, collaboration, and the innovative spirit fostered by platforms like Cultural Connector.

Redefining the Education Landscape

The education landscape is undergoing a profound transformation, driven by the integration of technology and innovative pedagogical approaches. This evolution is characterized by a shift from traditional, one-size-fits-all models of education to more personalized, flexible, and inclusive learning environments. The Cultural Connector platform, spearheaded by Riley Dubois, plays a pivotal role in this redefinition, addressing various challenges and harnessing opportunities to enhance educational outcomes.

Theoretical Frameworks

Several educational theories underpin the changes in the education landscape. Constructivism, as proposed by theorists such as Piaget and Vygotsky, emphasizes the importance of learners constructing their own understanding and knowledge through experiences. This theory advocates for active learning, where students engage in problem-solving and critical thinking activities.

Additionally, the principles of Universal Design for Learning (UDL) highlight the necessity of accommodating diverse learning needs and preferences. UDL posits that educational environments should be designed from the outset to provide multiple means of engagement, representation, and action/expression.

Challenges in Traditional Education

Traditional education systems often struggle with several key issues:
1. **Standardization**: The reliance on standardized testing can lead to a narrow focus on rote memorization rather than critical thinking and creativity. This approach often fails to account for the diverse abilities and interests of students.
2. **Accessibility**: Many students face barriers to accessing quality education, including socioeconomic factors, geographical limitations, and inadequate resources.
3. **Engagement**: The passive learning environment of traditional classrooms can lead to disengagement, particularly among students who thrive in interactive and collaborative settings.
4. **Equity**: Disparities in educational quality and resources can exacerbate existing inequalities, leaving marginalized groups at a disadvantage.

Innovative Solutions and Examples

The Cultural Connector platform addresses these challenges through several innovative strategies:

Personalized Learning Paths Riley Dubois's vision includes the implementation of personalized learning paths, where students can progress at their own pace and explore topics that resonate with their interests. For instance, adaptive learning technologies can analyze a student's performance and tailor the curriculum accordingly. Research shows that personalized learning can lead to improved student engagement and achievement [Smith, 2020].

Collaborative Learning Environments Cultural Connector promotes collaborative learning experiences that connect students from diverse backgrounds. For example, virtual exchange programs allow students to work on projects with peers from different countries, fostering cultural understanding and empathy. This not only enhances social skills but also prepares students for a globalized workforce.

Integration of Technology The use of technology in education has expanded significantly, with tools such as virtual reality (VR) and augmented reality (AR) providing immersive learning experiences. For instance, students can explore historical sites or scientific phenomena in a virtual environment, which enhances their understanding and retention of complex concepts. A study by Johnson et al.

(2021) found that students using VR in science classes scored 30% higher on assessments compared to those in traditional settings.

Focus on Social-Emotional Learning (SEL) Recognizing the importance of social-emotional skills, Cultural Connector integrates SEL into its educational framework. Programs that teach empathy, resilience, and teamwork are essential in preparing students for real-world challenges. Research indicates that SEL programs can lead to improved academic performance and better mental health outcomes [Durlak et al., 2011].

Embracing Lifelong Learning The redefined education landscape emphasizes the importance of lifelong learning. With the rapid pace of technological advancement, continuous education and skill development are crucial. Platforms like Cultural Connector offer resources for adult learners and professionals to upskill and adapt to changing job markets.

Conclusion

The redefinition of the education landscape through the Cultural Connector platform embodies a shift towards more inclusive, engaging, and effective learning experiences. By addressing the challenges of traditional education and leveraging innovative technologies and pedagogical approaches, Riley Dubois is not only transforming how education is delivered but also ensuring that it meets the diverse needs of all learners. As we move forward, the continued evolution of educational practices will be essential in preparing future generations for the complexities of a rapidly changing world.

Bibliography

[Smith, 2020] Smith, J. (2020). *Personalized Learning: A Guide for Engaging Students*. Education Press.

[Durlak et al., 2011] Durlak, J. A., Weissberg, R. P., Dymnicki, A. B., Taylor, R. D., & Schellinger, K. B. (2011). The impact of enhancing students' social and emotional learning: A meta-analysis of school-based universal interventions. *Child Development*, 82(1), 405-432.

[Johnson et al., 2021] Johnson, L., Adams Becker, S., Cummins, M., Estrada, V., & Freeman, A. (2021). *Horizon Report: 2021 Higher Education Edition*. EDUCAUSE.

bibliography

Cultural Connector's Impact on Social Connection

Bridging Cultural Divides

Fostering Understanding and Empathy

In an increasingly interconnected world, fostering understanding and empathy among individuals from diverse backgrounds is paramount. Riley Dubois's Cultural Connector platform serves as a catalyst for this essential human connection, leveraging technology to bridge cultural divides and promote meaningful interactions. This subsection delves into the theoretical underpinnings of empathy, the challenges faced in fostering understanding across cultures, and practical examples of how Cultural Connector addresses these issues.

Theoretical Framework

Empathy, defined as the ability to understand and share the feelings of another, is a cornerstone of social interaction and cohesion. According to [?], empathy involves two key components: cognitive empathy, which is the ability to understand another person's perspective, and affective empathy, which is the ability to share in another's emotional experience. This duality is crucial in fostering understanding across cultural boundaries.

The *Empathy-Altruism Hypothesis* proposed by [?] posits that empathetic concern for others leads to altruistic behavior. This suggests that enhancing empathy can lead to more compassionate actions and a greater willingness to engage with individuals from different backgrounds. Cultural Connector harnesses this potential by creating spaces that encourage users to share their stories and experiences, thereby cultivating empathy through shared narratives.

Challenges in Fostering Understanding

Despite the theoretical benefits of empathy, significant challenges remain in fostering understanding across cultures. These include:

- **Cultural Misunderstandings:** Different cultural norms and values can lead to misinterpretations and conflicts. For example, direct communication may be valued in some cultures, while others may prioritize indirect communication.

- **Stereotypes and Bias:** Preconceived notions about other cultures can hinder genuine understanding. Research by [?] illustrates how implicit biases can influence perceptions and interactions.

- **Digital Divide:** Access to technology is not uniform, which can create disparities in who can engage with platforms like Cultural Connector. This divide can perpetuate existing inequalities and limit the diversity of voices represented.

Cultural Connector's Approach

Cultural Connector addresses these challenges through various initiatives aimed at fostering understanding and empathy:

- **Storytelling Features:** The platform encourages users to share personal stories, which can humanize experiences and break down stereotypes. For instance, a user from a minority background might share their journey, allowing others to see the world through their eyes.

- **Interactive Workshops:** Cultural Connector hosts virtual workshops that bring together individuals from different backgrounds to discuss cultural norms and values. These sessions are designed to promote dialogue and understanding, allowing participants to learn from one another.

- **Empathy Training Modules:** The platform incorporates training modules focused on developing empathy skills. These modules utilize role-playing scenarios and reflective exercises to enhance users' ability to empathize with others.

- **Inclusive Design:** By prioritizing accessibility and inclusivity, Cultural Connector aims to bridge the digital divide. Features such as multilingual support and user-friendly interfaces ensure that diverse populations can engage with the platform.

Examples of Impact

Several case studies illustrate the effectiveness of Cultural Connector in fostering understanding and empathy:

1. **Global Dialogue Initiative:** A series of online discussions facilitated by Cultural Connector brought together young people from various countries to discuss their cultural identities. Participants reported a significant increase in their understanding of others' perspectives, highlighting the power of shared dialogue.

2. **Empathy Through Art:** Cultural Connector partnered with artists to create collaborative art projects that reflect diverse cultural narratives. One project involved artists from different backgrounds creating a mural that symbolizes unity. Participants noted that working together on a shared goal deepened their appreciation for each other's experiences.

3. **Language Exchange Programs:** The platform's language exchange feature connects users who wish to learn each other's languages. This initiative not only improves language skills but also fosters relationships that transcend cultural barriers. Users have reported forming lasting friendships through these exchanges, which have enriched their understanding of different cultures.

Conclusion

Fostering understanding and empathy is essential in a world marked by cultural diversity and technological advancement. Riley Dubois's Cultural Connector platform exemplifies how technology can be harnessed to bridge cultural divides and promote meaningful connections. By addressing the challenges of cultural misunderstandings, stereotypes, and the digital divide, and by implementing innovative solutions, Cultural Connector is paving the way for a more empathetic and understanding society. As users engage with diverse narratives and experiences, they cultivate a deeper appreciation for the richness of human diversity, ultimately contributing to a more harmonious global community.

Connecting Individuals from Different Backgrounds

The Cultural Connector platform has emerged as a transformative tool for fostering connections among individuals from diverse backgrounds. In an increasingly globalized world, the importance of understanding and appreciating cultural differences cannot be overstated. This subsection explores how Cultural Connector bridges gaps between individuals, encourages dialogue, and nurtures empathy across cultural divides.

Theoretical Framework

To understand the impact of Cultural Connector on connecting individuals from different backgrounds, we can draw upon the Intercultural Communication Theory, which posits that effective communication among individuals from diverse cultural backgrounds is essential for fostering mutual understanding and respect. According to Gudykunst (2004), the Anxiety/Uncertainty Management (AUM) theory suggests that individuals experience anxiety and uncertainty when interacting with people from different cultures. Cultural Connector aims to reduce this anxiety by providing a safe and structured environment for interaction.

$$AUM = f(Anxiety, Uncertainty) \qquad (28)$$

Where AUM represents the management of anxiety and uncertainty in intercultural interactions. Cultural Connector addresses these factors through its design, which promotes familiarity and comfort among users.

Addressing Barriers to Connection

Despite the potential for meaningful connections, individuals often face barriers when attempting to engage with those from different backgrounds. These barriers can include language differences, cultural misunderstandings, and preconceived notions or stereotypes. Cultural Connector effectively addresses these challenges through features such as:

- **Multilingual Support:** The platform offers translation tools that allow users to communicate in their preferred languages, facilitating understanding and reducing the language barrier.

- **Cultural Exchange Programs:** Users can participate in cultural exchange initiatives that promote shared experiences, such as virtual tours, cooking classes, and storytelling sessions, enabling them to learn about each other's cultures in an interactive manner.

- **Community Moderation:** Trained moderators help foster respectful dialogue and address any instances of bias or prejudice, ensuring a safe space for all participants.

Case Studies and Examples

Several success stories illustrate the effectiveness of Cultural Connector in connecting individuals from different backgrounds:

- **Global Classroom Initiative:** A program that connects classrooms from different countries, allowing students to collaborate on projects, share cultural traditions, and engage in discussions about global issues. For instance, a classroom in Brazil partnered with a classroom in Japan to explore environmental sustainability, resulting in a deeper understanding of each other's cultural perspectives on the topic.

- **Cultural Storytelling Circles:** These online events bring together individuals from various backgrounds to share personal stories and experiences related to their cultures. Participants often express newfound empathy and understanding after hearing diverse narratives, highlighting the platform's role in humanizing cultural differences.

- **Art and Music Collaborations:** Cultural Connector has facilitated collaborations between artists and musicians from different cultures, leading to innovative projects that blend diverse artistic traditions. For example, a hip-hop artist from the United States collaborated with a traditional folk musician from India to create a fusion album that celebrates their cultural heritage while appealing to a global audience.

Challenges and Considerations

While Cultural Connector has made significant strides in connecting individuals from diverse backgrounds, several challenges remain:

- **Digital Divide:** Access to technology and the internet is not uniform across the globe. Efforts must continue to ensure that individuals from underserved communities can participate in these connections.

- **Cultural Sensitivity:** It is crucial for users to approach intercultural interactions with an open mind and a willingness to learn. Cultural Connector emphasizes educational resources on cultural sensitivity to prepare users for meaningful exchanges.

- **Sustaining Engagement:** Maintaining long-term connections between users can be challenging. Cultural Connector encourages ongoing engagement through follow-up activities and community-building initiatives.

Conclusion

In conclusion, Cultural Connector serves as a powerful platform for connecting individuals from different backgrounds, fostering understanding, empathy, and collaboration. By addressing barriers to connection and promoting intercultural dialogue, it plays a vital role in creating a more inclusive and interconnected world. As we move forward, continued efforts to enhance accessibility, cultural sensitivity, and engagement will further strengthen the impact of Cultural Connector in bridging cultural divides.

Breaking Down Language Barriers

In an increasingly interconnected world, language barriers pose significant challenges to communication, collaboration, and understanding among diverse populations. Riley Dubois, through the Cultural Connector platform, has taken innovative steps to address these barriers, leveraging technology to foster inclusivity and cultural exchange. This section explores the theoretical frameworks, problems associated with language barriers, and practical examples of how Cultural Connector is making strides in this area.

Theoretical Framework

Language is not merely a tool for communication; it shapes our perceptions, influences our interactions, and reflects our cultural identities. According to *Sapir-Whorf Hypothesis*, the structure of a language affects its speakers' worldview and cognition. This theory underscores the importance of language in cultural exchange and highlights the challenges that arise when individuals from different linguistic backgrounds attempt to communicate.

The concept of *linguistic relativity* suggests that language influences thought processes and social interactions. When individuals encounter language barriers, they may struggle to express themselves fully, leading to misunderstandings and missed opportunities for connection. Thus, breaking down these barriers is essential for promoting empathy, understanding, and collaboration among diverse groups.

Identifying the Problems

Language barriers can manifest in various contexts, including education, business, and social interactions. Some common problems associated with language barriers include:

- **Miscommunication:** Differences in language can lead to misinterpretations of messages, resulting in confusion and conflict.

- **Exclusion:** Individuals who do not speak the dominant language may feel marginalized or excluded from social, educational, and professional opportunities.

- **Limited Access to Information:** Language barriers can restrict access to vital information, hindering individuals' ability to participate fully in society.

- **Cultural Misunderstanding:** Language is deeply intertwined with culture; thus, language barriers can prevent the sharing of cultural nuances and perspectives.

Innovative Solutions by Cultural Connector

Cultural Connector has implemented several innovative solutions to address language barriers:

1. **Real-time Translation Technology** Utilizing advanced machine learning algorithms, Cultural Connector offers real-time translation services that allow users to communicate seamlessly across languages. This technology not only translates text but also captures the context and intent behind messages, minimizing the risk of miscommunication. For example, during a virtual conference hosted on the platform, participants from various countries can engage in discussions without the hindrance of language differences, fostering a truly global dialogue.

2. **Collaborative Language Learning** Cultural Connector promotes collaborative language learning through community-driven initiatives. Users can connect with language partners who are native speakers of the language they wish to learn. This peer-to-peer learning model encourages cultural exchange and enhances language acquisition in a supportive environment. For instance, a user in Brazil can connect with a user in Japan to practice Portuguese and Japanese, respectively, while sharing insights about their cultures.

3. **Culturally Relevant Content Creation** To further bridge language gaps, Cultural Connector encourages the creation of culturally relevant content that resonates with diverse audiences. By partnering with local creators and influencers, the platform ensures that content is not only translated but also adapted to reflect

cultural contexts. This approach enhances engagement and fosters a sense of belonging among users from different backgrounds.

4. **Community Engagement Initiatives** Cultural Connector actively engages communities through events that celebrate linguistic diversity. Initiatives such as "Language Exchange Days" bring together individuals from various linguistic backgrounds to share their languages and cultures. These events not only promote language learning but also cultivate friendships and understanding among participants.

Case Studies and Examples

To illustrate the impact of Cultural Connector in breaking down language barriers, consider the following case studies:

Case Study 1: Global Classroom Initiative In a pilot program, Cultural Connector partnered with schools in multiple countries to create a global classroom experience. Students from diverse linguistic backgrounds collaborated on projects using the platform's real-time translation tools. Feedback from educators highlighted an increase in student engagement and a deeper understanding of global perspectives, demonstrating the effectiveness of breaking down language barriers in education.

Case Study 2: Social Justice Campaigns Cultural Connector played a crucial role in mobilizing social justice campaigns that transcended language barriers. By providing translation services for campaign materials and facilitating multilingual discussions, the platform empowered activists from different linguistic backgrounds to collaborate effectively. This initiative amplified marginalized voices and fostered a sense of solidarity among diverse groups advocating for change.

Challenges and Future Directions

Despite the advancements made by Cultural Connector, challenges remain in the quest to break down language barriers. Issues such as dialectical differences, cultural nuances, and the digital divide can hinder effective communication. Moreover, the reliance on technology raises ethical considerations regarding data privacy and the potential for algorithmic bias in translation services.

To address these challenges, Cultural Connector is committed to ongoing research and development. Future initiatives will focus on enhancing the accuracy of translation algorithms, expanding language offerings, and fostering partnerships with linguistic experts to ensure culturally sensitive communication.

Conclusion

Breaking down language barriers is essential for fostering understanding, empathy, and collaboration in an increasingly interconnected world. Through innovative solutions and community engagement, Cultural Connector is making significant strides in this area, empowering individuals to connect across linguistic divides. As we move forward, continued efforts to enhance language accessibility will play a crucial role in shaping a more inclusive and harmonious global society.

Promoting Cultural Exchange and Appreciation

The advent of digital platforms has revolutionized the way individuals interact across cultural boundaries, fostering an environment conducive to cultural exchange and appreciation. Riley Dubois's Cultural Connector plays a pivotal role in this transformation by creating spaces where diverse cultures can share their narratives, traditions, and values. This subsection explores the mechanisms through which Cultural Connector promotes cultural exchange and appreciation, the theoretical underpinnings of these initiatives, the challenges faced, and notable examples of successful cultural interactions facilitated by the platform.

Theoretical Framework

The promotion of cultural exchange can be grounded in several theoretical frameworks, including Cultural Relativism and Intercultural Communication Theory. Cultural Relativism posits that all cultures are of equal value and should be understood based on their own context rather than judged against the standards of another culture. This perspective encourages users of Cultural Connector to engage with diverse cultural practices without bias, fostering mutual respect and understanding.

Intercultural Communication Theory emphasizes the importance of communication in bridging cultural divides. It suggests that effective communication can lead to better understanding and appreciation of cultural differences. The Cultural Connector platform employs various tools—such as language translation features, multimedia storytelling, and user-generated content—to facilitate intercultural dialogue.

Mechanisms of Cultural Exchange

Cultural Connector employs several mechanisms to promote cultural exchange:

- **User-Generated Content:** The platform encourages users to share their cultural experiences, stories, and traditions through blogs, videos, and art. This democratization of content creation allows for a multitude of voices to be heard, enriching the cultural tapestry available to users.

- **Interactive Features:** Cultural Connector incorporates interactive elements such as forums, live discussions, and collaborative projects that enable users from different cultural backgrounds to engage in real-time dialogues. These interactions foster deeper understanding and appreciation of one another's cultures.

- **Cultural Events and Celebrations:** The platform organizes virtual cultural festivals, workshops, and exhibitions that highlight various cultural practices. These events not only showcase diverse cultures but also provide a space for users to participate in cultural activities, such as cooking classes or traditional dance workshops.

- **Educational Resources:** Cultural Connector offers educational materials that explore different cultures, including historical contexts, art forms, and social practices. This educational component empowers users to learn about and appreciate cultures beyond their own.

Challenges in Promoting Cultural Exchange

Despite its success, Cultural Connector faces several challenges in promoting cultural exchange:

- **Cultural Appropriation:** One significant concern is the potential for cultural appropriation, where elements of a culture are adopted without understanding or respect for their significance. Cultural Connector actively addresses this issue by providing guidelines on respectful cultural sharing and encouraging discussions on the ethics of cultural exchange.

- **Digital Divide:** Access to technology remains a barrier for many individuals, particularly in underrepresented communities. Cultural Connector strives to bridge this gap by developing mobile-friendly features and partnering with organizations that provide technology access to marginalized groups.

- **Misinformation and Stereotyping:** The platform must combat misinformation and stereotypes that can arise in online discussions. To address this, Cultural Connector implements moderation tools and promotes media literacy among its users to ensure that cultural representations are accurate and respectful.

Examples of Successful Cultural Exchange

Several successful examples illustrate the effectiveness of Cultural Connector in promoting cultural exchange and appreciation:

- **Global Storytelling Initiatives:** One notable initiative involved a storytelling project where users from various countries shared personal narratives about their cultural traditions. This project not only highlighted the richness of diverse cultures but also fostered empathy among participants, as they discovered shared experiences and values.

- **Cultural Exchange Workshops:** Cultural Connector hosted a series of virtual workshops that brought together artists from different backgrounds to collaborate on a joint art project. Participants learned about each other's techniques and cultural significances, resulting in a unique piece of art that blended various cultural elements, symbolizing unity in diversity.

- **Language Exchange Programs:** The platform initiated language exchange programs that paired users from different linguistic backgrounds. Participants engaged in conversations, helping each other learn new languages while sharing cultural insights, thereby enhancing their appreciation for each other's heritage.

Conclusion

In conclusion, Riley Dubois's Cultural Connector exemplifies how digital platforms can promote cultural exchange and appreciation in a globalized world. By leveraging user-generated content, interactive features, and educational resources, the platform fosters a vibrant community where diverse cultures can connect and thrive. While challenges such as cultural appropriation and the digital divide persist, the ongoing efforts to address these issues demonstrate a commitment to respectful and meaningful cultural exchange. As Cultural Connector continues to evolve, it holds the potential to redefine how individuals engage with and appreciate the rich tapestry of human culture.

Cultural Exchange = User Engagement + Respectful Interaction + Education
(29)

Encouraging Meaningful Dialogue

In an increasingly polarized world, the ability to engage in meaningful dialogue is essential for fostering understanding and empathy among individuals from diverse backgrounds. Riley Dubois's Cultural Connector platform has been instrumental in creating spaces where such dialogue can flourish. This section explores the theoretical underpinnings of meaningful dialogue, the challenges faced in its promotion, and the innovative strategies employed by Cultural Connector to encourage genuine conversations.

Theoretical Framework

Meaningful dialogue is rooted in several key theories, including Habermas's theory of communicative action, which posits that dialogue should be aimed at reaching mutual understanding rather than merely exchanging information [?]. According to Habermas, effective communication requires participants to engage in a process of rational discourse, where all voices are valued, and the goal is consensus-building. This aligns with the principles of deliberative democracy, which emphasizes the importance of public reasoning and dialogue in democratic decision-making [?].

Another relevant theory is the dialogical theory of education, which advocates for learning through dialogue rather than through transmission of knowledge. This theory, championed by thinkers such as Paulo Freire, highlights the importance of critical thinking and reflection in dialogue, allowing individuals to challenge assumptions and broaden their perspectives [?].

Challenges to Meaningful Dialogue

Despite the theoretical frameworks supporting meaningful dialogue, several challenges impede its practice in contemporary society:

- **Polarization:** Social media and digital communication often exacerbate divisions, leading to echo chambers where individuals are only exposed to viewpoints that reinforce their own beliefs [?]. This polarization makes it difficult for individuals to engage with opposing perspectives.

BRIDGING CULTURAL DIVIDES

- **Fear of Judgment:** Many individuals fear negative repercussions for sharing their thoughts, leading to self-censorship. This fear can stem from past experiences of ridicule or hostility in discussions about sensitive topics [?].

- **Lack of Skills:** Effective dialogue requires specific skills, such as active listening, empathy, and the ability to articulate thoughts clearly. Unfortunately, many individuals lack these skills, which can lead to misunderstandings and conflict [?].

Strategies for Encouraging Meaningful Dialogue

Cultural Connector employs several innovative strategies to promote meaningful dialogue among its users:

1. Facilitated Discussions Cultural Connector hosts facilitated discussions where trained moderators guide conversations on various topics. These moderators are skilled in creating an inclusive environment, encouraging participants to share their thoughts while ensuring that all voices are heard. This approach aligns with the principles of dialogical education, where the facilitator acts as a guide rather than an authority figure.

2. Interactive Features The platform incorporates interactive features such as polls, Q&A sessions, and breakout discussions that allow users to engage actively with one another. By fostering participation, Cultural Connector creates a sense of community and encourages individuals to express their views in a supportive environment.

3. Storytelling Initiatives Cultural Connector emphasizes the power of storytelling as a means of fostering empathy and understanding. Users are encouraged to share their personal stories, which can humanize complex issues and create connections among participants. This aligns with narrative theory, which posits that stories can bridge divides by allowing individuals to see the world through others' perspectives [?].

4. Educational Resources To address the skills gap, Cultural Connector provides educational resources on effective communication, active listening, and conflict resolution. By equipping users with these essential skills, the platform empowers them to engage in more productive and meaningful dialogues.

5. Diverse Perspectives Cultural Connector actively seeks to include diverse perspectives in its discussions. By inviting individuals from various backgrounds, cultures, and experiences, the platform ensures that conversations are rich and multifaceted. This diversity not only enhances the quality of dialogue but also helps to challenge stereotypes and biases.

Case Study: The Global Dialogue Initiative

One notable example of Cultural Connector's commitment to encouraging meaningful dialogue is the Global Dialogue Initiative, a series of online events designed to connect individuals from different countries and cultures. Participants engage in facilitated discussions around pressing global issues, such as climate change, social justice, and human rights.

The initiative has demonstrated significant success in fostering understanding and empathy among participants. For instance, during a discussion on climate change, participants from developed and developing nations shared their unique experiences and perspectives. This exchange not only highlighted the disparities in how climate change affects different communities but also fostered a sense of solidarity and shared responsibility among participants.

Conclusion

Encouraging meaningful dialogue is a cornerstone of Riley Dubois's vision for Cultural Connector. By employing innovative strategies grounded in theoretical frameworks, the platform not only facilitates conversations but also empowers individuals to engage with one another in a constructive and empathetic manner. As society continues to grapple with polarization and division, the importance of fostering meaningful dialogue cannot be overstated. Cultural Connector stands as a beacon of hope, demonstrating that through dialogue, understanding and connection can flourish.

Challenging Stereotypes and Bias

The digital age has transformed the landscape of communication and interaction, providing a platform for voices that have historically been marginalized. One of the most pressing challenges that Cultural Connector addresses is the pervasive issue of stereotypes and bias that permeate society. Stereotypes—oversimplified and generalized beliefs about a group—can lead to bias, discrimination, and social division. This subsection explores how Cultural Connector actively works to challenge these stereotypes and biases through various initiatives and strategies.

Understanding Stereotypes and Bias

Stereotypes are often formed through cultural narratives that are perpetuated over time, leading to a narrow understanding of diverse identities. According to social identity theory, individuals categorize themselves and others into groups, which can foster in-group favoritism and out-group discrimination [?]. This categorization can lead to the reinforcement of stereotypes, where individuals are judged based on preconceived notions rather than their unique qualities.

Bias, on the other hand, refers to the inclination to favor one group over another, which can manifest in various forms, including implicit bias. Implicit bias operates unconsciously, affecting decisions and behaviors in ways that individuals may not be aware of [?]. This phenomenon can have significant implications in areas such as education, employment, and social interactions, perpetuating inequality and injustice.

The Role of Cultural Connector

Cultural Connector employs a multifaceted approach to challenge stereotypes and biases by fostering understanding, empathy, and dialogue among users from diverse backgrounds. Below are key strategies utilized by Cultural Connector:

- **Promoting Diverse Narratives:** Cultural Connector amplifies the voices of individuals from various backgrounds, showcasing their stories and experiences. By highlighting diverse narratives, the platform helps to dismantle monolithic representations of cultures and identities. For example, campaigns featuring personal stories from LGBTQ+ individuals, people of color, and individuals with disabilities promote a more nuanced understanding of these communities.

- **Encouraging Empathy Through Interaction:** The platform facilitates interactive experiences that allow users to engage with different cultures and perspectives. Virtual reality (VR) experiences, for instance, can immerse users in the lives of individuals from diverse backgrounds, fostering empathy and understanding. Research indicates that VR can enhance empathy by allowing users to experience situations from another person's perspective [?].

- **Educational Resources and Workshops:** Cultural Connector offers educational resources and workshops aimed at raising awareness about stereotypes and bias. These resources include training on recognizing implicit bias, understanding cultural competence, and promoting allyship.

By equipping users with knowledge and tools, the platform empowers them to challenge their own biases and advocate for inclusivity.

- **Creating Safe Spaces for Dialogue:** The platform provides safe spaces for individuals to engage in meaningful conversations about stereotypes and bias. Discussion forums and moderated group chats allow users to share their experiences and perspectives, fostering a sense of community and understanding. Research shows that open dialogue can reduce prejudice and promote acceptance [?].

Case Studies and Examples

Cultural Connector has successfully implemented various initiatives that exemplify its commitment to challenging stereotypes and bias:

1. **The "Voices of Change" Campaign:** In 2022, Cultural Connector launched the "Voices of Change" campaign, which featured stories from individuals who have defied stereotypes in their communities. This campaign highlighted the achievements of women in STEM, immigrants who have contributed to their local economies, and activists fighting for social justice. By sharing these narratives, the campaign aimed to shift public perception and challenge the stereotypes associated with these groups.

2. **The Empathy Project:** The Empathy Project utilized VR technology to create immersive experiences that allowed users to walk in the shoes of individuals from different backgrounds. Participants reported increased empathy and understanding after engaging with the content. For instance, users experienced a day in the life of a refugee, gaining insight into the challenges and triumphs faced by displaced individuals. This project demonstrated the potential of technology to foster empathy and challenge stereotypes.

3. **Workshops on Implicit Bias:** Cultural Connector organized a series of workshops focused on recognizing and addressing implicit bias in various sectors, including education and hiring practices. Participants engaged in activities that revealed their own biases and learned strategies to counteract them. Feedback from attendees indicated that these workshops were instrumental in promoting self-awareness and encouraging proactive measures to challenge stereotypes in their workplaces.

Theoretical Frameworks and Implications

The initiatives of Cultural Connector align with several theoretical frameworks that underscore the importance of challenging stereotypes and bias:

- **Contact Hypothesis:** Proposed by Allport (1954), this theory posits that intergroup contact under appropriate conditions can reduce prejudice. Cultural Connector's emphasis on fostering connections among diverse individuals exemplifies this principle, as users engage with one another and learn from their experiences.

- **Social Learning Theory:** Bandura's social learning theory emphasizes the role of observation in learning behaviors. By showcasing diverse narratives and positive role models, Cultural Connector encourages users to adopt inclusive attitudes and challenge stereotypes within their own communities [?].

- **Critical Race Theory:** This framework highlights the systemic nature of racism and the importance of understanding the intersectionality of identities. Cultural Connector's commitment to amplifying marginalized voices aligns with the principles of critical race theory, as it seeks to address the complexities of identity and challenge the dominant narratives that perpetuate stereotypes.

Conclusion

Challenging stereotypes and bias is a crucial endeavor in fostering a more inclusive and equitable society. Cultural Connector plays a pivotal role in this process by promoting diverse narratives, encouraging empathy, providing educational resources, and creating safe spaces for dialogue. As the platform continues to grow, its commitment to challenging stereotypes and bias will remain integral to its mission of fostering understanding and connection among individuals from all walks of life.

Nurturing Global Citizens

In an increasingly interconnected world, the concept of global citizenship has emerged as a vital framework for understanding our responsibilities towards one another across borders. The Cultural Connector platform, founded by Riley Dubois, plays a pivotal role in nurturing global citizens by fostering empathy, understanding, and active participation in global issues. This subsection explores the theoretical foundations, challenges, and practical examples of nurturing global citizens through digital platforms.

Theoretical Foundations

Global citizenship is rooted in several key theories, including cosmopolitanism, social constructivism, and critical pedagogy. Cosmopolitanism posits that all individuals, regardless of nationality, belong to a single community based on shared morality and mutual respect. This perspective encourages individuals to transcend local identities and embrace a broader sense of belonging.

Social constructivism emphasizes the role of social interactions in shaping our understanding of global issues. It suggests that knowledge is constructed through engagement with diverse perspectives, which is essential for developing a nuanced understanding of global challenges. Critical pedagogy, championed by theorists such as Paulo Freire, advocates for education as a tool for social change, encouraging learners to question the status quo and engage in transformative action.

Challenges in Nurturing Global Citizens

Despite the potential for digital platforms to foster global citizenship, several challenges persist:

- **Digital Divide:** Access to technology remains unequal, with marginalized communities often lacking the resources to participate in global conversations. This divide can reinforce existing inequalities and limit the development of global citizens from underrepresented backgrounds.

- **Cultural Misunderstandings:** Engaging with diverse cultures can lead to misunderstandings and perpetuate stereotypes if not approached with sensitivity and respect. Without proper guidance, individuals may inadvertently reinforce biases rather than challenge them.

- **Information Overload:** The sheer volume of information available online can overwhelm users, making it difficult to discern credible sources and engage meaningfully with global issues. This can lead to apathy or disengagement from important social causes.

Practical Examples of Nurturing Global Citizens

Riley Dubois's Cultural Connector employs various strategies to address these challenges and nurture global citizens:

- **Interactive Learning Modules:** Cultural Connector offers interactive modules that engage users in global issues, such as climate change, social justice, and human rights. By participating in simulations and role-playing exercises, users gain empathy and a deeper understanding of the complexities involved in these issues.

- **Collaborative Projects:** The platform facilitates cross-cultural collaborations where individuals from different backgrounds can work together on projects that address global challenges. For example, a recent initiative brought together students from various countries to create a documentary on climate change impacts in their regions, fostering both awareness and solidarity.

- **Global Citizenship Education:** Cultural Connector partners with educational institutions to integrate global citizenship education into curricula. This approach encourages students to think critically about their roles as global citizens and equips them with the skills to advocate for change.

- **Storytelling Campaigns:** By highlighting personal stories from individuals around the world, Cultural Connector humanizes global issues and fosters empathy. Campaigns that showcase the lived experiences of refugees, climate activists, and marginalized communities encourage users to connect on a personal level and inspire action.

- **Mentorship Programs:** The platform connects young individuals with mentors who are experienced global citizens. These mentorship relationships provide guidance, support, and encouragement for young people to become active participants in their communities and beyond.

Conclusion

Nurturing global citizens is essential for addressing the complex challenges of our time. Through innovative strategies and a commitment to inclusivity, Riley Dubois's Cultural Connector not only fosters understanding and empathy among users but also empowers them to take meaningful action. By overcoming barriers and promoting cross-cultural dialogue, the platform paves the way for a generation of global citizens who are equipped to tackle the pressing issues of our world.

The journey towards nurturing global citizens is ongoing, requiring continuous reflection and adaptation. As the Cultural Connector evolves, its impact on fostering a sense of global responsibility and interconnectedness will undoubtedly shape the future of social engagement and activism.

Celebrating Diversity

The celebration of diversity is a fundamental aspect of cultural connection, and it plays a pivotal role in fostering understanding, empathy, and collaboration among individuals from different backgrounds. In this section, we will explore the significance of celebrating diversity within the framework of Cultural Connector, examining relevant theories, identifying problems, and presenting concrete examples of how this initiative has made an impact.

Theoretical Framework

Diversity can be understood through various theoretical lenses, including social identity theory, multiculturalism, and intersectionality. Social identity theory posits that individuals derive a sense of self from their group memberships, which can include race, ethnicity, gender, and other social categories [?]. This perspective highlights the importance of recognizing and valuing diverse identities as a means to promote inclusivity.

Multiculturalism, on the other hand, advocates for the coexistence of diverse cultures within a society, emphasizing the value of cultural pluralism and the need for equitable representation [?]. Intersectionality, introduced by Kimberlé Crenshaw, further expands this understanding by acknowledging that individuals may belong to multiple social categories simultaneously, leading to unique experiences of privilege and oppression [?].

Problems and Challenges

Despite the theoretical support for celebrating diversity, several challenges persist. One significant issue is the prevalence of stereotypes and biases, which can hinder genuine connections between individuals from different backgrounds. Stereotypes often lead to misinterpretations of behaviors and intentions, reinforcing existing prejudices [?].

Additionally, the lack of representation in various spheres—such as media, politics, and education—can perpetuate feelings of exclusion among marginalized groups. This underrepresentation not only affects individuals' sense of belonging but also limits the richness of perspectives that contribute to societal growth.

Examples of Celebrating Diversity in Cultural Connector

Cultural Connector has implemented several initiatives aimed at celebrating diversity and fostering a sense of belonging. One notable example is the "Cultural Exchange Program," which connects individuals from various cultural backgrounds through shared experiences, such as cooking classes, art workshops, and storytelling sessions. This program encourages participants to share their cultural heritage while learning about others, thus promoting mutual respect and understanding.

Another impactful initiative is the "Voices of Diversity" campaign, which amplifies the stories of individuals from underrepresented communities. By providing a platform for these voices, Cultural Connector challenges stereotypes and encourages dialogue, fostering a deeper appreciation for the complexities of diverse identities.

Moreover, Cultural Connector has leveraged technology to create virtual spaces where individuals can celebrate their cultural backgrounds. For instance, the use of augmented reality (AR) allows users to experience cultural festivals and traditions from around the world, promoting global awareness and appreciation for diversity.

The Role of Education in Celebrating Diversity

Education plays a crucial role in celebrating diversity, as it provides the foundation for understanding and appreciating different cultures. Cultural Connector has developed educational resources that highlight diverse perspectives, including lesson plans, multimedia content, and interactive activities. These resources aim to equip educators with the tools necessary to create inclusive classrooms that celebrate diversity.

Research indicates that inclusive education not only enhances students' academic performance but also fosters social-emotional learning and critical thinking skills [?]. By integrating diverse perspectives into the curriculum, educators can create a more equitable learning environment that prepares students for a multicultural world.

Conclusion

Celebrating diversity is essential for fostering cultural connections and creating a more inclusive society. Through initiatives such as the Cultural Exchange Program and the Voices of Diversity campaign, Cultural Connector exemplifies the power of embracing diverse identities. By addressing the challenges associated with stereotypes and underrepresentation, and by leveraging education as a tool for inclusivity, Cultural Connector is paving the way for a future where diversity is not only acknowledged but celebrated.

Building Bridges in a Divided World

In an era characterized by polarization and division, the role of platforms like Cultural Connector becomes increasingly vital. The ability to build bridges between disparate communities is not only a social imperative but also a necessity for fostering understanding and collaboration in a globalized world. This section explores the theoretical underpinnings, challenges, and practical examples of how Cultural Connector facilitates meaningful connections across cultural divides.

Theoretical Framework

The concept of bridging social capital, as articulated by sociologist Robert Putnam, emphasizes the importance of networks that connect individuals across diverse social groups. Bridging social capital fosters inclusivity and facilitates the exchange of ideas, experiences, and resources. In contrast, bonding social capital refers to the ties within a homogeneous group, which can reinforce division and isolation. Cultural Connector aims to create an environment that enhances bridging social capital through digital interactions.

$$BC = \frac{N_b}{N_t} \quad (30)$$

Where:

- BC = Bridging Capital

- N_b = Number of bridging connections

- N_t = Total number of connections

A higher BC value indicates a greater capacity for bridging social capital, which is essential for addressing societal divides.

Challenges in Building Bridges

Despite the potential for platforms like Cultural Connector to foster connections, several challenges persist:

- **Misinformation and Disinformation:** The digital landscape is rife with false information that can exacerbate divisions. Combatting misinformation requires robust fact-checking mechanisms and media literacy education.

- **Cultural Misunderstandings:** Differences in cultural norms and values can lead to misinterpretations and conflicts. Cultural Connector must prioritize cultural sensitivity and awareness in its initiatives.

- **Echo Chambers:** Social media algorithms often create echo chambers, where users are primarily exposed to perspectives that reinforce their own beliefs. This phenomenon can hinder the development of bridging connections.

Practical Examples

Cultural Connector has implemented several initiatives aimed at bridging divides:

- **Global Dialogue Forums:** These online forums bring together individuals from diverse backgrounds to discuss pressing global issues. By facilitating open dialogue, participants can share their perspectives and foster mutual understanding.

- **Cultural Exchange Programs:** Virtual exchange programs allow users to engage with peers from different cultures through collaborative projects. For instance, a program connecting students from the U.S. and Middle Eastern countries focused on environmental sustainability led to joint projects that addressed local ecological concerns while enhancing cultural appreciation.

- **Storytelling Campaigns:** Cultural Connector encourages users to share their personal narratives through multimedia storytelling. These campaigns highlight the commonalities among individuals from different backgrounds, promoting empathy and understanding.

Case Study: The "Unity in Diversity" Project

One notable example of Cultural Connector's impact is the "Unity in Diversity" project, which aimed to connect youth from conflict-affected regions. The project utilized a series of virtual workshops that focused on storytelling, art, and collaborative problem-solving.

- **Outcomes:** Participants reported increased awareness of cultural differences and a greater appreciation for diverse perspectives. The project successfully created a network of young leaders committed to peacebuilding and community development.
- **Feedback Mechanism:** Continuous feedback was solicited from participants to refine the program. The iterative process allowed for adjustments based on participant needs, enhancing the overall effectiveness of the initiative.

Conclusion

Building bridges in a divided world requires intentional efforts to create spaces for dialogue, understanding, and collaboration. Cultural Connector exemplifies how digital platforms can transcend geographical and cultural boundaries, fostering connections that promote peace and mutual respect. By addressing the challenges of misinformation, cultural misunderstandings, and echo chambers, Cultural Connector can continue to serve as a catalyst for building a more inclusive and interconnected global community.

Ultimately, the success of these initiatives hinges on the commitment of individuals to engage authentically with others, recognizing the shared humanity that binds us all together, despite our differences.

Empowering Individuals to Share Their Stories

In an increasingly interconnected world, the ability for individuals to share their stories has become paramount. The Cultural Connector platform has emerged as a vital tool in this narrative, enabling voices from diverse backgrounds to resonate across the globe. This subsection delves into the importance of storytelling, the challenges faced by individuals in sharing their narratives, and how Cultural Connector addresses these issues.

The Importance of Storytelling

Storytelling is a fundamental aspect of human culture, serving as a means of communication, cultural preservation, and personal expression. According to narrative theory, as posited by scholars such as Mikhail Bakhtin and Jerome Bruner, stories are not just a sequence of events but a way to construct meaning and identity. Bruner (1991) states that "narrative is the primary form by which human beings make sense of their experiences."

Through storytelling, individuals can articulate their unique experiences, fostering empathy and understanding among audiences. This is particularly crucial in a multicultural society where diverse perspectives are often overlooked. By providing a platform for storytelling, Cultural Connector empowers users to share their narratives, thereby promoting social cohesion and cultural appreciation.

Challenges in Sharing Stories

Despite the importance of storytelling, many individuals encounter significant barriers when attempting to share their narratives. These challenges can be categorized into several key areas:

- **Access to Technology:** Not everyone has equal access to the digital tools necessary for sharing stories online. This digital divide can inhibit marginalized groups from participating in the broader narrative landscape.

- **Cultural Sensitivity:** Individuals from different cultural backgrounds may fear misrepresentation or cultural appropriation, leading to reluctance in sharing their stories. This fear can stifle authentic voices and hinder cultural exchange.

- **Language Barriers:** Language differences can pose a significant challenge. Those who are not fluent in the dominant language of a platform may struggle to express their thoughts and experiences effectively.

- **Mental Health Considerations:** Sharing personal stories can be emotionally taxing, especially for individuals who have experienced trauma. The pressure to present a polished narrative can further exacerbate mental health issues.

Cultural Connector's Solutions

Cultural Connector addresses these challenges through a multifaceted approach designed to empower individuals to share their stories effectively:

- **User-Friendly Interface:** The platform features an intuitive interface that simplifies the process of story creation and sharing, making it accessible to users of all technological backgrounds. Tutorials and guides are available to assist users in navigating the platform.

- **Multilingual Support:** By offering multilingual capabilities, Cultural Connector breaks down language barriers, allowing users to share their stories in their native languages. This inclusivity fosters a richer tapestry of narratives and cultural exchange.

- **Cultural Sensitivity Training:** The platform provides resources and training on cultural sensitivity, encouraging users to engage with diverse narratives respectfully and thoughtfully. This training helps to create a supportive environment for sharing stories.

- **Mental Health Resources:** Recognizing the emotional weight of storytelling, Cultural Connector partners with mental health organizations to offer resources and support for users who may struggle with the implications of sharing personal narratives.

Examples of Empowered Storytelling

Numerous success stories illustrate the impact of Cultural Connector on empowering individuals to share their narratives. For instance, a young woman from a rural community in India utilized the platform to share her experiences with education and gender inequality. Her story resonated with audiences globally, sparking discussions on women's rights and inspiring others to advocate for change in their communities.

Another example is a group of refugees who collaborated on Cultural Connector to document their journeys. By sharing their stories, they not only found a sense of community but also raised awareness about the challenges faced by displaced individuals. Their narratives fostered empathy and understanding, challenging stereotypes and misconceptions.

Conclusion

Empowering individuals to share their stories is a crucial aspect of fostering social connection and cultural appreciation. Through its innovative approach, Cultural Connector addresses the barriers that many face in sharing their narratives, creating a platform that champions diversity and inclusivity. As individuals continue to share their stories, they contribute to a richer, more nuanced understanding of the human experience, ultimately shaping a more empathetic and connected world.

$$\text{Empowerment} = \text{Access} + \text{Support} + \text{Community} \tag{31}$$

In this equation, empowerment is achieved through the combination of access to technology, support from the platform and community, and a shared commitment to fostering an inclusive environment for storytelling. As Cultural Connector continues to evolve, its impact on individual empowerment and social connection will undoubtedly grow, ensuring that every voice has the opportunity to be heard.

Revolutionizing Social Media

Creating Safe Spaces Online

In the digital age, the concept of safe spaces online has become increasingly vital as individuals navigate a complex web of social interactions, information sharing, and community building. Safe spaces are environments—whether physical or virtual—where individuals can express themselves freely without fear of judgment, harassment, or discrimination. The emergence of safe spaces online is particularly crucial for marginalized groups, who often face systemic oppression and hostility in broader societal contexts.

Theoretical Framework

The theory of safe spaces is grounded in social justice and inclusive practices. According to [?], safe spaces enable individuals to engage in dialogue about their identities, experiences, and challenges without the pressure of external societal norms. This aligns with the principles of intersectionality, as articulated by [?], which emphasize the importance of recognizing overlapping social identities and the unique experiences that arise from them.

Creating safe spaces online requires an understanding of various psychological and sociological theories, including:

- **Social Identity Theory** [?]: This theory posits that individuals derive a sense of self from their group memberships. Online platforms that foster safe spaces can enhance individuals' social identities by providing a supportive community.

- **Cognitive Dissonance Theory** [?]: This theory suggests that individuals experience discomfort when holding conflicting beliefs or attitudes. Safe spaces can mitigate this discomfort by offering an environment where individuals can explore and reconcile their identities.

Challenges in Creating Safe Spaces Online

Despite the critical need for safe spaces, several challenges hinder their establishment and maintenance:

- **Cyberbullying and Harassment:** Online platforms often serve as breeding grounds for negative behavior. According to a study by [?], approximately 40% of internet users have experienced some form of online harassment. This pervasive issue undermines the creation of safe spaces, as individuals may feel threatened or unwelcome.

- **Trolling and Misinformation:** The rise of anonymous accounts and the spread of misinformation can disrupt discussions within safe spaces. As noted by [?], the presence of trolls can lead to a chilling effect, where individuals refrain from expressing their opinions due to fear of backlash.

- **Platform Policies and Moderation:** The effectiveness of safe spaces is often contingent upon the policies and moderation practices of online platforms. A lack of clear guidelines can result in inconsistent enforcement, leading to confusion and frustration among users [?].

Examples of Successful Safe Spaces Online

Several online platforms and communities have successfully established safe spaces, providing valuable examples for others to follow:

- **Reddit's r/AskWomen:** This subreddit serves as a safe space for women to share experiences and seek advice in a supportive environment. The community guidelines emphasize respect and empathy, fostering a culture of understanding.

- **The Trevor Project:** An organization dedicated to LGBTQ+ youth, The Trevor Project offers online chat and messaging services that provide a safe space for individuals to discuss their challenges and seek support. Their trained counselors create an environment of acceptance and understanding [?].

- **Facebook Groups for Marginalized Communities:** Various Facebook groups cater to specific marginalized groups, providing a platform for members to connect, share resources, and support one another. These groups often implement strict moderation policies to ensure a respectful atmosphere.

Strategies for Creating Safe Spaces Online

To effectively create and maintain safe spaces online, several strategies can be employed:

1. **Establish Clear Guidelines**: Creating a set of community guidelines that explicitly outline acceptable behavior is crucial. These guidelines should promote respect, empathy, and constructive dialogue.

2. **Implement Robust Moderation Practices**: Active moderation is essential to maintain a safe environment. This includes monitoring discussions, addressing conflicts promptly, and removing harmful content or users.

3. **Encourage Positive Interactions**: Promoting positive engagement through community-building activities, such as virtual events or discussions, can help foster a sense of belonging and support.

4. **Utilize Technology for Safety**: Leveraging technology, such as AI-driven moderation tools, can help identify and mitigate harmful behavior in real-time, enhancing the safety of online spaces.

Conclusion

Creating safe spaces online is a multifaceted challenge that requires a deep understanding of social dynamics, effective strategies, and a commitment to inclusivity. As digital interactions continue to evolve, the importance of fostering environments where individuals can express themselves freely and authentically cannot be overstated. By prioritizing the creation of safe spaces, we can empower individuals to share their stories, build connections, and contribute to a more inclusive online landscape.

Combating Cyberbullying and Online Harassment

Cyberbullying and online harassment have become pervasive issues in the digital age, particularly on social media platforms. As Riley Dubois's Cultural Connector seeks to foster positive social connections, it also recognizes the urgent need to combat these harmful behaviors. This subsection explores the theoretical frameworks surrounding cyberbullying, the problems it presents, and innovative strategies employed by Cultural Connector to create safer online spaces.

Theoretical Frameworks

Cyberbullying can be understood through several theoretical lenses, including social learning theory and the ecological systems theory. Social learning theory posits that individuals learn behaviors through observation and imitation. In the context of cyberbullying, users may observe aggressive behavior online and replicate it, believing it to be acceptable. This theory underscores the importance of modeling positive online interactions to counteract negative behaviors.

Ecological systems theory, developed by Urie Bronfenbrenner, emphasizes the multiple layers of influence on individual behavior, from immediate environments to broader societal norms. Cyberbullying can be viewed as a product of interactions within these systems, influenced by peer dynamics, parental guidance, and societal attitudes towards aggression. Understanding these frameworks is crucial for developing comprehensive strategies to combat cyberbullying.

Problems Associated with Cyberbullying

The impact of cyberbullying is profound and multifaceted. Victims often experience psychological distress, leading to anxiety, depression, and in severe cases, suicidal ideation. According to the Cyberbullying Research Center, approximately 20% of students have experienced cyberbullying, with a significant percentage reporting long-lasting effects on their mental health.

Furthermore, the anonymity afforded by the internet exacerbates the problem. Perpetrators may feel emboldened to engage in harmful behavior without fear of immediate repercussions. This anonymity can create a culture of silence among victims, who may feel powerless or ashamed to report incidents. The following equation illustrates the relationship between anonymity (A), aggression (G), and the likelihood of cyberbullying (C):

$$C = f(A, G) \text{ where } C \text{ increases as } A \text{ and } G \text{ increase.}$$

This equation demonstrates that as anonymity and aggression rise, so too does the likelihood of cyberbullying incidents.

Cultural Connector's Strategies

To address these challenges, Cultural Connector employs a multi-faceted approach to combat cyberbullying and online harassment. Key strategies include:

- **Education and Awareness:** Cultural Connector emphasizes the importance of educating users about the impact of cyberbullying. Through interactive campaigns and engaging content, the platform raises awareness about the signs of cyberbullying and encourages users to take action.

- **Safe Spaces:** The platform actively promotes the creation of safe spaces where individuals can express themselves without fear of harassment. This includes moderated forums and community guidelines that foster respectful dialogue.

- **Reporting Mechanisms:** Cultural Connector has integrated user-friendly reporting mechanisms that allow individuals to report incidents of cyberbullying quickly and anonymously. This encourages users to speak out against harassment and seek help.

- **Support Resources:** The platform provides access to mental health resources and support groups for victims of cyberbullying. By connecting users with professional help, Cultural Connector aims to mitigate the psychological effects of online harassment.

- **Community Engagement:** Engaging the community in discussions about cyberbullying is crucial. Cultural Connector hosts webinars and workshops that bring together experts, educators, and users to share experiences and solutions.

Examples of Impact

One notable initiative by Cultural Connector was the "#StandTogether" campaign, which encouraged users to share their stories of overcoming cyberbullying. This campaign not only raised awareness but also fostered a sense of community among participants. The hashtag trended on multiple platforms, garnering thousands of supportive comments and messages.

Additionally, Cultural Connector partnered with schools to implement anti-cyberbullying programs that educate students about responsible online behavior. Feedback from participating schools indicated a significant reduction in reported incidents of cyberbullying, highlighting the effectiveness of proactive education and community involvement.

Conclusion

Combating cyberbullying and online harassment is a critical component of Cultural Connector's mission. By leveraging theoretical frameworks, addressing the root problems, and implementing innovative strategies, the platform is making strides toward creating a safer and more inclusive online environment. As Riley

Dubois envisions a future where technology enhances social connection, the fight against cyberbullying remains a priority, ensuring that all users can engage in meaningful and respectful interactions.

Redefining Digital Identity

In the digital age, the concept of identity has evolved significantly, influenced by the rise of social media, online platforms, and virtual interactions. This transformation has led to a redefinition of what it means to have a digital identity, impacting individuals' self-perception, social interactions, and even their professional opportunities. Riley Dubois's Cultural Connector has played a pivotal role in this evolution, creating spaces where digital identities can be expressed authentically and safely.

Theoretical Framework

The redefinition of digital identity can be understood through several theoretical lenses, including Erving Goffman's concept of *presentation of self* (Goffman, 1959) and Sherry Turkle's ideas on *identity in the age of the internet* (Turkle, 2011). Goffman's theory posits that individuals manage their identities based on the social context, akin to actors performing on a stage. In the digital realm, this performance is amplified, as users curate their online personas through posts, images, and interactions.

Turkle emphasizes the multiplicity of identities that individuals can adopt online, suggesting that the internet allows for a more fluid and dynamic sense of self. This fluidity can empower individuals to explore different facets of their identity, yet it also raises concerns about authenticity and the potential for disconnection from one's true self.

Challenges in Digital Identity Formation

Despite the opportunities for self-expression, several challenges accompany the redefinition of digital identity:

- **Authenticity vs. Performance:** Individuals often grapple with the tension between presenting an authentic self and curating an idealized version of themselves. This can lead to feelings of inadequacy and anxiety, as users compare their lives to the seemingly perfect portrayals of others.

- **Privacy Concerns:** The digital footprint left by individuals can have lasting implications. Issues surrounding data privacy and the permanence of online content can hinder individuals from freely expressing themselves, as they may fear repercussions from employers or society.

- **Cyberbullying and Harassment:** The anonymity afforded by the internet can lead to negative behaviors, such as cyberbullying, which can severely impact an individual's mental health and sense of identity.

- **Digital Divide:** Access to technology and the internet is not uniform across populations. This disparity can create a divide in how different groups experience and express their digital identities, leading to a lack of representation for marginalized communities.

Cultural Connector's Role

Riley Dubois's Cultural Connector seeks to address these challenges by fostering environments that prioritize positive online interactions and authentic self-expression. The platform implements several strategies to redefine digital identity positively:

- **Creating Safe Spaces:** Cultural Connector emphasizes the importance of safety in online interactions. By establishing guidelines and moderation practices, the platform creates environments where individuals can share their identities without fear of harassment or judgment.

- **Encouraging Storytelling:** Users are empowered to share their personal stories, experiences, and cultural backgrounds. This encourages a more nuanced understanding of identity and fosters empathy among users from diverse backgrounds.

- **Promoting Digital Literacy:** The platform provides resources and workshops on digital literacy, helping users understand the implications of their online presence and how to manage their digital identities effectively.

- **Championing Diversity:** Cultural Connector actively promotes diverse voices and perspectives, ensuring that all users feel represented and valued. This not only enhances the richness of the community but also reinforces the idea that multiple identities can coexist and be celebrated.

Examples of Redefined Digital Identities

Numerous examples illustrate how Cultural Connector has successfully redefined digital identity for its users:

- **The Empowered Activist:** A young woman from a marginalized community uses Cultural Connector to share her experiences with social justice issues. By connecting with others who share her passion, she finds a supportive network that amplifies her voice and strengthens her identity as an activist.

- **The Creative Collaborator:** An artist utilizes the platform to showcase her work, engage with other creators, and collaborate on projects. Cultural Connector allows her to redefine her identity not just as an artist but as part of a vibrant community of innovators.

- **The Global Citizen:** A student studying abroad uses Cultural Connector to connect with peers from different cultures. Through shared experiences and discussions, he develops a multifaceted identity that transcends geographical boundaries, embracing his role as a global citizen.

Conclusion

The redefinition of digital identity is a complex and ongoing process that reflects broader societal changes. Cultural Connector, under the visionary leadership of Riley Dubois, is at the forefront of this transformation, fostering environments that empower individuals to explore and express their identities authentically. As technology continues to evolve, so too will the concept of digital identity, necessitating ongoing dialogue and adaptation to ensure that all voices are heard and valued in the digital landscape.

Bibliography

[1] Goffman, E. (1959). *The Presentation of Self in Everyday Life.* Edinburgh: University of Edinburgh Social Sciences Research Centre.

[2] Turkle, S. (2011). *Alone Together: Why We Expect More from Technology and Less from Each Other.* New York: Basic Books.

Promoting Positive Online Interactions

In the digital age, the nature of online interactions has transformed significantly, leading to both opportunities and challenges in how individuals communicate and connect. Promoting positive online interactions is essential to fostering a healthy digital environment. This section explores the theoretical frameworks, prevalent problems, and practical examples of initiatives aimed at enhancing online positivity.

Theoretical Framework

The promotion of positive online interactions can be grounded in several theoretical frameworks, including Social Exchange Theory, Social Capital Theory, and the Theory of Planned Behavior.

Social Exchange Theory posits that human relationships are formed by the use of a subjective cost-benefit analysis and the comparison of alternatives. In the context of online interactions, users weigh the potential rewards (such as social support and information) against the costs (such as time and emotional investment). Therefore, fostering positive interactions can increase perceived rewards, encouraging users to engage more constructively.

Social Capital Theory emphasizes the value of social networks and relationships. Positive online interactions contribute to social capital by enhancing trust and cooperation among users. When individuals engage positively, they build networks that can provide support, resources, and information, ultimately enhancing community resilience.

Theory of Planned Behavior suggests that an individual's intention to engage in a behavior is influenced by their attitudes, subjective norms, and perceived behavioral control. By promoting positive online interactions, platforms can shape users' attitudes towards constructive engagement and create norms that favor kindness and respect.

Problems with Online Interactions

Despite the potential for positive engagement, several problems persist in online interactions:

Cyberbullying remains a significant issue, with studies indicating that approximately 15-20% of students experience bullying online. The anonymity of the internet can embolden negative behaviors, leading to severe emotional and psychological consequences for victims.

Toxicity and Harassment are prevalent in many online communities, often resulting in users feeling unsafe or unwelcome. Research shows that toxic interactions can lead to increased anxiety and depression, as well as decreased participation in online platforms.

Echo Chambers and filter bubbles can exacerbate negativity by isolating users from diverse viewpoints. This phenomenon can lead to polarization, where individuals become entrenched in their beliefs, making constructive dialogue nearly impossible.

Promoting Positive Interactions: Practical Examples

To counteract the negative aspects of online interactions, various initiatives have emerged to promote positivity:

Safe Space Initiatives aim to create environments where users feel secure to express themselves without fear of harassment. For example, platforms like Reddit have implemented moderators and community guidelines to foster respectful discourse. Research indicates that well-moderated communities experience significantly lower levels of toxicity.

Digital Empathy Training programs encourage users to consider the impact of their words before posting. Initiatives like the "Kindness is Key" campaign have successfully raised awareness about the importance of empathy in online interactions, leading to a measurable decrease in negative comments on participating platforms.

Gamification of Positive Interactions has been employed by platforms such as Discord, which reward users for constructive contributions through points and badges. This approach not only incentivizes positive behavior but also fosters a sense of community among users.

Algorithmic Adjustments can also play a role in promoting positive interactions. Social media platforms like Facebook have begun to prioritize content that generates constructive engagement over sensationalist or negative posts. This shift has been shown to enhance the overall tone of discussions and reduce the visibility of harmful content.

Conclusion

Promoting positive online interactions is critical in creating a healthy digital landscape. By understanding the underlying theories, addressing prevalent problems, and implementing effective strategies, we can foster environments that encourage kindness, empathy, and constructive dialogue. As we navigate the complexities of online communication, the collective responsibility to promote positivity becomes increasingly vital for the well-being of individuals and communities alike.

$$\text{Positive Interaction} = \text{Social Capital} + \text{Empathy} - \text{Negativity} \quad (32)$$

This equation illustrates that the presence of social capital and empathy can enhance positive interactions, while negativity detracts from them. By focusing on these elements, we can work towards a more inclusive and supportive online environment.

An Ethical Approach to Data Privacy

In an era where data has become the new currency, the ethical implications surrounding data privacy have emerged as a critical concern for innovators like Riley Dubois and her platform, Cultural Connector. This section explores the theoretical frameworks, challenges, and real-world examples that illustrate the necessity of adopting an ethical approach to data privacy in social media and educational technologies.

Theoretical Frameworks

At the heart of data privacy ethics lies the concept of **informed consent**. According to *Mason's Principles of Information Ethics*, individuals should have the right to control their personal information. This principle emphasizes that users must be adequately informed about how their data will be used, shared, and stored before they agree to provide it.

Additionally, the **Fair Information Practices (FIPs)** provide a foundational framework for ethical data management. These practices include:

- **Transparency:** Organizations must clearly communicate their data collection practices.

- **Purpose Specification:** The purpose for collecting data must be explicitly stated.

- **Data Minimization:** Only the necessary data for the stated purpose should be collected.

- **Use Limitation:** Data should only be used for the purposes agreed upon by the user.

- **Security Safeguards:** Adequate security measures must be in place to protect data.

- **Access and Correction:** Users should have the ability to access their data and correct inaccuracies.

These principles serve as a guideline for ethical data practices and help build trust between users and platforms.

Challenges in Data Privacy

Despite the frameworks available, numerous challenges hinder the implementation of ethical data privacy practices. One significant issue is the **complexity of data policies**. Many users lack the technical understanding to navigate lengthy and convoluted privacy policies, leading to uninformed consent.

Moreover, the rise of **data monetization** poses a dilemma. Companies often prioritize profit over ethical considerations, collecting extensive data to sell to third parties. This practice raises concerns about user autonomy and the potential for exploitation.

Another challenge is the **data breach epidemic**. High-profile breaches, such as the 2017 Equifax breach, which exposed the personal information of over 147 million people, underscore the inadequacy of current security measures. As breaches become more frequent, the question of accountability arises—who is responsible for protecting user data?

Real-World Examples

Innovators like Riley Dubois can draw lessons from both positive and negative examples in the realm of data privacy. A notable case is that of **Apple**, which has made significant strides in prioritizing user privacy. Apple's approach includes features like *Sign in with Apple*, which allows users to create accounts without sharing their email addresses, thereby minimizing data exposure. Furthermore, Apple's transparency reports provide users with insights into how their data is handled, reinforcing trust.

Conversely, the case of **Facebook** illustrates the pitfalls of neglecting ethical data practices. The Cambridge Analytica scandal, where the personal data of millions of users was harvested without consent for political advertising, resulted in public outcry and regulatory scrutiny. This incident exemplifies the consequences of prioritizing data collection over ethical considerations, leading to a significant loss of user trust.

Towards an Ethical Future

To foster an ethical approach to data privacy, platforms like Cultural Connector must prioritize user education. By simplifying privacy policies and providing clear, accessible information about data practices, users can make informed choices. Additionally, implementing robust security measures and adhering to FIPs can help mitigate risks associated with data breaches and unauthorized access.

Furthermore, engaging users in the conversation about data privacy can empower them to take control of their information. This could involve regular surveys and feedback mechanisms to understand user concerns and preferences regarding data usage.

In conclusion, adopting an ethical approach to data privacy is not merely a regulatory obligation but a vital component of building trust and fostering meaningful connections in the digital age. As innovators continue to shape the future of social media and education, prioritizing ethical data practices will be essential in ensuring that technology serves as a tool for empowerment rather than exploitation.

Balancing Freedom of Expression and Responsible Use

The digital age has ushered in unprecedented opportunities for individuals to express themselves freely, transcending geographical boundaries and cultural barriers. However, this freedom comes with the weighty responsibility of ensuring that such expressions do not harm others or promote hate, misinformation, or violence. The challenge of balancing freedom of expression with responsible use is a complex issue that requires a nuanced understanding of both theoretical frameworks and practical implications.

Theoretical Frameworks

At the heart of the discussion on freedom of expression is the philosophical concept of *liberalism*, which posits that individuals should have the autonomy to express their thoughts and opinions without undue interference from authorities. This principle is enshrined in various international human rights documents, including Article 19 of the Universal Declaration of Human Rights, which states:

> *Everyone has the right to freedom of opinion and expression; this right includes freedom to hold opinions without interference and to seek, receive and impart information and ideas through any media and regardless of frontiers.*

However, liberalism must be tempered with the recognition of *social responsibility*, a concept that emphasizes the ethical obligations of individuals and organizations to consider the consequences of their expressions. This duality is echoed in John Stuart Mill's *harm principle*, which asserts that the actions of individuals should only be limited to prevent harm to others.

Mathematically, this can be represented as:

Freedom of Expression = Individual Autonomy − Social Responsibility

Where *Individual Autonomy* represents the unbridled right to express oneself, and *Social Responsibility* accounts for the ethical considerations that may restrict certain expressions.

Current Problems

The advent of social media has amplified the challenges associated with balancing these two principles. Misinformation, hate speech, and cyberbullying are rampant on various platforms, leading to real-world consequences that can harm individuals and communities. For instance, the spread of false information regarding vaccines has contributed to public health crises, illustrating how irresponsible expressions can have dire implications.

Moreover, the algorithms that govern social media platforms often prioritize engagement over accuracy, creating echo chambers where harmful ideologies can flourish. This phenomenon is exacerbated by the *filter bubble* effect, where users are only exposed to information that aligns with their pre-existing beliefs, further entrenching division and misunderstanding.

Examples of Balancing Acts

Several organizations and platforms have attempted to navigate this complex terrain by implementing policies aimed at promoting responsible use while upholding freedom of expression. For example, Twitter has instituted a policy of labeling tweets that contain misinformation, allowing users to make informed decisions about the information they consume while still permitting the original expression.

Similarly, Facebook has developed community standards that outline acceptable behavior, including prohibitions against hate speech and harassment. These guidelines are designed to protect users while still allowing a broad range of opinions to be shared. However, the enforcement of these policies often raises questions about bias and censorship, as users may perceive the removal of their content as an infringement on their rights.

The Role of Education and Media Literacy

To foster a culture of responsible expression, education plays a critical role. Promoting media literacy among users can empower individuals to critically evaluate the information they encounter online. This includes understanding the sources of information, recognizing bias, and distinguishing between fact and opinion. Educational initiatives that encourage open dialogue about the implications of free expression can also help cultivate a sense of responsibility among users.

Incorporating frameworks such as the *Digital Citizenship* model can further enhance understanding of responsible online behavior. This model emphasizes the importance of engaging in ethical communication, respecting diverse perspectives, and understanding the impact of one's digital footprint.

Conclusion

In conclusion, the balance between freedom of expression and responsible use is a delicate one that requires ongoing dialogue and collaboration among individuals, organizations, and policymakers. As we navigate the complexities of the digital landscape, it is imperative that we uphold the principles of autonomy while also recognizing our collective responsibility to foster a safe and inclusive environment for all. By embracing education, ethical guidelines, and critical engagement, we can work towards a future where freedom of expression is celebrated alongside responsible use.

Building Online Communities

Online communities have become an integral part of the digital landscape, serving as virtual spaces where individuals can connect, share experiences, and collaborate. The rise of social media platforms has facilitated the formation of these communities, enabling users to engage with like-minded individuals across geographic boundaries. This section explores the theory behind online community building, the challenges faced, and practical examples of successful community initiatives.

Theoretical Foundations of Online Communities

The concept of online communities is rooted in social identity theory, which posits that individuals derive part of their identity from their group memberships. According to Tajfel and Turner (1979), individuals categorize themselves and others into groups, leading to in-group favoritism and out-group discrimination. Online communities provide a platform for individuals to express their identity through shared interests, values, and goals.

Additionally, the Community of Practice (CoP) framework proposed by Wenger (1998) emphasizes the importance of shared learning and collaboration within a community. CoPs are characterized by mutual engagement, joint enterprise, and shared repertoire, which are essential for fostering a sense of belonging and collective knowledge.

Challenges in Building Online Communities

Despite the potential benefits, building and maintaining online communities presents several challenges:

- **Diversity and Inclusion:** Online communities often struggle with diversity and inclusion, leading to echo chambers where only similar voices are heard. This can stifle creativity and limit the scope of discussions.

- **Moderation and Governance:** Ensuring a safe and respectful environment is crucial for community health. However, the lack of effective moderation can lead to toxic behavior, harassment, and misinformation.

- **Sustaining Engagement:** Keeping community members actively engaged over time is a common challenge. As initial excitement wanes, community managers must find innovative ways to maintain interest and participation.

- **Technological Barriers:** Not all users have equal access to technology or digital literacy skills, which can create disparities in participation and limit community growth.

Successful Examples of Online Communities

Several online communities have successfully navigated these challenges, serving as models for effective community building:

- **Reddit:** Known as "the front page of the internet," Reddit hosts thousands of subreddits, each catering to specific interests. The platform's upvote/downvote system encourages quality content while user moderation helps maintain community standards. Reddit exemplifies how diverse interests can coexist within a larger framework.

- **Meetup:** Meetup.com facilitates the formation of local communities around shared interests, allowing users to organize events and meet in person. This hybrid model of online and offline interaction strengthens connections and fosters a sense of belonging.

- **Discord:** Originally designed for gamers, Discord has evolved into a platform for various communities, enabling real-time communication through text, voice, and video. Its customizable servers allow users to create spaces that reflect their unique identities and interests.

- **Facebook Groups:** Facebook Groups provide a space for people to connect based on shared interests, hobbies, or causes. The platform's features, such as polls and events, encourage interaction and engagement among members, making it easier to build a sense of community.

Strategies for Building Strong Online Communities

To build successful online communities, several strategies can be employed:

- **Establish Clear Guidelines:** Setting clear community guidelines helps create a respectful environment and informs members about acceptable behavior. This can reduce conflicts and promote positive interactions.

- **Foster Engagement:** Community managers should actively engage with members, encouraging participation through discussions, polls, and events. Recognizing and celebrating member contributions can further enhance engagement.

- **Encourage Diversity:** Actively promoting diversity within the community can lead to richer discussions and innovative ideas. This can be achieved by inviting diverse voices and perspectives and creating inclusive spaces for dialogue.

- **Utilize Technology:** Leveraging technology to facilitate communication, such as using chatbots for FAQs or analytics tools to understand member behavior, can enhance the community experience and streamline management.

In conclusion, building online communities requires a thoughtful approach that balances the theoretical foundations of social identity and collaborative learning with practical strategies for engagement and inclusion. By addressing the challenges and leveraging successful examples, community builders can create vibrant, supportive spaces that foster connection and collaboration in the digital age.

Navigating the Influence of Social Media on Mental Health

The rise of social media has transformed the way individuals interact, communicate, and perceive themselves and others. While these platforms offer opportunities for connection and community, they also present significant challenges to mental health. This subsection explores the complex relationship between social media use and mental health, drawing on relevant theories, empirical research, and real-world examples.

Theoretical Frameworks

Several theories provide insight into the influence of social media on mental health. The **Social Comparison Theory** posits that individuals determine their own social and personal worth based on how they stack up against others. Social media platforms, with their curated representations of life, exacerbate this tendency, leading users to engage in upward comparisons. This can result in feelings of inadequacy, anxiety, and depression, particularly among adolescents who are more susceptible to external validation.

Another relevant framework is the **Uses and Gratifications Theory**, which suggests that individuals actively seek out media to fulfill specific needs, such as social interaction, information seeking, or entertainment. While social media can satisfy these needs, it can also lead to compulsive usage patterns, where individuals feel compelled to engage with platforms even when it negatively impacts their mental well-being.

Problems Associated with Social Media Use

1. **Anxiety and Depression:** Numerous studies have linked excessive social media use to increased levels of anxiety and depression. For instance, a study published in *JAMA Psychiatry* found that individuals who spent more than three hours per day on social media were at a higher risk for mental health issues, including anxiety and depression [Twenge et al., 2019]. The constant exposure to idealized images and lifestyles can foster feelings of inadequacy and loneliness.

2. **Cyberbullying:** The anonymity of social media can lead to increased instances of cyberbullying, which is associated with severe mental health consequences. Victims of cyberbullying often experience heightened levels of stress, anxiety, and depression. According to a report by the Pew Research Center, 59% of U.S. teens have been bullied or harassed online, with long-lasting effects on their mental health [Pew Research Center, 2018].

3. **Fear of Missing Out (FOMO):** Social media platforms often induce FOMO, a phenomenon characterized by the anxiety that one is missing out on rewarding experiences that others are having. This can lead to compulsive checking of social media and a cycle of negative emotions. Research indicates that FOMO is strongly correlated with anxiety and depressive symptoms [Przybylski et al., 2013].

4. **Addictive Behaviors:** The design of social media platforms often encourages addictive behaviors. Features such as notifications, likes, and shares create a feedback loop that can lead to excessive use. The **Variable Reward Schedule** used by many platforms can trigger dopamine release, reinforcing the behavior and making it difficult for users to disengage [Kuss & Griffiths, 2017].

Examples of Mental Health Initiatives

Recognizing the impact of social media on mental health, various organizations and platforms have initiated programs to promote healthier usage:

1. **Instagram's Well-Being Features:** Instagram has introduced features aimed at reducing anxiety and promoting mental well-being, such as hiding like counts and providing users with resources for mental health support. These initiatives aim to alleviate the pressure associated with social validation and foster a healthier online environment.

2. **Mental Health Awareness Campaigns:** Campaigns such as #MentalHealthAwarenessMonth encourage open conversations about mental health on social media. These initiatives aim to destigmatize mental health issues and provide users with resources and support networks.

3. **Digital Well-Being Tools:** Many smartphones now include digital well-being tools that allow users to track their social media usage and set limits. These features empower users to take control of their online habits and prioritize their mental health.

Conclusion

Navigating the influence of social media on mental health requires a nuanced understanding of its complexities. While social media can foster connection and provide support, it also poses significant risks to mental well-being. By leveraging theoretical frameworks, recognizing the associated problems, and promoting positive initiatives, individuals and organizations can work towards creating a healthier digital landscape. As we continue to explore the evolving role of social media in our lives, it is essential to prioritize mental health and foster environments that support well-being in the digital age.

Bibliography

[Przybylski et al., 2013] Przybylski, A. K., Murayama, K., DeHaan, C. R., & Gladwell, V. (2013). Fear of missing out: A behavioral addiction. *Computers in Human Behavior*, 29(4), 1841-1848.

[Kuss & Griffiths, 2017] Kuss, D. J., & Griffiths, M. D. (2017). Social networking sites and addiction: A systematic review of the evidence. *International Journal of Mental Health and Addiction*, 15(3), 550-570.

[Pew Research Center, 2018] Pew Research Center. (2018). Teens, Social Media & Technology 2018. Retrieved from https://www.pewinternet.org/2018/05/31/teens-social-media-technology-2018/

[Twenge et al., 2019] Twenge, J. M., Joiner, T. E., Rogers, M. L., & Martin, G. N. (2019). Increases in depressive symptoms, suicide-related outcomes, and suicide rates among U.S. adolescents, 2010-2015. *JAMA Psychiatry*, 76(3), 1-8.

Leveraging Technology for Social Change

In the contemporary landscape, technology serves as a powerful catalyst for social change, enabling individuals and organizations to address systemic issues, mobilize communities, and create impactful movements. This section explores the theoretical frameworks, challenges, and real-world examples of how technology is leveraged to foster social change.

Theoretical Frameworks

Social change theory posits that societal transformation occurs through various mechanisms, including collective action, awareness-raising, and the redistribution of power. One significant framework is the *Diffusion of Innovations Theory*, proposed by Rogers (1962), which outlines how new ideas and technologies spread within and among communities. The theory identifies several stages: knowledge, persuasion, decision, implementation, and confirmation. Each stage is crucial for understanding how technology can be harnessed to promote social change.

Another relevant theory is the *Social Movement Theory*, which emphasizes the role of collective action in challenging social norms and injustices. Social movements often utilize technology to organize, communicate, and mobilize supporters. The advent of social media platforms has transformed traditional movement strategies, allowing for rapid information dissemination and grassroots mobilization.

Challenges in Leveraging Technology

Despite its potential, leveraging technology for social change is fraught with challenges:

1. **Digital Divide:** Access to technology is unevenly distributed, creating disparities in who can participate in digital activism. According to the Pew Research Center (2021), approximately 25% of Americans lack access to high-speed internet, which disproportionately affects marginalized communities.

2. **Misinformation:** The rapid spread of information online can lead to the dissemination of false narratives, undermining social movements. The rise of deepfake technology and manipulated media complicates the landscape, making it difficult for activists to maintain credibility.

3. **Surveillance and Privacy Concerns:** Governments and corporations often monitor online activities, posing risks to activists. The use of surveillance technologies can lead to repression, as seen in various authoritarian regimes where digital dissent is met with crackdowns.

4. **Sustainability:** While online campaigns can gain momentum quickly, maintaining engagement and translating online support into real-world action remains a challenge. Activists must develop strategies to sustain interest and commitment over time.

Examples of Technology for Social Change

Several notable examples illustrate how technology has been effectively leveraged for social change:

1. The Arab Spring The Arab Spring, a series of anti-government protests across the Arab world in 2010-2011, showcased the power of social media in mobilizing citizens. Platforms like Twitter and Facebook allowed activists to organize protests, share information, and document human rights abuses. The hashtag

#Jan25, associated with the Egyptian revolution, became a rallying cry for change, demonstrating the potential of technology to amplify voices and mobilize collective action.

2. **Black Lives Matter**   The Black Lives Matter (BLM) movement exemplifies how technology can be harnessed to address systemic racism and police violence. Following the murder of George Floyd in 2020, social media platforms became essential for organizing protests, sharing educational resources, and amplifying marginalized voices. The hashtag #BlackLivesMatter trended globally, fostering solidarity and raising awareness about racial injustice. The movement also utilized crowdfunding platforms to support legal defenses and community initiatives, showcasing the multifaceted ways technology can drive social change.

3. **Climate Change Activism**   Organizations like Fridays for Future, initiated by Greta Thunberg, have effectively used technology to mobilize youth around climate change. Social media campaigns and online petitions have garnered global attention, leading to mass protests and policy discussions. The movement's use of digital storytelling and visual content has engaged diverse audiences, emphasizing the urgency of climate action.

4. **Online Petitions and Crowdfunding**   Platforms like Change.org and GoFundMe have revolutionized grassroots activism by enabling individuals to create petitions and fundraise for social causes. These platforms empower ordinary citizens to advocate for change, bypassing traditional gatekeepers. For instance, the petition to remove Confederate statues in the United States gained significant traction, illustrating how technology can facilitate democratic participation and amplify collective demands.

Conclusion

Leveraging technology for social change presents both opportunities and challenges. By understanding the theoretical frameworks that underpin social movements and recognizing the obstacles that activists face, we can better appreciate the transformative potential of technology in fostering social justice. As we move forward, it is crucial to address the digital divide, combat misinformation, and ensure the safety of activists in the digital realm. Only then can technology serve as a true ally in the pursuit of a more equitable and just society.

$$\text{Impact} = \frac{\text{Engagement} \times \text{Access}}{\text{Barriers}} \qquad (33)$$

This equation illustrates that the impact of leveraging technology for social change is directly proportional to engagement and access while being inversely proportional to barriers. To maximize impact, efforts must focus on enhancing engagement and access while minimizing barriers.

In summary, the intersection of technology and social change is a dynamic and evolving landscape that holds great promise for the future. By harnessing the power of digital tools and platforms, we can continue to drive meaningful change and create a more inclusive world.

The Future of Social Connection

The future of social connection is poised to undergo transformative changes driven by advancements in technology, shifting societal norms, and the evolving landscape of digital interactions. As we navigate this uncharted territory, it is essential to explore the underlying theories, potential problems, and exemplary models that will shape our understanding of social connection in the years to come.

Theoretical Frameworks

To comprehend the future of social connection, we must consider several theoretical frameworks that have historically informed our understanding of social interactions. One such theory is *Social Capital Theory*, which posits that social networks have value and can be leveraged for individual and collective benefit. According to Bourdieu (1986), social capital comprises the resources available to individuals through their social networks, influencing their ability to access information, support, and opportunities.

$$\text{Social Capital} = \text{Network Size} \times \text{Network Quality} \qquad (34)$$

As digital platforms continue to evolve, the quality and nature of these networks will be critical in determining the effectiveness of social connections. The rise of *Networked Individualism* (Wellman, 2001) highlights a shift from traditional community-based interactions to personalized networks that individuals curate and manage. This shift raises questions about the depth and authenticity of connections made in digital spaces.

Challenges Ahead

Despite the promising potential of digital platforms to foster social connection, several challenges loom on the horizon. One of the most pressing issues is the phenomenon of *Digital Isolation*. While technology has the capacity to connect individuals across vast distances, it can also lead to feelings of loneliness and disconnection. A study by Primack et al. (2017) found a correlation between high social media usage and perceived social isolation, suggesting that increased online interactions do not necessarily equate to meaningful relationships.

Moreover, the rise of *Echo Chambers* and *Filter Bubbles* (Pariser, 2011) complicates the landscape of social connection. These phenomena occur when individuals are exposed primarily to information and perspectives that reinforce their existing beliefs, limiting exposure to diverse viewpoints. This can hinder constructive dialogue and exacerbate societal divisions.

Innovative Solutions

To combat these challenges, innovative solutions must be developed. One promising approach is the integration of *Artificial Intelligence* (AI) in social platforms to facilitate more meaningful interactions. AI can be employed to analyze user preferences and behaviors, curating content that encourages engagement with diverse perspectives and fostering a sense of community.

For example, platforms like *Meetup* utilize algorithms to suggest events and groups based on users' interests, helping individuals connect with like-minded people while also introducing them to new ideas and experiences. This model promotes the formation of *Bridging Social Capital*, which fosters connections between individuals from different backgrounds and experiences.

Case Studies

Several case studies exemplify the future of social connection. The platform *Nextdoor* serves as a hyperlocal social network that connects neighbors, enabling them to share resources, information, and support. By fostering local connections, Nextdoor addresses issues of community engagement and social cohesion, demonstrating the potential for technology to enhance social ties at the neighborhood level.

Similarly, initiatives like *The Empathy Project* leverage digital storytelling to encourage individuals to share their experiences and perspectives. By promoting empathy through narrative, these initiatives aim to bridge cultural divides and foster understanding among diverse populations.

Conclusion

In conclusion, the future of social connection is a complex interplay of technology, theory, and human behavior. As we embrace the opportunities presented by digital platforms, it is imperative to remain vigilant about the challenges they pose. By leveraging innovative solutions and fostering inclusive environments, we can cultivate meaningful social connections that transcend geographical boundaries and cultural divides. The future of social connection holds the promise of a more interconnected, empathetic, and engaged society, where individuals can thrive both online and offline.

References
- Bourdieu, P. (1986). The forms of capital. In J. Richardson (Ed.), *Handbook of Theory and Research for the Sociology of Education* (pp. 241-258). Greenwood. - Pariser, E. (2011). *The Filter Bubble: What the Internet Is Hiding from You.* Penguin Press. - Primack, B. A., Shensa, A., Sidani, J. E., Whaite, E. E., Lin, L., Rosen, D., ... & Colditz, J. (2017). Social Media Use and Perceived Social Isolation Among Young Adults in the U.S. *American Journal of Preventive Medicine*, 53(1), 1-8. - Wellman, B. (2001). Physical Place and Cyberplace: The Rise of Networked Individualism. *International Journal of Urban and Regional Research*, 25(2), 227-252.

The Power of Online Movements

Amplifying Marginalized Voices

In the digital age, the amplification of marginalized voices has become a critical aspect of social justice and equality. The Cultural Connector platform, spearheaded by Riley Dubois, serves as a powerful tool for individuals from underrepresented communities to share their stories, experiences, and perspectives. This subsection explores the theoretical frameworks, challenges, and real-world examples that illustrate the importance of amplifying marginalized voices.

Theoretical Frameworks

The concept of amplifying marginalized voices can be understood through various theoretical lenses, including Critical Theory, Intersectionality, and Social Constructivism.

Critical Theory Critical Theory posits that societal structures perpetuate inequalities and that marginalized groups must be empowered to challenge these structures. The Cultural Connector platform embodies this theory by providing a space where underrepresented individuals can express their realities, thereby challenging dominant narratives and fostering social change.

Intersectionality Intersectionality, coined by Kimberlé Crenshaw, highlights how various forms of identity (such as race, gender, sexuality, and class) intersect to create unique experiences of oppression and privilege. By amplifying marginalized voices, Cultural Connector recognizes and validates these diverse experiences, promoting a more nuanced understanding of social issues.

Social Constructivism Social Constructivism emphasizes the role of social interactions in shaping knowledge and understanding. The platform facilitates dialogue among users from different backgrounds, fostering a community where marginalized voices can influence collective knowledge and cultural narratives.

Challenges in Amplifying Marginalized Voices

Despite the potential of platforms like Cultural Connector, several challenges persist in the effort to amplify marginalized voices:

Access and Digital Divide One of the primary challenges is the digital divide, which refers to the gap between those who have easy access to digital technology and those who do not. Marginalized communities often face barriers such as limited internet access, lack of digital literacy, and economic constraints. These barriers can hinder their ability to participate fully in online platforms.

Tokenism and Misrepresentation Another significant challenge is the risk of tokenism, where marginalized voices are included superficially without genuine engagement or support. This can lead to misrepresentation and the perpetuation of stereotypes. It is crucial for platforms to not only amplify these voices but also ensure that they are represented authentically and respectfully.

Online Harassment and Safety Concerns Individuals from marginalized groups often face heightened risks of online harassment and abuse. The fear of backlash can deter individuals from sharing their stories and engaging in conversations. Cultural Connector must prioritize creating safe spaces where users feel protected and supported.

Real-World Examples

Numerous initiatives and movements illustrate the successful amplification of marginalized voices through digital platforms:

#BlackLivesMatter The #BlackLivesMatter movement is a prime example of how social media can amplify marginalized voices. Originating as a hashtag, it has evolved into a global movement advocating for racial justice and police reform. Through social media, individuals have shared personal stories of racial discrimination, mobilizing support and raising awareness about systemic injustices.

Me Too Movement Similarly, the Me Too movement has utilized digital platforms to amplify the voices of survivors of sexual harassment and assault. By sharing their experiences, individuals have challenged societal norms and demanded accountability from perpetrators. The movement has highlighted the prevalence of sexual violence, particularly against marginalized women, and has sparked critical conversations about consent and power dynamics.

Indigenous Voices on Social Media Indigenous communities have also leveraged social media to amplify their voices and advocate for their rights. Campaigns such as #NoDAPL (No Dakota Access Pipeline) have brought attention to issues affecting Indigenous lands and sovereignty. Through these platforms, Indigenous individuals have shared their stories, cultural practices, and perspectives, fostering greater awareness and solidarity.

Conclusion

Amplifying marginalized voices is essential for fostering social justice and equity in our increasingly interconnected world. The Cultural Connector platform, through its commitment to inclusivity and representation, plays a vital role in this endeavor. By addressing the challenges of access, tokenism, and online safety, and by learning from successful real-world examples, the platform can continue to empower individuals from underrepresented communities to share their stories and shape the cultural landscape. As we move forward, it is imperative to recognize the value of diverse voices in creating a more equitable society.

Harnessing the Power of Online Activism

In the digital age, online activism has emerged as a powerful tool for social change, enabling individuals and groups to mobilize resources, raise awareness, and advocate for various causes. This phenomenon, often referred to as "clicktivism," leverages social media platforms, websites, and other online tools to facilitate collective action. The rise of online activism has transformed traditional methods of protest and advocacy, presenting both opportunities and challenges.

Theoretical Framework

The theoretical underpinnings of online activism can be explored through several lenses, including social movement theory, networked individualism, and the concept of digital citizenship.

Social Movement Theory posits that social movements arise in response to perceived injustices and mobilize individuals around shared grievances. Online activism fits into this framework by providing a platform for individuals to express their concerns, organize protests, and engage in collective action. According to Tilly and Tarrow (2015), social movements are characterized by sustained campaigns of claim-making, where activists use various forms of communication to articulate their demands.

Networked Individualism, introduced by Wellman (2001), emphasizes the shift from traditional, community-based social networks to more individualized, online connections. This shift allows activists to form loose, decentralized networks that can quickly mobilize in response to emerging issues. The ability to connect with like-minded individuals across geographical boundaries enhances the reach and impact of online activism.

Digital Citizenship highlights the responsibilities and rights of individuals in the digital realm. As citizens of the online world, individuals are empowered to engage in activism, participate in discussions, and advocate for change. This concept underscores the importance of digital literacy and ethical engagement in online spaces.

Challenges of Online Activism

Despite its potential, online activism faces several challenges that can hinder its effectiveness:

Information Overload is a significant barrier, as the sheer volume of content shared online can overwhelm individuals, making it difficult to discern credible information from misinformation. This phenomenon can dilute the impact of genuine activism, as users may become desensitized to calls for action.

Digital Divide exacerbates inequalities in online activism. Not all individuals have equal access to the internet or digital tools, which can limit participation and representation in online movements. Marginalized communities may face additional barriers, such as lack of resources or digital literacy, which can hinder their ability to engage in activism effectively.

Slacktivism is another concern, where individuals may feel that signing an online petition or sharing a post constitutes meaningful action, leading to complacency rather than sustained engagement. This phenomenon can create a false sense of accomplishment, diverting attention from the need for more substantial, on-the-ground efforts.

Examples of Successful Online Activism

Numerous examples illustrate the power of online activism in effecting social change:

#BlackLivesMatter is a prominent movement that gained traction through social media platforms, particularly Twitter. The hashtag emerged in response to the killing of Trayvon Martin in 2012 and has since evolved into a global movement advocating for racial justice and police reform. The ability to share experiences, organize protests, and mobilize supporters online has amplified the voices of marginalized communities and brought attention to systemic injustices.

#MeToo is another example of successful online activism, highlighting the prevalence of sexual harassment and assault. Founded by Tarana Burke and popularized by Alyssa Milano, the movement encouraged individuals to share their stories and experiences, creating a powerful collective narrative. The viral nature of the hashtag allowed for widespread awareness and led to significant discussions around accountability in various industries.

Climate Strikes initiated by Greta Thunberg, exemplify the intersection of online activism and environmental advocacy. Thunberg's social media presence galvanized youth around the world to participate in climate strikes, demanding action from governments and institutions. The movement's ability to mobilize millions demonstrates the effectiveness of online platforms in fostering global solidarity for urgent causes.

Conclusion

Harnessing the power of online activism requires a nuanced understanding of its potential and limitations. By leveraging digital tools and platforms, activists can amplify their messages, connect with diverse audiences, and mobilize for change. However, it is crucial to address challenges such as misinformation, the digital divide, and the risk of slacktivism to ensure that online activism translates into meaningful action. As society continues to navigate the complexities of the digital age, the role of online activism will remain pivotal in shaping social movements and advocating for justice.

Bibliography

[Tilly and Tarrow(2015)] Tilly, C., & Tarrow, S. (2015). *Contentious performances.* Cambridge University Press.

[Wellman(2001)] Wellman, B. (2001). The networked community: An introduction. In *Networked sociology* (pp. 1-18). University of Toronto Press.

Promoting Social Justice and Equality

In an era where social media platforms have the power to mobilize individuals and amplify voices, the role of Cultural Connector in promoting social justice and equality is both critical and transformative. This subsection explores how the platform harnesses technology to foster awareness, advocate for marginalized communities, and create a more equitable society.

Theoretical Framework

The promotion of social justice and equality can be grounded in various theoretical frameworks, including Critical Theory and Social Identity Theory. Critical Theory emphasizes the need to challenge societal structures that perpetuate inequality, suggesting that social media can serve as a tool for resistance and empowerment. Meanwhile, Social Identity Theory posits that individuals derive a sense of identity from their group memberships, which can lead to in-group favoritism and out-group discrimination. Cultural Connector addresses these dynamics by creating inclusive spaces that encourage dialogue and understanding across diverse groups.

Identifying Problems

Despite the potential for social media to promote justice, several challenges persist:

- **Echo Chambers:** Social media can reinforce existing beliefs, leading to polarization and a lack of understanding between different groups.

- **Misinformation:** The rapid spread of false information can undermine social justice efforts and perpetuate stereotypes.

- **Digital Divide:** Access to technology remains unequal, hindering the ability of marginalized communities to participate in online advocacy.

- **Tokenism:** There is a risk of organizations engaging in performative allyship rather than committing to substantive change.

Strategies for Promoting Social Justice

Cultural Connector employs several strategies to combat these challenges and promote social justice:

1. **Amplifying Marginalized Voices:** The platform prioritizes giving voice to those often silenced in traditional media. For example, campaigns that highlight the stories of underrepresented communities not only raise awareness but also foster empathy and understanding among users.

2. **Educational Initiatives:** Cultural Connector offers resources and workshops aimed at educating users about social justice issues. By providing access to information and critical discussions, the platform empowers individuals to become advocates for change.

3. **Collaborative Campaigns:** Partnering with organizations focused on social justice, Cultural Connector facilitates campaigns that mobilize users around specific issues, such as racial equality, gender rights, and environmental justice. These campaigns often utilize hashtags and viral challenges to engage broader audiences.

4. **Creating Safe Spaces:** The platform implements features that foster respectful dialogue and protect users from harassment. This includes moderation tools that help maintain a supportive environment for discussions on sensitive topics.

5. **Utilizing Data for Advocacy:** By analyzing user engagement and sentiment, Cultural Connector can identify key issues affecting communities and tailor campaigns accordingly. This data-driven approach ensures that advocacy efforts are relevant and impactful.

Case Studies

Several successful initiatives demonstrate Cultural Connector's commitment to promoting social justice:

- **#VoicesUnheard Campaign:** This campaign featured stories from individuals in marginalized communities, highlighting their experiences and challenges. The campaign went viral, leading to increased awareness and discussions around systemic inequality.

- **Digital Ally Program:** A collaboration with various NGOs, this program trained users on how to effectively advocate for social justice online. Participants learned to identify misinformation, engage in constructive dialogue, and mobilize their networks for action.

- **Community Grants:** Cultural Connector established a grant program to support grassroots organizations working toward social justice. This initiative not only provides financial assistance but also encourages collaboration among community leaders.

Measuring Impact

The impact of Cultural Connector's efforts can be assessed through various metrics:

- **Engagement Rates:** Increased interactions on posts related to social justice indicate growing awareness and interest in these issues.

- **User Feedback:** Surveys and feedback forms allow users to express how the platform has influenced their understanding of social justice topics.

- **Campaign Reach:** Analyzing the reach of specific campaigns provides insight into the effectiveness of messaging and the ability to mobilize users.

Conclusion

Promoting social justice and equality through Cultural Connector is an ongoing journey that requires continuous effort, reflection, and adaptation. By leveraging technology to amplify marginalized voices, educate users, and facilitate meaningful dialogue, Cultural Connector plays a pivotal role in shaping a more just and equitable society. As we move forward, it is essential to remain vigilant against the challenges that arise and to embrace the opportunities that technology presents in the pursuit of social justice.

$$\text{Social Justice Impact} = \frac{\text{Engagement} \times \text{Awareness}}{\text{Barriers}} \tag{35}$$

This equation illustrates that the impact of social justice initiatives can be enhanced by increasing engagement and awareness while simultaneously addressing the barriers that hinder progress.

Mobilizing Global Networks

In an increasingly interconnected world, mobilizing global networks has become a pivotal strategy for social movements, activism, and cultural exchange. The Cultural Connector platform, spearheaded by Riley Dubois, exemplifies how digital tools can facilitate the creation and mobilization of these networks, enabling individuals and communities to unite around shared causes and goals.

Theoretical Framework

The mobilization of global networks can be understood through the lens of social movement theory, particularly the concepts of resource mobilization and networked activism. Resource mobilization theory posits that the success of social movements depends on the availability of resources—financial, human, and informational—and the ability to utilize these resources effectively. Networked activism, on the other hand, emphasizes the role of digital technologies in connecting individuals across geographical boundaries, allowing for rapid dissemination of information and coordination of collective action.

$$R = f(H, F, I) \tag{36}$$

Where:

- R = Resources mobilized

- H = Human resources (volunteers, activists)

- F = Financial resources (funding, donations)

- I = Informational resources (data, communication tools)

This equation illustrates the interdependence of various resource types in mobilizing networks effectively.

Challenges in Mobilizing Global Networks

Despite the potential of digital platforms to connect people, several challenges persist in mobilizing global networks:

- **Digital Divide:** Access to technology remains uneven across different regions, limiting participation from marginalized communities. According to the International Telecommunication Union (ITU), approximately 3.7 billion people still lack internet access, which hinders their ability to engage in global dialogues and movements.

- **Cultural Barriers:** Differences in language, customs, and social norms can create misunderstandings and hinder collaboration among diverse groups. As highlighted by cultural theorist Edward Said, the misrepresentation of cultures can lead to stereotyping and conflict.

- **Misinformation:** The rapid spread of misinformation through social media can undermine the credibility of movements and create divisions among participants. A study by the MIT Media Lab found that false news stories are 70% more likely to be retweeted than true stories, complicating efforts to mobilize support.

- **Security and Privacy Concerns:** Activists often face threats to their safety and privacy, particularly in authoritarian regimes. The use of surveillance technologies can deter individuals from participating in movements, as they fear repercussions for their involvement.

Examples of Successful Mobilization

Despite these challenges, several global movements have successfully mobilized networks to drive change:

- **#MeToo Movement:** Originating in 2006 and gaining momentum in 2017, the #MeToo movement harnessed social media to connect survivors of sexual harassment and assault across the globe. The hashtag became a rallying cry, leading to widespread discussions about consent, accountability, and systemic inequalities. The movement's ability to transcend borders exemplifies the power of global networks in addressing shared issues.

- **Climate Strikes:** Initiated by Greta Thunberg in 2018, the Fridays for Future movement mobilized millions of young people worldwide to advocate for climate action. Utilizing social media platforms, participants organized strikes, shared educational resources, and amplified their demands for policy changes. The movement's global reach demonstrates the effectiveness of digital networks in fostering collective action on pressing issues.

- **Black Lives Matter (BLM):** Founded in 2013, the BLM movement gained international recognition following the murder of George Floyd in 2020. Through social media campaigns, protests, and global solidarity actions, BLM mobilized a diverse coalition of activists advocating for racial justice and police reform. The movement's ability to connect individuals across various contexts highlights the significance of global networks in addressing systemic injustices.

Strategies for Effective Mobilization

To enhance the effectiveness of mobilizing global networks, several strategies can be employed:

- **Building Inclusive Platforms:** Creating accessible digital spaces that accommodate diverse languages and cultural contexts can foster greater participation. Platforms should prioritize user-friendly interfaces and provide resources that cater to various demographics.

- **Fostering Collaboration:** Encouraging partnerships between organizations, activists, and communities can amplify efforts and resources. Cross-sector collaboration can lead to innovative solutions and a stronger collective impact.

- **Utilizing Data Analytics:** Leveraging data analytics tools can help identify trends, measure engagement, and optimize strategies for mobilization. Understanding audience behavior and preferences can inform targeted outreach efforts.

- **Promoting Digital Literacy:** Educating individuals about digital tools, security measures, and critical media consumption can empower them to navigate the online landscape effectively. Initiatives aimed at enhancing digital literacy can bridge the gap for marginalized communities.

- **Prioritizing Safety:** Establishing protocols for protecting the privacy and safety of participants is crucial. Activist organizations should provide resources on digital security and create safe spaces for dialogue and expression.

Conclusion

Mobilizing global networks is essential for addressing complex social issues and fostering meaningful change. By leveraging digital platforms, activists can connect individuals across borders, share experiences, and collaborate on solutions. Despite the challenges that persist, the examples of successful movements demonstrate the transformative potential of global networks in shaping the future of social connection and activism. As Riley Dubois's Cultural Connector continues to innovate and expand, the ability to mobilize these networks will remain a cornerstone of its mission to empower individuals and communities worldwide.

The Role of Technology in Political Activism

The landscape of political activism has undergone a profound transformation due to the advent of technology. From social media platforms to mobile applications, technology has become an indispensable tool for activists seeking to mobilize support, disseminate information, and effect change. This section explores the multifaceted role of technology in political activism, examining its benefits, challenges, and real-world examples.

The Empowerment of the Grassroots

Technology has democratized access to information and communication, empowering grassroots movements across the globe. Social media platforms like Twitter, Facebook, and Instagram have enabled activists to bypass traditional media gatekeepers, allowing them to share their narratives directly with the public. This shift has led to the emergence of decentralized movements, where individuals can organize and mobilize without relying on established political structures.

For example, the Black Lives Matter (BLM) movement gained momentum through social media, where hashtags like #BlackLivesMatter became rallying cries for justice and equality. The movement's ability to quickly mobilize protests and raise awareness about systemic racism exemplifies how technology can amplify grassroots activism.

The Speed of Information Dissemination

The rapid dissemination of information is another critical aspect of technology's role in political activism. In the past, activists relied on print media and word of mouth to spread their messages. Today, a single tweet or post can reach millions within seconds, allowing for real-time updates on protests, rallies, and political developments.

During the Arab Spring, for instance, platforms like Facebook and Twitter were instrumental in organizing protests and sharing information about government crackdowns. Activists used these platforms to coordinate actions and inform the world about the struggles they faced, leading to widespread international support and attention.

Mobilization and Fundraising

Technology has also revolutionized the way activists mobilize supporters and raise funds. Crowdfunding platforms such as GoFundMe and Kickstarter allow individuals to contribute financially to causes they care about, enabling movements to sustain their efforts without relying solely on large donations from wealthy benefactors.

The Women's March, which took place in January 2017, serves as a prime example of successful mobilization through technology. Organizers utilized social media to promote the event, resulting in millions of participants worldwide. Furthermore, the movement raised significant funds through online donations, showcasing how technology can facilitate both mobilization and financial support.

Challenges and Risks

Despite the benefits, the role of technology in political activism is not without challenges. The digital landscape is fraught with risks, including misinformation, online harassment, and surveillance. Activists must navigate a complex environment where their messages can be distorted or weaponized against them.

Misinformation campaigns, often amplified by social media algorithms, can undermine the credibility of movements. For instance, during the COVID-19 pandemic, various conspiracy theories spread rapidly online, leading to confusion and division among the public. Activists must be vigilant in combating misinformation while maintaining their message's integrity.

Moreover, activists face the threat of surveillance from governments and corporations. Digital tools that facilitate communication can also be used to track and monitor individuals involved in political activism. The rise of authoritarian regimes has led to increased scrutiny of online activities, as seen in countries like China and Iran, where dissent is often met with harsh repercussions.

The Future of Technology in Activism

Looking ahead, the role of technology in political activism is likely to evolve further. Emerging technologies such as artificial intelligence (AI) and blockchain hold the potential to enhance activism in various ways. AI can analyze large datasets to identify trends and sentiments, helping activists tailor their strategies more effectively. Blockchain technology can ensure transparency and security in fundraising efforts, providing a trust framework for donors.

However, as technology continues to advance, activists must remain aware of its implications. Ethical considerations surrounding data privacy, algorithmic bias, and the digital divide must be addressed to ensure that technology serves as a tool for empowerment rather than oppression.

Conclusion

In conclusion, technology plays a crucial role in shaping the landscape of political activism. By empowering grassroots movements, facilitating rapid information dissemination, and enabling mobilization and fundraising, technology has transformed the way activists operate. However, challenges such as misinformation and surveillance pose significant risks that must be navigated carefully. As technology continues to evolve, activists must harness its potential while remaining vigilant about its ethical implications, ensuring that it remains a force for positive change in society.

Inspiring Real-World Change

In the digital age, the capacity for online movements to inspire real-world change has become a significant focus for innovators like Riley Dubois and her platform, Cultural Connector. This section delves into the mechanisms through which online activism translates into tangible societal impact, examining both theoretical frameworks and practical examples.

Theoretical Frameworks

Understanding the dynamics of online activism requires a solid theoretical foundation. Two prominent theories in this realm are the **Mobilization Theory** and the **Networked Publics Theory**.

Mobilization Theory posits that social movements are successful when they can effectively mobilize resources, including people, money, and information. According to this theory, online platforms serve as critical tools for mobilization by providing a space for organizing, recruiting, and disseminating information. The equation for successful mobilization can be expressed as:

$$M = R + A + C \qquad (37)$$

where M represents mobilization, R stands for resources, A is for activism, and C denotes communication.

Networked Publics Theory emphasizes the role of social media in creating new forms of public engagement. It suggests that online platforms allow for the formation of *networked publics*, where individuals can connect, share, and engage in discussions that transcend geographical boundaries. This theory highlights the potential for collective action in ways that traditional forms of activism may not achieve.

Challenges in Online Activism

Despite the potential for real-world change, online activism faces several challenges:

- **Fragmentation of Movements:** Online platforms can lead to the fragmentation of movements, where various groups pursue different agendas, diluting the overall impact.

- **Echo Chambers:** Social media algorithms often create echo chambers, where individuals are only exposed to viewpoints that reinforce their beliefs, limiting the potential for broader societal dialogue.

- **Sustainability:** Many online movements struggle to maintain momentum after initial successes, leading to short-lived campaigns that fail to translate into lasting change.

- **Digital Divide:** Access to technology remains a barrier for many, limiting participation in online movements and exacerbating existing inequalities.

Case Studies of Successful Real-World Change

To illustrate the potential of online activism to inspire real-world change, we can examine several case studies that exemplify the effectiveness of Cultural Connector's approach.

BIBLIOGRAPHY

1. The Black Lives Matter Movement The Black Lives Matter (BLM) movement is a prime example of how online activism can lead to significant societal change. Originating from a hashtag on social media, BLM grew into a global movement advocating for racial justice and police reform. Through the use of social media, activists were able to:

- Raise awareness about systemic racism and police brutality.
- Organize protests and rallies across the globe.
- Influence policy changes at local, state, and national levels.

The movement's ability to mobilize large numbers of people and sustain momentum over time demonstrates the power of networked publics in driving real-world change.

2. The Me Too Movement Another significant movement is the Me Too campaign, which highlights the prevalence of sexual harassment and assault. Founded by activist Tarana Burke and popularized by social media, Me Too has:

- Empowered survivors to share their stories, leading to greater awareness of sexual violence.
- Resulted in legislative changes aimed at protecting victims and holding perpetrators accountable.
- Fostered a cultural shift in how society views and addresses issues of consent and harassment.

The Me Too movement exemplifies how online platforms can amplify marginalized voices and inspire collective action for systemic change.

3. Climate Change Activism Climate change activism has also seen a surge in online engagement, particularly among youth. Movements like Fridays for Future, initiated by Greta Thunberg, have utilized social media to:

- Mobilize millions of young people for climate strikes worldwide.
- Pressure governments and corporations to adopt more sustainable practices.
- Foster a global dialogue on the urgency of climate action.

Through the strategic use of digital platforms, these activists have successfully brought climate issues to the forefront of political agendas globally.

Conclusion

The impact of online movements on real-world change is profound, as demonstrated by the successes of BLM, Me Too, and climate activism. While challenges remain, the potential for platforms like Cultural Connector to inspire collective action and drive societal transformation is immense. By leveraging the principles of Mobilization Theory and Networked Publics Theory, innovators can continue to harness the power of technology to create lasting change in communities worldwide.

In summary, inspiring real-world change through online activism is not only possible but essential in our interconnected world. As we move forward, it will be crucial to address the challenges of fragmentation, echo chambers, and sustainability to ensure that online movements can achieve their full potential in effecting real change.

Cultivating a Sense of Agency

In an era where digital platforms dominate communication and social interaction, cultivating a sense of agency among individuals is paramount. Agency, defined as the capacity of individuals to act independently and make their own choices, is crucial for empowerment and social change. This subsection explores the role of Cultural Connector in fostering agency, the theoretical frameworks that support this initiative, the challenges faced, and real-world examples that illustrate its impact.

Theoretical Frameworks

The concept of agency is deeply rooted in various psychological and sociological theories. One significant framework is Bandura's Social Cognitive Theory, which posits that individuals learn and develop a sense of agency through observation, imitation, and modeling. Bandura (1986) emphasizes the importance of self-efficacy—belief in one's ability to succeed in specific situations—as a critical component of agency.

$$\text{Self-efficacy} = \frac{\text{Successes}}{\text{Total Attempts}} \qquad (38)$$

This equation illustrates that as individuals experience success, their self-efficacy increases, reinforcing their sense of agency. Additionally, the Capability Approach, developed by Amartya Sen, highlights the importance of providing individuals with the tools and opportunities to achieve their potential. This approach underscores the need for cultural connectors to create environments that foster agency by expanding access to resources and opportunities.

Challenges to Cultivating Agency

Despite the potential for digital platforms to enhance agency, several challenges must be addressed:

- **Digital Divide:** Access to technology remains uneven, with marginalized communities often lacking the resources necessary to engage fully in digital spaces. This gap can hinder their ability to exercise agency.

- **Information Overload:** The vast amount of information available online can overwhelm individuals, making it difficult for them to discern credible sources and make informed decisions. This can diminish their sense of agency.

- **Algorithmic Bias:** Algorithms that govern social media platforms can perpetuate biases and limit exposure to diverse perspectives, constraining individuals' ability to engage with a broad range of ideas and communities.

Strategies for Cultivating Agency

Cultural Connector employs several strategies to cultivate a sense of agency among users:

- **Empowerment through Education:** By providing educational resources that enhance digital literacy, Cultural Connector enables individuals to navigate online spaces confidently. Workshops and webinars focused on critical thinking and media literacy help users evaluate information effectively.

- **Encouraging Participation:** Cultural Connector fosters a participatory culture by encouraging users to share their stories and engage in discussions. This not only amplifies diverse voices but also reinforces individuals' belief in their ability to influence change.

- **Creating Safe Spaces:** By establishing online communities that prioritize respect and inclusivity, Cultural Connector cultivates environments where individuals feel safe to express their opinions and explore their identities without fear of judgment or harassment.

Real-World Examples

Several initiatives within Cultural Connector exemplify the cultivation of agency:

- **Storytelling Campaigns:** Cultural Connector has launched storytelling campaigns that invite individuals from diverse backgrounds to share their experiences. These campaigns not only empower participants but also foster a sense of community and shared understanding among users.

- **Collaborative Projects:** Initiatives that encourage collaboration among users, such as community art projects or social justice campaigns, allow individuals to take ownership of their contributions. This collaborative spirit enhances their sense of agency and belonging.

- **Mentorship Programs:** By connecting experienced professionals with emerging voices, Cultural Connector facilitates mentorship opportunities that empower individuals to pursue their passions and develop their skills, further reinforcing their agency.

Conclusion

Cultivating a sense of agency is essential for empowering individuals and fostering social change. Cultural Connector plays a pivotal role in this process by providing the tools, resources, and supportive environments necessary for users to exercise their agency. By addressing the challenges associated with digital engagement and implementing effective strategies, Cultural Connector not only enhances individual agency but also contributes to a more equitable and inclusive digital landscape. As we continue to navigate the complexities of the digital age, the importance of agency in shaping a just society cannot be overstated.

Bibliography

[1] Bandura, A. (1986). *Social Foundations of Thought and Action: A Social Cognitive Theory*. Prentice-Hall.

[2] Sen, A. (1999). *Development as Freedom*. Oxford University Press.

The Future of Online Movements

The evolution of online movements has become a defining characteristic of contemporary social activism. As technology continues to advance, the future of these movements will be shaped by various factors, including the integration of new platforms, the role of artificial intelligence, and the increasing importance of digital literacy among participants.

The Role of Technology in Amplifying Voices

Online movements have historically relied on social media platforms to amplify marginalized voices. For instance, the #BlackLivesMatter movement gained traction through Twitter and Instagram, where users shared personal stories, videos, and artwork to highlight systemic racism and police brutality. As we look toward the future, the integration of advanced technologies such as artificial intelligence (AI) and machine learning will play a crucial role in shaping how these movements operate.

AI can analyze vast amounts of data to identify trends and sentiments within social media conversations. This capability allows activists to tailor their messages more effectively and reach wider audiences. For example, algorithms can help identify the most influential users within a network, enabling movements to focus their outreach efforts on those who have the potential to mobilize others.

Challenges of Digital Surveillance

However, the future of online movements is not without challenges. As governments and corporations increasingly monitor digital spaces, issues of privacy and surveillance become paramount. The use of AI for tracking online behavior raises ethical questions about the balance between security and freedom of expression. The chilling effect of surveillance can deter individuals from participating in movements, fearing repercussions for their activism.

A notable example of this concern is the response to the Hong Kong protests, where activists utilized encrypted messaging apps to communicate and organize while evading government surveillance. As technology evolves, so too must the strategies employed by activists to protect their privacy and ensure the safety of their digital communications.

The Importance of Digital Literacy

To navigate these complexities, digital literacy will be essential for participants in future online movements. Understanding how to effectively use technology, recognize misinformation, and advocate for data privacy will empower individuals to engage more meaningfully in activism. Educational initiatives focused on digital literacy can help equip activists with the tools they need to discern credible information from false narratives, ultimately strengthening the integrity of online movements.

Moreover, fostering digital literacy can also promote inclusivity within movements. Many marginalized groups lack access to technology or the skills necessary to engage online effectively. Ensuring equitable access to digital resources will be critical in creating a diverse and representative activist landscape.

The Future of Online Activism: A Hybrid Approach

Looking ahead, the future of online movements may adopt a hybrid approach, combining digital activism with traditional forms of protest. The COVID-19 pandemic demonstrated the potential for virtual gatherings and campaigns, yet it also underscored the importance of in-person actions. Movements may increasingly utilize digital platforms for organization and outreach while mobilizing supporters for physical demonstrations when possible.

For example, the global climate strikes led by youth activists utilized social media to coordinate events and spread awareness, culminating in large-scale protests worldwide. This synergy between online and offline activism can create a more robust and resilient movement, capable of adapting to changing circumstances.

Conclusion: A Dynamic Landscape

In conclusion, the future of online movements will be shaped by technological advancements, ethical considerations, and the ongoing struggle for digital equity. As activists harness the power of AI and social media, they must also remain vigilant against the challenges posed by surveillance and misinformation. By prioritizing digital literacy and fostering inclusive practices, the next generation of online movements can continue to amplify marginalized voices and drive meaningful social change.

The landscape of online activism is dynamic and ever-evolving, reflecting the complexities of our interconnected world. As we move forward, the lessons learned from past movements will inform the strategies employed by future activists, ensuring that the fight for justice and equality remains at the forefront of the digital age.

$$\text{Future Impact} = \text{Technology} \times \text{Digital Literacy} \times \text{Inclusivity} \quad (39)$$

This equation encapsulates the multifaceted nature of online movements, suggesting that their future impact will depend on the interplay between technological advancements, the level of digital literacy among participants, and the inclusivity of the movements themselves.

Ethical Considerations in Online Advocacy

In the age of digital activism, ethical considerations have emerged as a critical aspect of online advocacy. The ease of sharing information and mobilizing support through social media platforms has led to a proliferation of online movements, each with its unique set of ethical dilemmas. This section explores the ethical implications of online advocacy, drawing on relevant theories, potential problems, and illustrative examples.

Theoretical Frameworks

Several ethical theories can be applied to online advocacy, each offering a different lens through which to analyze the actions and motivations of digital activists.

1.1 Utilitarianism Utilitarianism posits that the best action is one that maximizes overall happiness or utility. In the context of online advocacy, this theory raises questions about the outcomes of digital campaigns. For example, a campaign aimed at raising awareness for climate change may gain significant traction online, but if it inadvertently leads to misinformation or division among supporters, the negative consequences may outweigh the intended benefits.

1.2 Deontological Ethics Deontological ethics focuses on the morality of actions themselves rather than their consequences. This framework emphasizes the importance of principles such as honesty, integrity, and respect for individuals. In online advocacy, this could mean ensuring that information shared is accurate and that the privacy of individuals involved in a movement is respected. For instance, sharing personal stories of marginalized individuals without their consent can violate ethical standards, regardless of the campaign's overall goals.

1.3 Virtue Ethics Virtue ethics emphasizes the character and intentions of the individual advocating for a cause. This perspective encourages advocates to reflect on their motivations and the ethical implications of their actions. An advocate who promotes a cause purely for personal gain or recognition, rather than genuine concern, may be seen as lacking the virtues necessary for ethical advocacy.

Ethical Problems in Online Advocacy

While online advocacy has the potential to drive significant social change, it also presents several ethical challenges that need to be addressed.

2.1 Misinformation and Disinformation One of the most pressing ethical issues in online advocacy is the spread of misinformation and disinformation. The rapid sharing of information can lead to the dissemination of false or misleading content, which can undermine the credibility of a movement. For instance, during the Black Lives Matter protests, various false narratives circulated online, which created confusion and detracted from the movement's objectives.

2.2 Privacy Concerns Advocates often share personal stories or sensitive information to garner support for their causes. However, this raises ethical concerns regarding privacy and consent. For example, activists may share stories of individuals affected by systemic injustice without obtaining their explicit consent, potentially exposing them to further harm or backlash.

2.3 Online Harassment and Toxicity The digital landscape can be hostile, with many activists facing online harassment or threats. This toxicity can discourage individuals from participating in advocacy efforts and can disproportionately affect marginalized voices. Ethical considerations must include creating safe spaces for discussion and ensuring that advocates are protected from harm.

2.4 The Ethics of Amplification In online advocacy, the act of amplification—sharing and promoting content from others—can raise ethical dilemmas. Advocates must consider whose voices they are amplifying and whether they are inadvertently sidelining marginalized perspectives. For example, a well-meaning advocate may share content from a prominent figure while neglecting grassroots activists who have been working on the issue for years.

Examples of Ethical Considerations in Action

Several case studies illustrate the ethical challenges faced by online advocates.

3.1 The #MeToo Movement The #MeToo movement highlights the complexities of online advocacy. While it successfully raised awareness about sexual harassment and assault, it also faced criticism for the potential for false accusations and the public shaming of individuals without due process. Advocates within the movement have had to navigate these ethical waters carefully, balancing the need for accountability with respect for individual rights.

3.2 The Ice Bucket Challenge The Ice Bucket Challenge, which aimed to raise funds for ALS research, serves as an example of ethical considerations in advocacy. While it successfully raised millions of dollars, critics pointed out that it often overshadowed the voices of those living with ALS and did not address the underlying issues of healthcare accessibility. This raises questions about the ethics of fundraising methods and the importance of centering the voices of those most affected by the issues at hand.

Conclusion

As online advocacy continues to evolve, ethical considerations must remain at the forefront of discussions surrounding digital activism. Advocates should strive to adhere to ethical principles that prioritize accuracy, respect for individuals, and the amplification of diverse voices. By doing so, they can foster a more inclusive and effective online advocacy landscape that drives meaningful social change.

In summary, the ethical landscape of online advocacy is complex and multifaceted. By engaging with various ethical theories and addressing the potential problems inherent in digital activism, advocates can navigate this terrain more effectively. Ultimately, the goal of online advocacy should be to create a just and equitable society, where the voices of all individuals are heard and respected.

Shaping the Social Landscape

The advent of the digital age has significantly transformed the social landscape, altering the way individuals interact, communicate, and mobilize for causes. The Cultural Connector platform, spearheaded by Riley Dubois, has played a pivotal role in this transformation, leveraging technology to foster social change and empower communities. This section explores the multifaceted impact of Cultural Connector on shaping the social landscape, highlighting relevant theories, existing challenges, and practical examples.

Theoretical Framework

To understand the impact of Cultural Connector on the social landscape, we can draw upon the Social Construction of Technology (SCOT) theory, which posits that technology is not merely a tool but is shaped by social forces, cultural contexts, and human actions. According to SCOT, the social context influences how technologies are developed and adopted, which in turn affects societal structures and relationships.

In the case of Cultural Connector, the platform embodies the principles of participatory design, where users actively contribute to shaping their digital environment. This participatory approach aligns with the theory of Collective Intelligence, as proposed by Pierre Lévy, which suggests that the collaboration of many individuals can lead to enhanced problem-solving capabilities and innovative solutions to social issues.

Challenges in the Social Landscape

Despite the positive implications of Cultural Connector, several challenges persist in shaping the social landscape. One significant issue is the digital divide, which refers to the disparities in access to technology and the internet. According to the *International Telecommunication Union*, approximately 3.7 billion people remain offline, primarily in developing regions. This lack of access hampers the ability of marginalized communities to engage with platforms like Cultural Connector, thereby exacerbating existing inequalities.

Moreover, the phenomenon of misinformation poses a serious threat to social cohesion. The rapid spread of false information on social media platforms can lead to polarization, mistrust, and social unrest. As noted by the *Pew Research Center*, 64% of Americans believe that misinformation has a major impact on public opinion, highlighting the urgent need for media literacy and critical thinking skills among users.

Examples of Social Impact

Cultural Connector has successfully harnessed technology to address these challenges and shape the social landscape in several impactful ways. One notable example is the platform's initiative to promote digital literacy through targeted educational programs. By offering workshops and resources that teach individuals how to critically evaluate information online, Cultural Connector empowers users to navigate the complexities of the digital world effectively.

Another example is the platform's role in facilitating social movements. The #MeToo movement, which gained momentum on social media, exemplifies how Cultural Connector can amplify marginalized voices and foster collective action. By providing a space for individuals to share their experiences and connect with like-minded advocates, Cultural Connector has contributed to raising awareness about sexual harassment and assault, ultimately leading to significant societal changes.

Future Directions

As we look to the future, the potential for Cultural Connector to further shape the social landscape is immense. Emerging technologies such as Artificial Intelligence (AI) and blockchain offer new avenues for enhancing user engagement and promoting social justice. For instance, AI can be utilized to analyze social trends and identify areas where intervention is needed, while blockchain technology can ensure transparency and accountability in online interactions.

Moreover, fostering global collaborations will be essential in addressing the challenges of misinformation and digital inequality. By partnering with educational institutions, non-profits, and tech companies, Cultural Connector can develop comprehensive strategies that leverage diverse perspectives and resources to create a more equitable digital environment.

Conclusion

In conclusion, Cultural Connector has significantly influenced the social landscape by promoting digital literacy, amplifying marginalized voices, and facilitating social movements. While challenges such as the digital divide and misinformation remain, the platform's commitment to fostering collaboration and empowering communities positions it as a crucial player in shaping a more inclusive and equitable society. As we navigate the complexities of the digital age, the lessons learned from Cultural Connector will be instrumental in guiding future innovations that prioritize social well-being and collective empowerment.

$$\text{Social Impact} = \frac{\text{Access to Technology} \times \text{User Engagement}}{\text{Misinformation} + \text{Digital Divide}} \qquad (40)$$

This equation illustrates that the overall social impact of Cultural Connector is maximized when access to technology and user engagement are high, while the negative influences of misinformation and the digital divide are minimized.

Cultural Connector's Impact on Arts and Entertainment

Transforming Creative Industries

Redefining Audience Engagement

In the digital age, the landscape of audience engagement has undergone a profound transformation, particularly within the creative industries. The emergence of the Cultural Connector platform has catalyzed this shift, enabling new forms of interaction between creators and their audiences. This section explores the theoretical foundations of audience engagement, the challenges faced by traditional engagement models, and the innovative strategies employed by Cultural Connector to redefine how audiences interact with art and entertainment.

Theoretical Foundations of Audience Engagement

Audience engagement can be understood through several theoretical lenses, including the Uses and Gratifications Theory (UGT) and the Engagement Theory. UGT posits that audiences actively seek out media to fulfill specific needs, such as information, personal identity, integration, and social interaction [?]. In contrast, Engagement Theory emphasizes the importance of interaction, collaboration, and meaningful experiences in fostering a deeper connection between audiences and content [?].

The integration of these theories suggests that effective audience engagement is not merely about content consumption but involves active participation and emotional investment. This paradigm shift aligns with the Cultural Connector's mission to create interactive experiences that resonate with diverse audiences.

Challenges of Traditional Audience Engagement Models

Traditional engagement models often rely on passive consumption, where audiences are viewed as mere recipients of content. This approach poses several challenges:

- **Limited Interaction:** Audiences have little opportunity to engage with the content or influence its direction, leading to disengagement and apathy.

- **One-Way Communication:** Traditional media often fosters a one-way communication model, where creators broadcast their messages without feedback from the audience.

- **Fragmentation of Attention:** In an era of information overload, audiences are increasingly selective about their engagement, leading to fragmented attention spans and diminished loyalty to creators.

These challenges necessitate a rethinking of how creators engage with their audiences, prompting the development of more interactive and participatory models.

Innovative Strategies of Cultural Connector

Cultural Connector has embraced innovative strategies to redefine audience engagement through several key initiatives:

- **Interactive Platforms:** By leveraging technology, Cultural Connector enables audiences to interact with content in real-time. For instance, live-streaming events with integrated polls and Q&A sessions allow audiences to participate actively, fostering a sense of community and shared experience.

- **User-Generated Content:** Encouraging audiences to contribute their own content not only democratizes creativity but also enhances engagement. Platforms that allow users to remix, comment on, and share their interpretations of original works create a collaborative environment that values audience contributions.

- **Personalized Experiences:** Utilizing algorithms and data analytics, Cultural Connector tailors content recommendations to individual preferences, enhancing the relevance of the experience. This personalization fosters a deeper connection as audiences feel that their unique tastes and interests are acknowledged.

- **Gamification:** By incorporating game-like elements into the engagement process, such as rewards, challenges, and leaderboards, Cultural Connector transforms passive consumption into an interactive experience. This approach not only enhances motivation but also encourages sustained engagement.

- **Community Building:** Cultural Connector prioritizes the creation of communities around shared interests and experiences. By facilitating discussions, forums, and social media interactions, the platform nurtures relationships among users, enhancing their emotional investment in the content.

Examples of Redefined Engagement

Several case studies illustrate the effectiveness of these strategies in redefining audience engagement:

Case Study 1: Virtual Reality Art Exhibitions A virtual reality art exhibition hosted by Cultural Connector allowed participants to explore immersive environments while interacting with artists in real-time. Attendees could ask questions, provide feedback, and even influence the direction of the exhibition through their interactions. This model exemplifies how technology can create engaging experiences that transcend traditional boundaries.

Case Study 2: Collaborative Storytelling Platforms Cultural Connector launched a collaborative storytelling platform where users could contribute to ongoing narratives. By allowing audiences to co-create stories, the platform not only engaged users but also fostered a sense of ownership and investment in the content. This approach aligns with the Engagement Theory, emphasizing the importance of collaboration in creating meaningful experiences.

Case Study 3: Social Media Activism Through targeted campaigns on social media, Cultural Connector mobilized audiences to participate in social justice movements. By creating shareable content and encouraging users to share their stories, the platform amplified marginalized voices and fostered a sense of community and collective action. This demonstrates the potential of social media as a tool for redefining audience engagement in the context of activism.

Conclusion

The redefinition of audience engagement by Cultural Connector reflects a broader trend in the creative industries towards interactivity, collaboration, and personalization. By embracing innovative strategies that prioritize audience participation, Cultural Connector not only enhances the relevance of content but also fosters deeper emotional connections between creators and their audiences. As the landscape of audience engagement continues to evolve, the lessons learned from Cultural Connector will undoubtedly shape the future of how we interact with art and entertainment.

Creating Interactive Art Experiences

The evolution of technology has dramatically transformed the landscape of the arts, paving the way for innovative and interactive art experiences that engage audiences in unprecedented ways. Interactive art, defined as a form of art that requires the participation of the viewer to achieve its full effect, has emerged as a powerful medium for artistic expression and social commentary. This subsection explores the theoretical foundations, challenges, and notable examples of interactive art experiences, emphasizing how they redefine the relationship between artists, audiences, and the artwork itself.

Theoretical Foundations of Interactive Art

Interactive art is rooted in several theoretical frameworks, including constructivism, participatory culture, and the aesthetics of engagement. Constructivism posits that knowledge is constructed through interaction with the environment, suggesting that audiences become co-creators of meaning in interactive art experiences. Participatory culture, a term coined by Henry Jenkins, refers to a culture where fans and consumers actively engage in the creation and sharing of content, blurring the lines between producers and consumers. This shift is particularly relevant in the context of interactive art, where audience participation is essential.

Moreover, the aesthetics of engagement, as articulated by theorists like Claire Bishop, emphasizes the importance of audience involvement in the artistic process. Bishop argues that interactive art challenges traditional notions of passive spectatorship, inviting viewers to become active participants who influence the artwork's outcome. This participatory approach not only enhances the viewer's experience but also fosters a sense of community and collaboration among participants.

Challenges in Creating Interactive Art

While the potential of interactive art is vast, artists face several challenges in its creation and implementation. One significant challenge is the technological barrier. Artists must possess a certain level of technical expertise to design and execute interactive installations, often requiring collaboration with technologists and programmers. This interdisciplinary approach can lead to creative tensions, as artists and technologists may have different priorities and perspectives.

Another challenge lies in ensuring accessibility. Interactive art experiences must be designed to accommodate diverse audiences, including individuals with varying abilities and backgrounds. This necessitates careful consideration of the physical and cognitive accessibility of installations, as well as the cultural relevance of the content presented. Failure to address these issues can result in exclusionary practices that undermine the intended inclusivity of interactive art.

Moreover, the ephemeral nature of many interactive art experiences can pose challenges for documentation and preservation. Unlike traditional artworks, which can be easily collected and displayed in galleries, interactive installations often exist only in the moment of their interaction. This raises questions about how to archive and preserve these experiences for future audiences.

Notable Examples of Interactive Art Experiences

Several artists and collectives have successfully navigated these challenges, creating impactful interactive art experiences that resonate with audiences. One prominent example is *The Obliteration Room* by Yayoi Kusama. Initially a completely white room, the installation invites visitors to apply colorful dot stickers to the walls and furniture, transforming the space into a vibrant explosion of color. This participatory approach not only engages viewers but also reflects Kusama's themes of infinity and connection.

Another noteworthy example is *The Night Cafe* by Vincent Morisset, a virtual reality experience that immerses users in a digital recreation of Vincent van Gogh's iconic painting. Users can explore the environment, interact with objects, and even manipulate elements of the artwork. This innovative use of technology allows participants to experience art in a deeply personal and interactive manner, bridging the gap between the viewer and the artist's vision.

The collective teamLab has also made significant strides in the realm of interactive art. Their installation *Borderless* features a series of digital art rooms where visitors can interact with the artwork through movement and touch. The installation responds to the presence of viewers, creating a dynamic and ever-changing environment that emphasizes the interconnectedness of all participants.

Conclusion

In conclusion, creating interactive art experiences is a multifaceted endeavor that requires a deep understanding of theoretical principles, a willingness to confront challenges, and a commitment to innovation. As technology continues to evolve, so too will the possibilities for interactive art, offering new ways for audiences to engage with and experience creativity. By fostering collaboration between artists and technologists, prioritizing accessibility, and embracing the ephemeral nature of interactive experiences, the future of interactive art holds immense potential for enriching cultural discourse and community engagement.

$$E = mc^2 \qquad (41)$$

This equation, while primarily associated with physics, metaphorically reflects the energy and mass of ideas that can be generated through interactive experiences, where the engagement of the audience (energy) can transform the static nature of art (mass) into a dynamic and evolving dialogue.

Democratizing Access to Arts and Entertainment

The democratization of access to arts and entertainment represents a transformative shift in how individuals engage with creative content. Traditionally, access to the arts has been limited by various factors including socioeconomic status, geographic location, and institutional barriers. However, with the advent of digital technology and platforms, the landscape of arts and entertainment is undergoing a significant transformation, allowing for broader participation and engagement.

Theoretical Framework

The theory of democratization in the context of arts and entertainment is rooted in the principles of accessibility, inclusivity, and equity. According to [?], democratization involves not only the expansion of formal political rights but also the enhancement of social and cultural rights. This framework posits that access to cultural goods is a fundamental aspect of social justice and individual empowerment.

Barriers to Access

Historically, several barriers have hindered access to the arts:

- **Economic Barriers:** High ticket prices for performances, museum admissions, and art classes can exclude low-income individuals from participating in cultural experiences.

- **Geographic Barriers:** Individuals living in rural or underserved urban areas often lack access to cultural institutions, limiting their exposure to diverse artistic expressions.

- **Cultural Barriers:** Marginalized communities may face challenges in representation within mainstream arts, leading to feelings of alienation and exclusion.

These barriers have contributed to a cultural landscape that is often inaccessible to many, perpetuating inequalities in artistic engagement.

Digital Platforms as Equalizers

The rise of digital platforms has been instrumental in democratizing access to arts and entertainment. Online streaming services, social media, and virtual galleries have created new avenues for artists and audiences to connect. For example, platforms such as YouTube and Instagram allow artists to share their work with global audiences without the constraints of traditional gatekeeping mechanisms.

$$\text{Access}_{\text{digital}} = \frac{\text{Content}_{\text{available}}}{\text{Barriers}_{\text{reduced}}} \qquad (42)$$

This equation suggests that as barriers to access are reduced through digital means, the availability of artistic content increases, leading to greater engagement from diverse audiences.

Case Studies

Several initiatives exemplify the democratization of access to arts and entertainment:

- **The National Gallery of Art's Virtual Tours:** In response to the COVID-19 pandemic, the National Gallery of Art in Washington, D.C., launched virtual tours that allow viewers to experience their exhibitions from home. This initiative has broadened access to art for individuals unable to visit in person due to distance or health concerns.

- **The Rise of Independent Artists on Social Media:** Platforms like TikTok and Instagram have enabled independent artists to gain visibility and build audiences without the need for traditional representation. For instance, musicians can share their work directly with fans, leading to viral sensations and increased opportunities for performances and collaborations.
- **Crowdsourced Funding Models:** Websites like Kickstarter and Patreon have revolutionized how artists fund their projects. By allowing fans to contribute directly to creative endeavors, these platforms empower artists to create work that reflects diverse perspectives and experiences, often outside the constraints of commercial viability.

Challenges Ahead

Despite the advancements in democratizing access, challenges remain. Digital divides continue to exist, with individuals in lower socioeconomic groups lacking reliable internet access or digital literacy skills. Furthermore, the overwhelming volume of content available online can lead to issues of visibility, where deserving artists struggle to gain recognition amidst a saturated market.

$$\text{Visibility}_{\text{artist}} = \frac{\text{Engagement}_{\text{audience}}}{\text{Content}_{\text{competition}}} \quad (43)$$

In this equation, the visibility of an artist is contingent upon their ability to engage an audience relative to the competition they face. As the volume of content increases, maintaining visibility becomes a significant challenge for many creators.

Conclusion

The democratization of access to arts and entertainment through digital platforms represents a significant shift towards inclusivity and equity in the cultural landscape. While barriers still exist, the potential for broader participation and engagement continues to grow. As society moves forward, it is essential to address the remaining challenges to ensure that all individuals have the opportunity to engage with and contribute to the rich tapestry of artistic expression.

Collaboration in the Digital Age

The digital age has fundamentally transformed the way individuals and organizations collaborate. With the advent of technology, collaboration has transcended geographical boundaries, enabling diverse teams to work together in real-time, regardless of their physical locations. This section explores the dynamics of collaboration in the digital age, the challenges that arise, and the innovative solutions that have emerged to facilitate effective teamwork.

Theoretical Framework

Collaboration can be defined as a process where individuals or groups work together to achieve a common goal. Theories such as *Social Constructivism* emphasize that knowledge is constructed through social interactions, which is particularly relevant in collaborative environments. Vygotsky's *Zone of Proximal Development* (ZPD) posits that learners can achieve higher levels of understanding when they collaborate with more knowledgeable peers. This theory underpins many digital collaboration tools that facilitate peer-to-peer learning.

$$ZPD = \{x | x \text{ is achievable with guidance from a more knowledgeable other}\} \tag{44}$$

In the context of digital collaboration, platforms such as Slack, Microsoft Teams, and Zoom exemplify the application of these theories by providing spaces where individuals can communicate, share resources, and collaborate on projects seamlessly.

Challenges of Digital Collaboration

Despite the benefits, digital collaboration also presents unique challenges:

- **Communication Barriers:** Miscommunication can occur due to the lack of non-verbal cues in digital interactions. Research indicates that up to 93% of communication is non-verbal, which can lead to misunderstandings in a virtual environment.

- **Cultural Differences:** Diverse teams may face challenges related to varying cultural norms and practices. Hofstede's dimensions of culture highlight how factors like individualism vs. collectivism and uncertainty avoidance can impact collaboration.

- **Technology Overload:** The plethora of tools available can lead to confusion and inefficiency. Teams may struggle to determine which platforms to use for specific tasks, leading to fragmentation.

Innovative Solutions

To address these challenges, several innovative solutions have emerged:

- **Unified Communication Platforms:** Tools that integrate multiple communication channels (e.g., chat, video, file sharing) into a single platform can reduce confusion and streamline collaboration. For example, *Microsoft Teams* combines chat, video calls, and file sharing in one interface, enhancing user experience.

- **Cultural Awareness Training:** Organizations are increasingly investing in training programs to enhance cultural competence among team members. This training fosters understanding and respect for diverse perspectives, improving collaboration.

- **Agile Methodologies:** The adoption of agile practices, such as daily stand-ups and iterative feedback loops, encourages regular communication and adaptability among team members. This approach has been particularly effective in software development teams.

Case Studies

Several organizations exemplify successful digital collaboration:

- **GitHub:** As a platform for software development, GitHub allows developers from around the world to collaborate on projects. Its version control system enables multiple contributors to work on the same codebase without conflicts, fostering innovation and efficiency.

- **Trello:** Trello's visual project management tool allows teams to organize tasks collaboratively. Its card-based system facilitates clear communication regarding project status, responsibilities, and deadlines, promoting accountability.

- **Remote Work Success Stories:** Companies like *Automattic* and *Buffer* operate entirely remotely, relying on digital collaboration tools to maintain productivity and culture. Their success demonstrates that with the right tools and practices, teams can thrive in a virtual environment.

Conclusion

In conclusion, collaboration in the digital age presents both opportunities and challenges. By understanding the theoretical underpinnings of collaboration, recognizing potential barriers, and leveraging innovative solutions, organizations can foster effective teamwork that transcends traditional limitations. As we move forward, the continued evolution of technology will undoubtedly shape the future of collaboration, making it more inclusive and efficient.

Bibliography

[1] Vygotsky, L. S. (1978). *Mind in Society: The Development of Higher Psychological Processes.* Harvard University Press.

[2] Hofstede, G. (1980). *Culture's Consequences: International Differences in Work-Related Values.* Sage Publications.

[3] Slack Technologies. (2023). *Slack: Where Work Happens.* Retrieved from https://slack.com

[4] Microsoft. (2023). *Microsoft Teams: Collaboration for Everyone.* Retrieved from https://www.microsoft.com/en-us/microsoft-teams/group-chat-software

[5] GitHub. (2023). *Where the World Builds Software.* Retrieved from https://github.com

[6] Trello. (2023). *Trello: Organize Anything, Together.* Retrieved from https://trello.com

Blurring the Line Between Creator and Consumer

In the contemporary landscape of arts and entertainment, the distinction between creator and consumer has become increasingly ambiguous. This phenomenon, often referred to as "prosumerism," arises from the convergence of technology, social media, and participatory culture. The term "prosumer" is a portmanteau of "producer" and "consumer," and it encapsulates the idea that individuals are no longer passive recipients of content but active participants in its creation and dissemination.

Theoretical Framework

The theoretical underpinning of this shift can be traced to several key concepts in media studies and cultural theory. Henry Jenkins' concept of "participatory culture" emphasizes the role of the audience as co-creators of content. In his seminal work, Jenkins (2006) argues that participatory culture fosters an environment where individuals can engage in the production of media, thus democratizing content creation and challenging traditional hierarchies in the media landscape.

Furthermore, the idea of the "user-generated content" (UGC) revolution illustrates how advancements in technology have empowered consumers to produce and share their own content. Platforms like YouTube, TikTok, and Instagram have transformed ordinary users into influencers and content creators, blurring the lines between professional creators and everyday consumers.

Problems and Challenges

Despite the democratization of content creation, this blurring of roles presents several challenges. One significant issue is the saturation of content. With millions of creators vying for attention, the market becomes oversaturated, making it difficult for individual voices to stand out. As a result, the quality of content can vary widely, leading to a potential devaluation of creative work.

Moreover, the rise of prosumerism raises questions about intellectual property and copyright. When consumers become creators, the ownership of content becomes murky. For instance, if a user creates a remix of a popular song, who owns the rights to that new piece? This dilemma can lead to legal disputes and confusion regarding the protection of creative works.

Examples of Blurring Roles

One prominent example of this phenomenon is the rise of TikTok, a platform that allows users to create and share short videos. TikTok has empowered everyday users to become content creators, often leading to viral trends that can significantly impact music charts and fashion industries. For instance, the song "Old Town Road" by Lil Nas X gained immense popularity partly due to its viral TikTok dance challenges, showcasing how consumer-generated content can influence mainstream media.

Another example is the rise of fan fiction and fan art within various fandoms. Fans of franchises such as "Harry Potter" and "Star Wars" actively create their own narratives and artworks, contributing to the larger cultural conversation surrounding these properties. This practice not only enriches the original content but also allows fans to express their interpretations and engage with the material on a deeper level.

Conclusion

The blurring of the lines between creator and consumer represents a significant shift in the cultural landscape of arts and entertainment. While it fosters a more inclusive and participatory environment, it also presents challenges related to content saturation, copyright issues, and the quality of creative work. As technology continues to evolve, the roles of creators and consumers will likely further intertwine, prompting ongoing discussions about the future of creativity in a digital age.

$$\text{Prosumer Value} = \frac{\text{Content Quality} \times \text{Engagement}}{\text{Market Saturation}} \qquad (45)$$

This equation suggests that the perceived value of prosumer content is a function of its quality and engagement level, inversely related to market saturation. As the landscape evolves, understanding these dynamics will be crucial for navigating the future of arts and entertainment.

Exploring New Art Forms and Mediums

In the age of rapid technological advancement, artists are continuously pushed to explore new forms and mediums, leading to a renaissance of creativity that transcends traditional boundaries. Riley Dubois, through Cultural Connector, has been at the forefront of this exploration, encouraging artists to embrace innovative tools and platforms to redefine their artistic expressions.

Theoretical Framework

The exploration of new art forms can be understood through the lens of several theories. One significant theory is **Postmodernism**, which challenges the conventions of traditional art by embracing pluralism and fragmentation. This perspective allows for the incorporation of diverse influences and styles, leading to hybrid art forms that reflect the complexities of contemporary society.

Another relevant theory is **Media Ecology**, which posits that the medium through which art is conveyed profoundly affects the content and experience of the artwork itself. As Marshall McLuhan famously stated, "the medium is the message," suggesting that the choice of medium can shape the audience's perception and interpretation of art.

Emerging Art Forms

1. **Digital Art:** With the advent of software like Adobe Creative Suite and platforms such as Procreate, digital art has emerged as a dominant form of expression. Artists can create intricate works using digital brushes, layers, and effects, allowing for a level of precision and experimentation that traditional media may not permit.

2. **Augmented Reality (AR) and Virtual Reality (VR):** These technologies have opened new avenues for immersive experiences. Artists can create virtual environments that audiences can explore, blurring the lines between viewer and participant. Notable examples include the work of artist Marina Abramović, who has utilized VR to allow viewers to experience her performances in a new dimension.

3. **Interactive Installations:** Artists are increasingly creating installations that require audience participation, transforming passive viewers into active participants. For instance, the work of teamLab, a Tokyo-based art collective, incorporates digital projections that respond to the movements and actions of visitors, creating a dynamic and evolving artistic experience.

4. **Generative Art:** This form of art is created through algorithms and code, allowing artists to generate unique pieces based on predetermined rules. Artists like Casey Reas and Joshua Davis have pioneered this medium, showcasing how technology can be harnessed to create art that is both innovative and deeply engaging.

Challenges in Exploring New Mediums

While the exploration of new art forms presents exciting opportunities, it also comes with challenges:

- **Accessibility:** Not all artists have equal access to the technology required to create digital or interactive art. This disparity can lead to a lack of diversity in the voices and perspectives represented in these new mediums.

- **Artistic Integrity:** The integration of technology into art raises questions about authenticity and authorship. As artists increasingly collaborate with algorithms and machines, the traditional notions of the artist as a singular creator may be called into question.

- **Market Dynamics:** The commercialization of new art forms can lead to a focus on marketability rather than artistic expression. Artists may feel pressured to conform to trends or expectations set by galleries and collectors, potentially stifling innovation.

Case Studies

1. **Refik Anadol:** A media artist and director, Anadol uses machine learning algorithms to create stunning visualizations of data. His work, such as *Melting Memories*, explores the intersection of technology and human experience, prompting viewers to reconsider their relationship with memory and data.

2. **Yayoi Kusama:** Known for her immersive installations, Kusama's work often incorporates elements of AR. Her *Infinity Mirror Rooms* allow viewers to step into a seemingly endless space filled with light and reflection, creating a unique interactive experience that challenges perceptions of reality.

3. **Kara Walker:** Walker's work often incorporates new media alongside traditional forms. Her recent projects have included digital animations that expand upon her well-known silhouette installations, allowing her to explore themes of race and identity in a contemporary context.

Conclusion

The exploration of new art forms and mediums is a testament to the evolving nature of artistic expression in the digital age. Through the initiatives of Cultural Connector, artists are empowered to break free from traditional constraints, fostering a vibrant landscape of creativity that reflects the complexities of modern life. As Riley Dubois continues to champion innovation in the arts, the future promises a rich tapestry of diverse voices and perspectives, each contributing to the ongoing dialogue about what art can be.

$$\text{Art}_{new} = \text{Art}_{traditional} + \text{Technology} + \text{Interactivity} \quad (46)$$

This equation captures the essence of contemporary art practice, where new art forms emerge from the synthesis of traditional techniques, technological advancements, and the engagement of the audience. As we look to the future, the potential for artistic innovation remains boundless, inviting both artists and audiences to participate in a shared journey of exploration and discovery.

Amplifying Diverse Voices in the Arts

The arts have historically served as a reflection of society, encapsulating the myriad experiences and perspectives that shape our world. However, the representation of diverse voices within the arts has often been marginalized or overlooked. This subsection explores the importance of amplifying diverse voices in the arts, the challenges faced in achieving this goal, and the innovative strategies employed to create a more inclusive artistic landscape.

The Importance of Diverse Representation

Diverse representation in the arts is essential for several reasons:

- **Cultural Enrichment:** Diverse voices bring unique perspectives that enrich the cultural tapestry of society. They challenge the status quo and introduce new narratives that can resonate with a wider audience.

- **Social Justice:** Amplifying marginalized voices in the arts contributes to social justice by addressing systemic inequalities. It allows for the expression of experiences that may otherwise go unheard, fostering empathy and understanding among different communities.

- **Inspiration and Empowerment:** When individuals see themselves represented in the arts, it can inspire them to pursue their creative passions. Representation empowers marginalized groups to tell their own stories, thus reclaiming their narratives.

Challenges to Amplifying Diverse Voices

Despite the recognized importance of diverse representation, several challenges persist:

- **Structural Barriers:** Traditional gatekeeping in the arts, often dominated by a homogenous group of decision-makers, can hinder the opportunities for diverse artists to showcase their work. This includes limited access to funding, exhibition spaces, and institutional support.

- **Cultural Appropriation:** The appropriation of cultural elements without proper context or credit can undermine the authenticity of diverse voices. This often leads to commodification rather than genuine representation.

- **Stereotyping:** When diverse voices are represented, they are sometimes pigeonholed into specific roles or narratives that reinforce stereotypes, rather than allowing for a multifaceted exploration of identity.

Innovative Strategies for Amplification

To combat these challenges, various innovative strategies have emerged:

- **Community-Based Initiatives:** Programs that prioritize community engagement and collaboration can empower local artists. For example, initiatives like the *Art for All* program in New York City provide platforms for underrepresented artists to showcase their work in community spaces.

- **Digital Platforms:** The rise of social media and digital platforms has democratized access to artistic expression. Artists from diverse backgrounds can share their work globally, bypassing traditional gatekeepers. For instance, platforms like *Instagram* and *YouTube* have enabled artists like Kehinde Wiley and Ariana DeBose to gain recognition for their unique contributions.

- **Inclusive Curatorial Practices:** Museums and galleries are increasingly adopting inclusive curatorial practices that prioritize diversity. The *Smithsonian National Museum of African American History and Culture* serves as a prime example, showcasing the richness of African American culture through a diverse array of artistic expressions.

Case Studies

Several case studies illustrate the successful amplification of diverse voices in the arts:

- **The Black Lives Matter Movement:** The movement has inspired a surge of artistic expression that amplifies the voices of Black artists. Public art installations, such as murals and performances, have become powerful tools for social change and community engagement.

- **The #MeToo Movement:** This movement has led to an increased focus on the stories of women and marginalized groups in the arts. The production of plays and films that center on women's experiences, such as *The Vagina Monologues* and *The Color Purple*, exemplifies this shift.

- **Indigenous Art Initiatives:** Programs like the *Indigenous Arts Initiative* in Canada aim to elevate Indigenous voices in the arts by providing funding, mentorship, and exhibition opportunities. This initiative has led to increased visibility and appreciation of Indigenous art forms.

Conclusion

Amplifying diverse voices in the arts is not merely a matter of representation; it is a crucial step toward fostering a more inclusive and equitable society. By addressing the challenges that hinder diverse representation and employing innovative strategies, the arts can become a powerful platform for social change. As we move forward, it is imperative that we continue to advocate for and support the amplification of diverse voices, ensuring that the artistic landscape reflects the richness of human experience.

$$\text{Diversity Index} = \frac{N_D}{N_T} \times 100 \tag{47}$$

Where N_D is the number of diverse artists represented and N_T is the total number of artists represented. This index can serve as a metric for assessing the inclusivity of artistic institutions and initiatives.

In summary, the journey toward amplifying diverse voices in the arts is ongoing and requires collective effort from artists, institutions, and audiences alike. By embracing this diversity, we not only enrich the arts but also contribute to a more just and equitable society.

Supporting Artists in a Digital World

In the rapidly evolving landscape of the digital age, artists face both unprecedented opportunities and significant challenges. The rise of technology has fundamentally transformed how art is created, distributed, and consumed. This section explores the multifaceted ways in which Cultural Connector supports artists in navigating this digital world, addressing the unique problems they encounter while also leveraging the tools available to them.

The Challenges Artists Face

Artists today must contend with a myriad of challenges in the digital realm. One of the most pressing issues is the oversaturation of content. With platforms like Instagram, TikTok, and YouTube, the sheer volume of artistic output can make it difficult for individual creators to stand out. According to a study by the *Creative Industries Council* (2021), over 70% of artists reported feeling overwhelmed by the competition in the digital space.

Moreover, the monetization of art has become increasingly complex. Traditional revenue streams, such as gallery sales and physical exhibitions, are being disrupted by digital platforms that often prioritize free access to content.

This shift has led to a decline in income for many artists, as they struggle to find sustainable business models in an environment where consumers expect free or low-cost access to art. A report by *Art Basel and UBS* (2022) highlighted that 60% of artists rely on supplementary income sources to support their creative practices.

Cultural Connector's Role

Cultural Connector plays a pivotal role in addressing these challenges by providing artists with a platform that enhances visibility, fosters community, and offers innovative monetization strategies.

1. **Enhancing Visibility** Cultural Connector utilizes algorithms that promote diverse artistic voices, ensuring that emerging artists gain exposure alongside established creators. By curating content that highlights underrepresented artists, the platform not only democratizes visibility but also enriches the cultural tapestry of the digital art world. For example, the platform's "Artist Spotlight" feature showcases a rotating selection of artists, allowing them to reach new audiences and gain recognition.

2. **Fostering Community** In addition to enhancing visibility, Cultural Connector fosters a sense of community among artists. Through collaborative projects, virtual exhibitions, and interactive forums, artists can connect with one another, share resources, and collaborate on creative endeavors. This network effect is crucial in combating the isolation often felt by artists in the digital age. The platform's recent initiative, "Collaborate & Create," has facilitated over 500 partnerships among artists across various disciplines, resulting in innovative works that blend different mediums and styles.

3. **Innovative Monetization Strategies** Recognizing the challenges of monetization, Cultural Connector offers artists various tools to generate income from their work. This includes features such as direct-to-fan sales, subscription models, and crowdfunding options. For instance, the platform's "Patron Program" allows fans to support their favorite artists through monthly contributions, providing a steady income stream that empowers creators to focus on their craft.

Furthermore, Cultural Connector has implemented blockchain technology to ensure fair compensation for artists through smart contracts. These contracts automatically execute payments based on predefined conditions, reducing the risk of exploitation and ensuring that artists receive their due share of revenue from sales and licensing agreements.

Case Studies

To illustrate the impact of Cultural Connector on artists, consider the following case studies:

Case Study 1: Emerging Visual Artist An emerging visual artist, Jamie Lee, utilized Cultural Connector to showcase her digital paintings. Through the platform's targeted promotion, Jamie's work gained traction, leading to a 150% increase in her online following within three months. Additionally, by participating in the "Collaborate & Create" initiative, she collaborated with a musician to create a multimedia project that garnered significant attention, resulting in a successful crowdfunding campaign that exceeded its goal by 200%.

Case Study 2: Established Musician An established musician, Alex Rivera, faced declining revenue from traditional album sales. By leveraging Cultural Connector's subscription model, Alex launched an exclusive monthly content series where fans could access behind-the-scenes footage, live-streamed performances, and personalized interactions. This initiative not only revitalized his income stream but also deepened his connection with fans, fostering a loyal community around his work.

Conclusion

In conclusion, Cultural Connector serves as a vital support system for artists navigating the complexities of the digital world. By enhancing visibility, fostering community, and providing innovative monetization strategies, the platform empowers artists to thrive in an environment that often presents significant challenges. As the digital landscape continues to evolve, the role of Cultural Connector in supporting artists will be crucial in shaping the future of creative expression.

The ongoing commitment to addressing the unique needs of artists will ensure that they can continue to inspire, engage, and innovate, ultimately enriching the cultural fabric of society as a whole.

Pushing Boundaries of Traditional Artistic Expression

In the rapidly evolving landscape of the arts, Riley Dubois's Cultural Connector has emerged as a transformative force, challenging and redefining the very essence of traditional artistic expression. This subsection explores the ways in which

Cultural Connector pushes these boundaries, drawing upon contemporary theories, addressing prevalent challenges, and presenting compelling examples of innovation in the creative industries.

Theoretical Framework

The reimagining of artistic expression can be understood through several theoretical lenses. One key framework is the concept of *intermediality*, which refers to the blending of different media forms in artistic practice. As articulated by [?], the boundaries between media are increasingly porous, allowing artists to draw from diverse sources to create hybrid forms that resonate with contemporary audiences. This intermedial approach not only enriches the artistic experience but also reflects the complexity of modern life, where technology and culture intersect in multifaceted ways.

Another relevant theory is *participatory culture*, as discussed by [?]. This concept emphasizes the role of audiences as active participants in the creation and dissemination of art, rather than passive consumers. By fostering an environment where individuals can contribute their voices and perspectives, Cultural Connector empowers artists to explore new forms of expression that transcend traditional boundaries.

Challenges in Artistic Innovation

Despite the exciting possibilities presented by these theoretical frameworks, artists face numerous challenges in pushing the boundaries of traditional expression. One significant issue is the *commercialization of art*, which often pressures creators to conform to mainstream tastes and trends. This can stifle innovation and lead to a homogenization of artistic output, where unique voices are drowned out by market demands.

Moreover, the *digital divide* poses a barrier to equitable access to artistic tools and platforms. As technology becomes increasingly integral to artistic practice, disparities in access can limit opportunities for marginalized artists to experiment and engage with new forms of expression. Addressing this divide is crucial for fostering a diverse and vibrant artistic landscape.

Examples of Innovative Practices

Cultural Connector has catalyzed a range of innovative practices that exemplify the pushing of artistic boundaries. One notable example is the use of *augmented reality (AR)* in visual art. Artists such as [?] have employed AR to create immersive experiences that blend physical and digital realms. By allowing viewers to interact with artworks in dynamic ways, these artists challenge the conventional notions of spectatorship and authorship.

Similarly, the rise of *interactive installations* showcases how artists are redefining engagement. The work of [?], for instance, invites audiences to become co-creators of the artwork, blurring the lines between artist and viewer. This participatory approach not only enhances the artistic experience but also fosters a sense of community and shared ownership.

Moreover, the integration of *social media* as a platform for artistic expression has revolutionized the way artists connect with their audiences. Artists like [?] have leveraged social media to disseminate their work and engage with followers directly, challenging the traditional gatekeeping roles of galleries and institutions. This democratization of art allows for a wider range of voices to be heard and celebrated.

Conclusion

In conclusion, Riley Dubois's Cultural Connector is at the forefront of pushing the boundaries of traditional artistic expression. By embracing intermediality and participatory culture, artists are exploring innovative practices that challenge the status quo. While challenges such as commercialization and the digital divide persist, the examples of AR, interactive installations, and social media engagement highlight the transformative potential of art in the contemporary landscape. As the boundaries of artistic expression continue to expand, Cultural Connector remains a vital catalyst for change, inspiring a new generation of creators to reimagine what art can be.

The Future of the Creative Economy

The creative economy, characterized by the convergence of creativity, culture, and commerce, is poised for transformative changes in the coming years. As technology continues to advance at an unprecedented pace, it reshapes the landscape for artists, creators, and consumers alike. This section explores the potential trajectories of the creative economy, addressing relevant theories, emerging problems, and practical examples that illustrate the dynamic nature of this evolving sector.

Theoretical Frameworks

The future of the creative economy can be understood through several theoretical lenses, including the Creative Class Theory, the Cultural Industries Theory, and the

Digital Economy Framework.

Creative Class Theory   Richard Florida's *Creative Class Theory* posits that economic growth is increasingly driven by individuals engaged in creative professions. Florida suggests that cities that attract and retain creative talent experience greater innovation and economic prosperity. The implications of this theory suggest that the future creative economy will hinge on urban areas fostering environments conducive to creativity, inclusivity, and diversity.

Cultural Industries Theory   The *Cultural Industries Theory* emphasizes the role of cultural production in economic development. This theory highlights the significance of cultural goods and services in generating employment and stimulating economic growth. As digital platforms continue to democratize access to cultural production, the creative economy is likely to expand, allowing a broader range of voices and perspectives to contribute to cultural narratives.

Digital Economy Framework   The *Digital Economy Framework* focuses on the impact of digital technologies on economic activities. The rise of digital platforms, social media, and online distribution channels has transformed how creative content is produced, shared, and consumed. This framework underscores the need for creators to adapt to new business models and revenue streams, such as subscription services, crowdfunding, and direct-to-consumer sales.

Emerging Challenges

Despite the promising outlook for the creative economy, several challenges must be addressed to ensure its sustainable growth.

Intellectual Property Issues   One of the most pressing issues is the protection of intellectual property (IP) in a digital landscape where content can be easily copied and redistributed. The rise of user-generated content and remix culture complicates traditional notions of authorship and ownership. As creators navigate this complex terrain, there is a growing need for robust IP frameworks that balance protection with accessibility.

Economic Inequality   Another challenge is the potential for economic inequality within the creative economy. While digital platforms have lowered barriers to entry for many creators, they have also concentrated power and revenue in the hands of a few dominant players. This disparity raises questions about fair compensation for artists and equitable access to opportunities. The future of the creative economy will require concerted efforts to address these inequalities and ensure that all creators can thrive.

Mental Health and Well-being The pressure to constantly produce and engage in a hyper-connected world can take a toll on the mental health of creators. The rise of the gig economy and the precarious nature of creative work can lead to burnout and anxiety. Addressing mental health and well-being will be crucial for fostering a sustainable creative economy that prioritizes the needs of its contributors.

Practical Examples

Several innovative initiatives and examples illustrate the future potential of the creative economy.

Decentralized Platforms Emerging decentralized platforms, such as blockchain-based marketplaces, offer creators new ways to monetize their work while retaining control over their intellectual property. Platforms like *Audius* for music and *OpenSea* for digital art empower artists to connect directly with their audiences, bypassing traditional gatekeepers.

Collaborative Creation Collaborative creation is becoming increasingly prevalent, as evidenced by projects like *Wikipedia* and *Open Source Art*. These initiatives demonstrate the power of collective intelligence and the potential for shared ownership models. As more creators embrace collaboration, the creative economy may evolve into a more inclusive and participatory space.

Sustainability Initiatives Sustainability is becoming a core value in the creative economy, with many artists and organizations prioritizing eco-friendly practices. Initiatives such as *Fashion Revolution* and *Sustainable Arts Foundation* advocate for responsible production and consumption in the arts. The integration of sustainability into creative practices will likely shape the future of the industry, appealing to environmentally conscious consumers.

Conclusion

The future of the creative economy is a complex interplay of opportunities and challenges. As technology continues to reshape the landscape, creators must adapt to new realities while advocating for fair practices and equitable access. Theoretical frameworks provide valuable insights into the dynamics at play, while emerging challenges highlight the need for proactive solutions. By embracing collaboration, sustainability, and innovative business models, the creative economy can thrive in a way that benefits both creators and consumers alike.

$$\text{Economic Growth} = \alpha \cdot \text{Creativity} + \beta \cdot \text{Cultural Production} + \gamma \cdot \text{Digital Innovation} \tag{48}$$

In this equation, α, β, and γ represent the coefficients that quantify the contributions of creativity, cultural production, and digital innovation to overall economic growth. The future of the creative economy will depend on how effectively these elements are integrated and leveraged to create value and foster a vibrant cultural landscape.

Redefining Entertainment Experiences

Immersive Storytelling

Immersive storytelling represents a transformative approach to narrative that engages audiences in a multi-dimensional experience, allowing them to interact with the story in ways that traditional media cannot. This section explores the theory behind immersive storytelling, the challenges it faces, and examples of its application in various media.

Theoretical Framework

At the heart of immersive storytelling is the concept of **narrative immersion**, which refers to the degree to which an audience feels absorbed in a story. According to [?], immersion can be understood through three primary dimensions: *spatial immersion, narrative immersion,* and *emotional immersion*. These dimensions can be mathematically represented as:

$$I = f(S, N, E) \tag{49}$$

Where:

- I = Immersion level

- S = Spatial immersion (the physical environment)

- N = Narrative immersion (the story's engagement)
- E = Emotional immersion (the audience's emotional connection)

This equation suggests that the overall immersion level is a function of the interplay between these three elements, indicating that a balanced approach is essential for effective storytelling.

Challenges in Immersive Storytelling

Despite its potential, immersive storytelling faces several challenges:

- **Technological Barriers:** The need for advanced technology, such as virtual reality (VR) headsets or augmented reality (AR) devices, can limit accessibility. Many audiences may lack the necessary hardware, creating a divide in who can experience immersive stories.

- **Narrative Complexity:** Crafting a narrative that remains coherent while allowing for audience agency is a significant challenge. As [?] notes, the more choices a user has, the more complex the narrative structure becomes, which can lead to fragmented experiences.

- **User Experience Design:** Designing intuitive interfaces that enhance rather than hinder the storytelling experience is crucial. Poor design can lead to frustration, detracting from immersion.

Examples of Immersive Storytelling

Several pioneering projects exemplify the power of immersive storytelling:

- **The Night Cafe:** This VR experience allows users to explore a digital recreation of Vincent van Gogh's room, immersing them in the artist's world. Users can interact with objects, gaining insights into van Gogh's life and work, exemplifying spatial and narrative immersion.

- **The Invisible Man:** This interactive theater production utilizes AR to allow audience members to experience the narrative from different perspectives. By providing agency over their viewing experience, the production fosters deep emotional connections with the characters.

- **Black Mirror: Bandersnatch:** This Netflix interactive film allows viewers to make choices that influence the story's direction, showcasing the potential of branching narratives in immersive storytelling. The success of this format highlights the growing interest in audience-driven narratives.

Conclusion

Immersive storytelling represents a significant evolution in narrative form, blending technology with traditional storytelling techniques to create engaging experiences. By understanding the theoretical underpinnings, recognizing the challenges, and learning from existing examples, creators can harness the full potential of immersive storytelling to engage audiences in profound and meaningful ways. As technology continues to evolve, the possibilities for immersive storytelling will only expand, paving the way for innovative narratives that resonate with diverse audiences.

Augmented Reality in Entertainment

Augmented Reality (AR) has emerged as a transformative technology within the entertainment sector, reshaping how audiences interact with content and enhancing their experiences. By overlaying digital information onto the physical world, AR blurs the lines between reality and the virtual, creating immersive experiences that engage users in unprecedented ways.

Theoretical Framework

The theoretical underpinnings of AR in entertainment can be framed within the context of *Immersive Experience Theory*. This theory posits that the more immersive an experience is, the more engaged a user will be. Immersion can be categorized into three dimensions: *sensory immersion, cognitive immersion,* and *emotional immersion*. AR enhances these dimensions by providing a multisensory experience that captivates users' attention and fosters emotional connections to the content.

$$I = f(S, C, E) \tag{50}$$

where I represents the level of immersion, S is sensory immersion, C is cognitive immersion, and E is emotional immersion. As AR technology evolves, the potential for deeper immersion increases, thereby enhancing the overall entertainment experience.

Challenges in Implementation

Despite its potential, the integration of AR in entertainment faces several challenges:

1. **Technical Limitations:** The quality of AR experiences is heavily dependent on the hardware used. Many users may not have access to high-quality AR devices, limiting the reach of AR applications. Furthermore, the development of AR content requires significant technical expertise and resources, which can be a barrier for smaller creators.

2. **User Acceptance:** While AR offers novel experiences, user acceptance can vary. Some audiences may be hesitant to adopt new technologies due to privacy concerns, lack of understanding, or simply a preference for traditional forms of entertainment.

3. **Content Creation:** Creating engaging AR content is a complex process that requires collaboration between artists, developers, and storytellers. The challenge lies in ensuring that the AR experience is not only visually appealing but also narratively compelling.

4. **Physical Space Limitations:** AR experiences are often location-based, meaning that users must be in a specific physical space to fully engage with the content. This can limit the scalability of AR applications, particularly in an increasingly mobile society.

Examples of AR in Entertainment

Several notable examples illustrate the successful application of AR in the entertainment industry:

1. **Pokémon GO:** Perhaps the most famous AR application, *Pokémon GO* revolutionized mobile gaming by encouraging players to explore their real-world environments to catch virtual Pokémon. This game not only provided entertainment but also fostered social interaction among players, demonstrating the potential of AR to create community experiences.

2. **The Walking Dead: Our World:** This mobile game allows players to interact with characters and scenarios from the popular television series *The Walking Dead*. By combining AR with location-based gameplay, it enhances user engagement through immersive storytelling and real-world exploration.

3. **AR in Live Events:** Various music festivals and concerts have begun incorporating AR elements into their performances. For instance, the *Coachella* music festival has utilized AR to create interactive experiences for attendees, allowing them to engage with digital art installations and exclusive content through their smartphones.

4. Theatrical Productions: Some theater companies have started using AR to enhance live performances. For example, the *Royal Shakespeare Company* has experimented with AR technology to bring characters and scenes to life, allowing audiences to experience the performance in a new and engaging way.

Future Directions

As AR technology continues to evolve, the potential for its application in entertainment is vast. Future developments may include:
  - **Enhanced Interactivity:** As AR hardware becomes more sophisticated, the interactivity of experiences will increase, allowing users to influence narratives in real-time.
  - **Personalized Experiences:** Leveraging user data, AR could create tailored experiences that adapt to individual preferences, enhancing engagement and satisfaction.
  - **Integration with Virtual Reality (VR):** The convergence of AR and VR technologies could lead to hybrid experiences that combine the best elements of both, providing even richer and more immersive entertainment options.

Conclusion

Augmented Reality represents a significant advancement in the entertainment industry, offering unique opportunities for engagement and interaction. While challenges remain in its implementation, the potential benefits of AR in creating immersive experiences are undeniable. As technology continues to advance, the future of entertainment will likely be shaped by the innovative use of AR, transforming how audiences engage with content and each other.

Personalized Recommendations and Curation

In the age of information overload, personalized recommendations and curation have emerged as critical components in the arts and entertainment landscape. With countless options available at our fingertips, individuals often struggle to discover content that resonates with their unique tastes and preferences. Personalized recommendations leverage algorithms and user data to streamline this process, ensuring that users receive tailored suggestions that enhance their engagement and satisfaction.

Theoretical Foundations

The theoretical framework behind personalized recommendations is largely rooted in collaborative filtering and content-based filtering. Collaborative filtering relies on the behavior and preferences of similar users to recommend items. For example, if User A and User B have similar tastes in movies, and User A enjoys a specific film, it is likely that User B will also appreciate that film. This can be mathematically represented as follows:

$$R_{ui} = \frac{\sum_{v \in N(u)} (R_{vi} \cdot sim(u,v))}{\sum_{v \in N(u)} sim(u,v)} \tag{51}$$

where R_{ui} is the predicted rating for user u on item i, $N(u)$ represents the set of users similar to u, and $sim(u,v)$ is the similarity score between users u and v.

Content-based filtering, on the other hand, recommends items based on the attributes of the items themselves and the user's past preferences. For instance, if a user enjoys action films, the system will recommend other action films based on their genre, director, or cast. The recommendation can be represented as:

$$R_{ui} = \sum_{j \in I} (w_j \cdot f_{ji}) \tag{52}$$

where R_{ui} is the predicted rating for user u on item i, I is the set of items, w_j is the weight assigned to feature j, and f_{ji} is the feature value of item i for feature j.

Challenges in Personalized Recommendations

Despite the advantages of personalized recommendations, several challenges persist. One significant issue is the *cold start problem*, which occurs when there is insufficient user data to make accurate recommendations. This can happen with new users who have not yet provided enough information about their preferences or with new items that have not been rated by enough users.

Additionally, the algorithms can inadvertently reinforce existing biases, leading to a phenomenon known as the *filter bubble*. Users may find themselves repeatedly exposed to similar content, limiting their exposure to diverse viewpoints and genres. This can stifle creativity and prevent users from discovering new interests.

Examples of Personalized Recommendations in Practice

Numerous platforms have successfully implemented personalized recommendations to enhance user experience. For instance, Netflix employs sophisticated algorithms that analyze viewing history, ratings, and user behavior to curate personalized movie and series suggestions. The platform's recommendation engine accounts for over 80% of the content watched on the service, demonstrating its effectiveness in engaging users.

Similarly, Spotify utilizes a combination of collaborative filtering and natural language processing to create personalized playlists, such as "Discover Weekly," which introduces users to new music based on their listening habits. The success of these personalized playlists has significantly contributed to user retention and satisfaction.

Future Directions

As technology continues to evolve, the future of personalized recommendations and curation holds immense potential. Emerging techniques such as deep learning and reinforcement learning are being explored to improve recommendation systems further. These advanced methods can analyze vast amounts of data more effectively, enabling even more accurate and nuanced recommendations.

Moreover, ethical considerations surrounding data privacy and algorithmic transparency are becoming increasingly important. Users must be informed about how their data is being used and the potential biases inherent in recommendation algorithms. Striking a balance between personalization and user privacy will be crucial in shaping the future landscape of personalized recommendations and curation.

In conclusion, personalized recommendations and curation play a pivotal role in transforming the arts and entertainment industry. By leveraging sophisticated algorithms and user data, platforms can enhance user experience, foster engagement, and promote the discovery of diverse content. However, addressing the challenges of cold starts, filter bubbles, and ethical considerations will be essential for the continued evolution of this vital aspect of digital culture.

Live-Streaming and Virtual Concerts

The rise of live-streaming and virtual concerts marks a transformative moment in the arts and entertainment landscape. With the advent of technology and the increasing ubiquity of high-speed internet, artists and audiences have been able to connect in real-time, transcending geographical barriers. This section explores the implications of this phenomenon, the challenges it presents, and notable examples that illustrate its impact.

Theoretical Framework

Live-streaming can be understood through the lens of media convergence theory, which posits that the merging of previously distinct media forms creates new opportunities for content creation and consumption. According to Jenkins (2006), media convergence results in a participatory culture where audiences are not just passive consumers but active participants in the content they engage with. This participatory culture is particularly evident in live-streaming, where viewers can interact with performers through comments, reactions, and even live chats.

The equation for audience engagement in live-streaming can be represented as:

$$E = \frac{I + R + C}{T} \tag{53}$$

where:

- E = Engagement level
- I = Interactions (likes, shares)
- R = Real-time responses (comments, reactions)
- C = Content quality (production value, artist performance)
- T = Time spent watching

This equation illustrates that higher engagement levels are achieved through a combination of content quality and active viewer participation.

Challenges of Live-Streaming and Virtual Concerts

Despite the advantages, live-streaming and virtual concerts come with their own set of challenges:

- **Technical Issues:** Buffering, lag, and connectivity problems can detract from the viewer experience. A study by Pew Research Center (2021) noted that 45% of users experienced technical difficulties during live streams, which can lead to viewer frustration and disengagement.
- **Monetization:** Artists often struggle with monetizing their virtual performances. Traditional revenue streams, such as ticket sales and merchandise, may not translate effectively to the online space. According to a report by the International Federation of the Phonographic Industry

(IFPI, 2020), only 30% of musicians reported earning significant income from live-streaming events.

- **Audience Fatigue:** With the proliferation of live-streamed events, audiences may experience fatigue, leading to reduced attendance and engagement. A survey by Eventbrite (2021) revealed that 65% of respondents felt overwhelmed by the number of virtual events available.

- **Intimacy and Connection:** While virtual concerts allow for global reach, they can lack the intimate atmosphere of in-person performances. The absence of physical presence can make it challenging for artists to forge a personal connection with their audience.

Notable Examples of Live-Streaming and Virtual Concerts

Several artists and platforms have successfully navigated the challenges of live-streaming, creating memorable experiences for audiences:

- **Travis Scott's Fortnite Concert:** In April 2020, Travis Scott performed a virtual concert within the popular video game Fortnite, attracting over 12 million simultaneous viewers. The event showcased innovative use of technology, blending gaming and music, and included interactive elements where players could engage with the performance in real-time.

- **Billie Eilish's Live-Streamed Concert:** Billie Eilish hosted a live-streamed concert titled "Where Do We Go? The Livestream" in October 2020. The event featured stunning visuals and interactive elements, including a Q&A session with fans. The concert generated significant revenue through ticket sales and merchandise, demonstrating the potential for successful monetization in virtual formats.

- **NPR's Tiny Desk Concerts:** NPR's Tiny Desk series transitioned to virtual formats during the pandemic, allowing artists to perform intimate sets from their homes. This series has become a beloved platform for emerging and established artists, showcasing the power of simplicity and authenticity in live-streamed performances.

Conclusion

Live-streaming and virtual concerts represent a significant evolution in the way artists connect with their audiences. While challenges remain, the potential for engagement, global reach, and innovation continues to drive this trend forward. As technology evolves, it is essential for artists and industry stakeholders to adapt, finding new ways to monetize and enhance the virtual concert experience. The future of live entertainment may very well depend on the continued exploration of these digital avenues, fostering a dynamic and inclusive cultural landscape.

Bibliography

[1] Jenkins, H. (2006). *Convergence Culture: Where Old and New Media Collide.* New York: New York University Press.

[2] Pew Research Center. (2021). *The State of Online Events: A Survey of Users and Trends.* Retrieved from https://www.pewresearch.org

[3] International Federation of the Phonographic Industry. (2020). *Global Music Report 2020.* Retrieved from https://www.ifpi.org

[4] Eventbrite. (2021). *The Future of Live Events: A Survey of Attendees.* Retrieved from https://www.eventbrite.com

Creating Unique Audience Experiences

In an era where attention spans are dwindling and audiences are craving more engaging content, the need for unique audience experiences has never been more crucial. This section explores how Cultural Connector is redefining audience engagement through innovative strategies and technologies, ultimately transforming how audiences interact with art and entertainment.

Theoretical Framework

The concept of unique audience experiences draws from several theoretical frameworks, including the Experience Economy proposed by Pine and Gilmore (1998), which posits that businesses must create memorable events for their customers. In the context of arts and entertainment, this means moving beyond traditional consumption to immersive experiences that evoke emotions and foster connections.

$$E = f(M, I, C) \tag{54}$$

where E represents the audience experience, M is the emotional engagement, I is the interactivity level, and C is the context of the experience. This equation suggests that a successful unique audience experience is a function of these three variables, emphasizing the importance of emotional and interactive components in creating memorable moments.

Challenges in Audience Engagement

Despite the potential for creating unique experiences, several challenges persist:

1. **Diverse Audience Needs**: Audiences come from varied backgrounds, each with unique preferences and expectations. Catering to this diversity can be challenging, as what resonates with one demographic may not with another.

2. **Technological Limitations**: While technology offers numerous tools for engagement, not all audiences have equal access to these resources. This digital divide can limit the effectiveness of innovative experiences.

3. **Content Saturation**: With the proliferation of content available online, audiences are often overwhelmed, making it difficult for creators to capture and retain attention.

4. **Measuring Engagement**: Quantifying the success of unique audience experiences can be complex. Traditional metrics may not adequately capture the emotional and experiential aspects of engagement.

Innovative Strategies for Engagement

To overcome these challenges, Cultural Connector employs several innovative strategies to create unique audience experiences:

1. Immersive Environments Utilizing augmented and virtual reality technologies, Cultural Connector crafts immersive environments that transport audiences into the heart of the experience. For example, a virtual reality art exhibit allows users to explore a digital gallery, interact with artworks, and even engage with the artists in real-time. This level of immersion fosters a deeper connection between the audience and the content.

2. Personalized Content Delivery Leveraging data analytics and machine learning algorithms, Cultural Connector tailors content delivery to individual audience preferences. By analyzing user behavior, the platform can recommend personalized experiences that align with users' interests, thereby enhancing engagement and satisfaction.

3. Interactive Storytelling By incorporating interactive elements into narratives, Cultural Connector empowers audiences to influence the direction of the story. This approach not only captivates attention but also encourages active participation. For instance, a live-streamed performance might allow viewers to vote on plot developments, making them co-creators of the experience.

4. Community Engagement Creating a sense of community is essential for fostering unique audience experiences. Cultural Connector facilitates online forums and discussion groups where audiences can share their thoughts, experiences, and interpretations. This collective engagement enriches the experience and builds a loyal community around the content.

Case Studies

Several notable examples illustrate the effectiveness of these strategies:

1. The Virtual Art Gallery In 2022, Cultural Connector launched a virtual art gallery featuring works from emerging artists worldwide. By utilizing VR technology, visitors could navigate the gallery, interact with digital installations, and attend live Q&A sessions with the artists. Feedback indicated that 85% of participants felt more connected to the art and artists compared to traditional galleries.

2. Interactive Theater Production A theater company collaborated with Cultural Connector to create an interactive production where audience members could choose different storylines. The result was a multi-layered experience that engaged audiences on multiple levels, leading to a 40% increase in ticket sales compared to previous productions.

3. Personalized Music Recommendations Cultural Connector's music platform uses AI to analyze listening habits and recommend curated playlists tailored to individual tastes. This personalization has led to a 30% increase in user engagement, as listeners are more likely to explore and enjoy content that resonates with them.

Conclusion

Creating unique audience experiences is not just about leveraging technology; it is about fostering connections and evoking emotions. By embracing innovative strategies that prioritize interactivity, personalization, and community engagement, Cultural Connector is redefining how audiences experience art and entertainment. As we move forward, the challenge will be to continually adapt and evolve these strategies to meet the ever-changing needs of diverse audiences, ensuring that the experiences created are not only memorable but also meaningful.

Bibliography

[1] Pine, B. J., & Gilmore, J. H. (1998). *The Experience Economy: Work Is Theatre & Every Business a Stage*. Harvard Business Review Press.

Empowering Independent Artists

In the rapidly evolving landscape of arts and entertainment, independent artists face unique challenges that can inhibit their creative expression and financial stability. The advent of digital platforms and the Cultural Connector has provided unprecedented opportunities for these artists to thrive, enabling them to reach wider audiences, monetize their work, and maintain creative control. This section explores the mechanisms through which independent artists are empowered, the theoretical frameworks that support this empowerment, and examples of successful independent artists who have leveraged the Cultural Connector.

Theoretical Frameworks

Empowerment theory posits that individuals gain power and control over their lives through access to resources, knowledge, and networks. In the context of independent artists, empowerment can be analyzed through three primary lenses: economic empowerment, creative autonomy, and community support.

    1. **Economic Empowerment:** This refers to the ability of independent artists to generate income from their work without relying on traditional gatekeepers such as record labels or galleries. Economic empowerment is facilitated by platforms that allow artists to sell their work directly to consumers, thereby increasing their revenue share.

    2. **Creative Autonomy:** Independent artists often operate outside the constraints of mainstream commercial expectations. This autonomy allows them to explore innovative artistic expressions and themes that may not align with commercial viability. The Cultural Connector provides tools and platforms that

allow artists to showcase their unique voices without compromising their artistic integrity.

3. **Community Support:** The rise of online communities has created networks where independent artists can collaborate, share resources, and promote each other's work. This sense of community fosters an environment of mutual support and encouragement, which is vital for the sustainability of independent art practices.

Challenges Faced by Independent Artists

Despite the opportunities presented by the Cultural Connector, independent artists still encounter significant challenges:

1. **Market Saturation:** With the democratization of content creation, the market is flooded with independent works, making it difficult for artists to stand out. According to the theory of *information overload*, consumers may struggle to navigate the vast array of options, leading to decision fatigue.

2. **Financial Instability:** Many independent artists face unpredictable income streams, which can make it challenging to sustain their practice. The lack of traditional funding sources, such as grants or sponsorships, exacerbates this issue.

3. **Access to Resources:** While digital platforms have lowered barriers to entry, not all artists have equal access to the necessary tools and technology to produce and promote their work. This digital divide can hinder the ability of certain groups, particularly marginalized communities, to fully participate in the cultural economy.

Examples of Empowerment through Cultural Connector

Several independent artists have successfully navigated these challenges by leveraging the Cultural Connector:

1. **Musician Example: Amanda Lee** - Amanda Lee, an independent musician, utilized social media platforms to build a following and connect with fans directly. By releasing her music on streaming services and engaging with her audience through live-streamed performances, she has created a sustainable income model that allows her to retain creative control over her work. Her success illustrates the economic empowerment aspect of the Cultural Connector.

2. **Visual Artist Example: Malik Thompson** - Malik Thompson, a visual artist, has embraced online galleries and social media to showcase his art. By participating in virtual exhibitions and collaborating with other artists through the Cultural Connector, he has gained visibility and access to new markets. His story

highlights the importance of community support and creative autonomy in empowering independent artists.

3. **Filmmaker Example: Sarah Kim** - Sarah Kim, an independent filmmaker, utilized crowdfunding platforms to finance her projects. By engaging her audience through social media and providing behind-the-scenes content, she built a loyal community that supported her work financially. Her experience demonstrates how independent artists can leverage community support to overcome financial instability.

Conclusion

The Cultural Connector has played a pivotal role in empowering independent artists by providing them with the tools, resources, and networks necessary to thrive in a competitive landscape. By addressing the challenges of market saturation, financial instability, and access to resources, independent artists can harness the power of digital platforms to amplify their voices and achieve their artistic visions. The ongoing evolution of these platforms promises to further enhance the opportunities for independent artists, ensuring that diverse and innovative artistic expressions continue to flourish in the cultural landscape.

$$P = \frac{R}{C} \qquad (55)$$

Where:

- P = Profitability
- R = Revenue generated by the artist
- C = Costs associated with production and distribution

This equation illustrates the financial dynamics that independent artists must navigate to achieve sustainability in their creative endeavors. As the Cultural Connector continues to evolve, it will be essential to monitor its impact on the empowerment of independent artists and the broader cultural economy.

Exploring the Intersection of Technology and Performance

The intersection of technology and performance has increasingly become a fertile ground for innovation within the arts. This synergy not only transforms how performances are created and experienced but also challenges traditional notions of artistry and audience engagement.

Theoretical Framework

The integration of technology into performance can be understood through several theoretical lenses, including *media theory, performance studies,* and *cultural studies.* Media theory, particularly the work of Marshall McLuhan, posits that "the medium is the message," suggesting that the technology used in performance fundamentally alters the way content is perceived. In performance studies, theorists like Richard Schechner emphasize the importance of the performance environment, which can be profoundly influenced by technological elements such as lighting, sound, and digital projections.

Problems and Challenges

Despite the exciting possibilities that technology offers, several challenges arise when merging it with performance. One major issue is the risk of *over-reliance* on technology, which can detract from the human element of performance. For instance, performances that heavily utilize visual effects may lead to a diminished emotional connection between the performers and the audience. Additionally, the rapid pace of technological advancement can create disparities in access. Not all artists or institutions can afford the latest tools, leading to a divide between those who can innovate and those who cannot.

Another challenge is the potential for *technical failures.* A reliance on complex technological setups can result in disruptions during live performances, which may alienate audiences. The infamous incident during the 2017 Academy Awards, where the wrong film was announced as Best Picture due to a technical error, exemplifies the precarious nature of technology in live performances.

Case Studies

Several notable examples illustrate the successful integration of technology in performance:

- **The Lion King on Broadway:** The use of puppetry and digital projections in Disney's adaptation of *The Lion King* showcases how technology can enhance storytelling. The innovative use of projections to create the African savanna backdrop allows for a more immersive experience, blurring the lines between reality and performance.

- **The Wooster Group:** This experimental theater company is known for its avant-garde approach to performance, utilizing video projections and live feeds to create a layered narrative. Their production of *Hamlet* incorporated real-time video manipulation, allowing the audience to experience the play through multiple perspectives simultaneously.

- **Cirque du Soleil:** Known for its breathtaking acrobatics and theatrical flair, Cirque du Soleil integrates technology in various forms, such as augmented reality and interactive projections. Their show, O, features a massive water stage with synchronized multimedia elements, creating a unique blend of physical performance and digital artistry.

The Future of Technology in Performance

Looking ahead, the possibilities for technology in performance are vast. Innovations such as *virtual reality (VR)* and *augmented reality (AR)* are set to redefine audience engagement. For instance, VR can transport audiences to different worlds, allowing them to experience performances from within the narrative itself. This immersive experience challenges the traditional role of the spectator, transforming them into active participants.

Moreover, the rise of *live streaming* technology has made performances accessible to global audiences, breaking geographical barriers. Artists can now reach viewers who may not have the means to attend live events, democratizing access to the arts.

Conclusion

In conclusion, the intersection of technology and performance represents a dynamic and evolving landscape. While challenges exist, the potential for innovation and redefinition of artistic expression is immense. As artists continue to explore this intersection, they will not only push the boundaries of performance but also enrich the cultural fabric of society. The future promises an exciting fusion of creativity and technology, where the stage becomes a canvas for limitless possibilities.

Redefining the Film and Television Industry

The film and television industry has undergone a significant transformation in recent years, driven largely by advancements in technology and the emergence of new platforms for content distribution. This subsection explores how Cultural Connector has played a pivotal role in redefining the landscape of film and television, addressing key theories, challenges, and real-world examples that illustrate this evolution.

Theoretical Framework

To understand the changes within the film and television industry, we can reference the **Media Ecology Theory**, which posits that media environments shape human experiences and societal structures. As new forms of media emerge, they alter the way audiences consume content, interact with creators, and perceive narratives. Cultural Connector exemplifies this theory by fostering an environment where diverse voices can flourish, leading to a richer tapestry of storytelling.

Challenges in the Traditional Film and Television Model

Historically, the film and television industry has been characterized by a few dominant players controlling production and distribution. This oligopoly has led to several challenges:

- **Gatekeeping:** Traditional studios often act as gatekeepers, deciding which stories are worth telling and which voices are amplified. This has resulted in a lack of diversity in narratives and representation.

- **Content Saturation:** With the rise of streaming services, audiences are inundated with content, leading to a phenomenon known as *choice paralysis*. Viewers often struggle to find quality content amidst the overwhelming options.

- **Monetization Issues:** The traditional revenue models, reliant on box office sales and advertising, have been disrupted by the proliferation of ad-free streaming services, leading to a reevaluation of how content creators are compensated.

Cultural Connector's Innovations

Cultural Connector has emerged as a transformative force in the film and television industry by addressing these challenges head-on. Its innovative platform allows for the democratization of content creation and distribution, enabling creators from diverse backgrounds to share their stories with a global audience.

Democratization of Content Creation

Cultural Connector provides tools and resources that empower independent filmmakers and content creators. By lowering the barriers to entry, the platform encourages a wider range of voices to participate in the storytelling process. For instance, through collaborative projects and workshops, emerging filmmakers can access funding, mentorship, and distribution channels that were previously unavailable to them.

Interactive and Immersive Experiences

The integration of augmented reality (AR) and virtual reality (VR) into film and television production has redefined audience engagement. Cultural Connector has pioneered projects that allow viewers to immerse themselves in narratives, transforming passive consumption into active participation. For example, the interactive series *Beyond the Screen* invites viewers to make choices that affect the storyline, creating a personalized viewing experience.

User-Generated Content and Community Engagement

In a departure from traditional content models, Cultural Connector champions user-generated content (UGC) as a legitimate form of storytelling. By hosting competitions and showcasing UGC on its platform, Cultural Connector not only amplifies diverse voices but also fosters community engagement. The success of the short film competition *Voices Unheard* illustrates this point, where submissions from aspiring filmmakers were curated into a widely viewed anthology.

New Revenue Models

Cultural Connector has also explored alternative monetization strategies that benefit creators. By implementing a subscription-based model, the platform allows audiences to support their favorite creators directly. This shift challenges the traditional advertising-based model and promotes a more sustainable ecosystem for independent filmmakers.

Case Studies

Several case studies illustrate the impact of Cultural Connector on the film and television industry:

- **The Documentary Project:** *Voices of Change*: This documentary series, produced through Cultural Connector, highlights grassroots movements around the world. By utilizing crowdfunding and community engagement, the project raised over $500,000, showcasing the power of collective storytelling.

- **The Interactive Film:** *Choose Your Path*: This innovative film allows viewers to make decisions that affect the narrative outcome. Released exclusively on Cultural Connector, it garnered critical acclaim for its unique approach to storytelling and audience engagement, leading to discussions about the future of interactive media.

- **The Global Film Festival:** *Cultural Connect*: This annual festival, hosted by Cultural Connector, showcases films from around the world, emphasizing underrepresented voices. The festival has become a platform for networking and collaboration, further solidifying Cultural Connector's role as a cultural hub.

Conclusion

Cultural Connector is redefining the film and television industry by challenging traditional norms and embracing innovative practices. Through democratization, interactive experiences, community engagement, and new revenue models, the platform is paving the way for a more inclusive and diverse media landscape. As we move forward, it is essential to continue exploring the potential of technology to enhance storytelling and foster connections among creators and audiences.

The future of the film and television industry lies in its ability to adapt to these changes and to embrace the myriad of voices that contribute to the rich tapestry of human experience. Cultural Connector stands at the forefront of this evolution, shaping the narrative for generations to come.

Navigating the Copyright Landscape

In the digital age, the copyright landscape has become increasingly complex, particularly in the realms of arts and entertainment. As creators leverage new technologies to produce and distribute their work, the implications of copyright law evolve, prompting both opportunities and challenges. This section explores the nuances of copyright in the context of the Cultural Connector platform, examining the theoretical frameworks, practical problems, and real-world examples that shape the current landscape.

Theoretical Frameworks of Copyright

Copyright law is fundamentally designed to protect the rights of creators while promoting the progress of science and useful arts. The U.S. Constitution grants

Congress the power to enact copyright laws, which aim to balance the interests of creators and the public. The key principles of copyright theory include:

- **Originality:** Copyright protects original works of authorship, meaning that the work must be independently created and possess a minimal degree of creativity.

- **Fixation:** A work must be fixed in a tangible medium of expression to qualify for copyright protection. This includes written works, recorded music, and digital content.

- **Duration:** Copyright protection lasts for a limited time, after which the work enters the public domain. As of now, the duration of copyright for individual authors is the life of the author plus 70 years.

The theoretical underpinnings of copyright can be articulated through the following equation, representing the balance between creator rights and public access:

$$C = R - P \qquad (56)$$

Where:

- C = Creator's rights
- R = Rights granted by copyright law
- P = Public access to works

This equation highlights the ongoing negotiation between protecting the creator's rights and ensuring public access to creative works.

Problems in the Copyright Landscape

Despite the theoretical framework, several practical problems arise in navigating the copyright landscape:

- **Infringement Issues:** With the rise of digital content sharing, unauthorized use of copyrighted material has become rampant. This raises questions about fair use and the extent to which users can engage with copyrighted works without infringing on the creator's rights.

- **Global Variability:** Copyright laws vary significantly across countries, complicating enforcement for creators who wish to distribute their work internationally. The lack of uniformity can lead to confusion and potential exploitation of creators in jurisdictions with weaker protections.

- **Digital Rights Management (DRM):** While DRM technologies aim to protect digital content, they can also restrict legitimate uses and access, leading to frustration among consumers and creators alike. The balance between protection and accessibility remains a contentious issue.

- **Misinformation and Misattribution:** In a digital landscape where content can be easily manipulated and shared, misinformation regarding copyright ownership can lead to misattribution of works, undermining the rights of original creators.

Real-World Examples

Real-world examples illustrate the challenges and evolving nature of copyright in the digital age:

- **The Case of "Blurred Lines":** The 2015 court case involving Robin Thicke's "Blurred Lines" highlighted the complexities of copyright infringement. The court ruled that Thicke and his co-writer had infringed on Marvin Gaye's "Got to Give It Up," emphasizing the subjective nature of originality and inspiration in music creation.

- **YouTube's Content ID System:** YouTube's Content ID system represents an attempt to navigate copyright issues in user-generated content. While it allows copyright holders to claim and monetize their content, it has also faced criticism for its automated nature, which can lead to wrongful takedowns and disputes over fair use.

- **The Rise of Creative Commons:** Creative Commons provides a licensing framework that allows creators to share their work while retaining certain rights. This initiative has gained traction among artists seeking to navigate copyright restrictions while promoting collaboration and access to creative content.

The Future of Copyright in the Digital Age

As technology continues to evolve, so too must copyright law. The Cultural Connector platform exemplifies the need for adaptive strategies to address the challenges of copyright in the digital landscape. Potential developments include:

- **Revising Copyright Laws:** Legislators may need to reconsider existing copyright laws to better reflect the realities of digital content creation and distribution, including clearer guidelines on fair use and the implications of remix culture.

- **Enhancing Digital Literacy:** Educating creators and consumers about copyright laws and their rights can empower individuals to navigate the landscape more effectively, fostering a culture of respect for intellectual property.

- **International Cooperation:** Collaborative efforts among countries to harmonize copyright laws could mitigate the challenges posed by jurisdictional discrepancies, ensuring creators are better protected on a global scale.

In conclusion, navigating the copyright landscape in the context of the Cultural Connector platform requires a nuanced understanding of the theoretical principles, practical problems, and real-world implications of copyright law. As creators continue to innovate and push the boundaries of artistic expression, the conversation surrounding copyright must evolve to foster a more equitable and accessible creative ecosystem.

Pushing the Boundaries of Imagination

In the rapidly evolving landscape of arts and entertainment, the concept of pushing the boundaries of imagination has become a critical focal point for creators, innovators, and audiences alike. This section explores how the integration of technology, collaboration, and new creative processes is reshaping the ways in which art is conceived, produced, and experienced.

The Role of Technology in Expanding Creative Horizons

Technology serves as a catalyst for artistic innovation, allowing creators to explore previously uncharted territories. The advent of virtual reality (VR), augmented reality (AR), and artificial intelligence (AI) has provided artists with tools to transcend traditional mediums. For instance, VR enables immersive storytelling experiences that engage audiences in a multi-sensory manner. One notable example is the VR installation "The Night Cafe," which allows users to step into a digital recreation of Vincent van Gogh's famous painting, experiencing the artwork in a three-dimensional space. This interactive approach not only enhances viewer engagement but also invites them to participate in the narrative of the artwork.

Collaboration Across Disciplines

Pushing the boundaries of imagination often requires collaboration across various disciplines. Artists, technologists, and scientists are increasingly joining forces to create hybrid works that challenge conventional definitions of art. An exemplary case is the collaboration between visual artists and data scientists in projects that visualize complex data sets through artistic expression. One such project is "Data-Driven Art," where data related to climate change is transformed into dynamic visual installations. This intersection of art and science not only raises awareness about pressing global issues but also encourages audiences to engage with data in a more visceral and emotional way.

Interactive and Participatory Art

The shift towards interactive and participatory art forms represents another significant trend in pushing the boundaries of imagination. Artists are now inviting audiences to become co-creators, blurring the lines between artist and viewer. This participatory approach can be seen in projects like "The Obliteration Room" by Yayoi Kusama, where visitors are given colorful dot stickers to place throughout a white room, transforming it into a vibrant explosion of color over time. Such experiences empower audiences to take an active role in the artistic process, fostering a sense of community and shared ownership of the artwork.

Theoretical Frameworks: Imagination and Creativity

The exploration of imagination in art can be grounded in several theoretical frameworks. Theories of creativity, such as the Componential Theory of Creativity proposed by Amabile (1983), emphasize the importance of intrinsic motivation, domain-relevant skills, and creativity-relevant processes. This framework suggests that when artists are provided with the right environment and tools, they are more likely to push the boundaries of their imagination.

Moreover, Csikszentmihalyi's (1996) concept of "flow" describes the state of complete immersion and engagement that artists experience during the creative process. This state is often characterized by heightened creativity and innovation, as artists lose themselves in their work, allowing their imaginations to run free.

Challenges in Expanding Imagination

While the potential for pushing the boundaries of imagination is vast, several challenges remain. One significant issue is the accessibility of technology. Not all artists have equal access to cutting-edge tools and resources, which can create disparities in who gets to innovate and redefine artistic boundaries. Furthermore, the rapid pace of technological change can lead to a sense of overwhelm, where artists may struggle to keep up with new tools and platforms, potentially stifling their creative processes.

Additionally, the commercialization of art in the digital age raises ethical questions about the commodification of creativity. As art becomes increasingly intertwined with technology, concerns about authenticity and originality emerge. The rise of AI-generated art, for instance, challenges traditional notions of authorship and creativity, prompting debates about the role of human intuition and emotion in the artistic process.

Conclusion: The Future of Imagination in Arts and Entertainment

As we look to the future, the potential for pushing the boundaries of imagination in arts and entertainment is both exciting and complex. The integration of technology, collaborative practices, and participatory experiences will continue to redefine the landscape of creativity. Artists who embrace these changes and adapt to the evolving environment will likely lead the charge in exploring new forms of expression and connection.

In summary, pushing the boundaries of imagination is not merely an artistic endeavor; it is a reflection of our collective desire to explore, innovate, and connect in an increasingly complex world. As we continue to navigate the intersections of art and technology, the possibilities for creative expression are boundless.

> **Theorem**
>
> Let C represent the creative potential of an artist, T the technological tools available, and E the environment in which the artist operates. The relationship can be expressed as:
>
> $$C = f(T, E)$$
>
> where f is a function that indicates that increased access to technology and a supportive environment enhance creative potential.

The Impact of Cultural Connector on Media

The Rise of User-Generated Content

User-generated content (UGC) has transformed the landscape of media and communication, serving as a cornerstone for the Cultural Connector platform pioneered by Riley Dubois. This section delves into the emergence of UGC, its theoretical underpinnings, inherent challenges, and notable examples that illustrate its profound impact on the creative economy.

Theoretical Framework

The rise of UGC can be contextualized within several theoretical frameworks, including the **Participatory Culture** model posited by Henry Jenkins. Jenkins argues that participatory culture allows individuals to engage in creative expression and community-building, challenging traditional notions of media consumption. According to Jenkins, this shift democratizes content creation, enabling a diverse array of voices to be heard.

Additionally, the **Long Tail Theory** proposed by Chris Anderson elucidates how UGC allows niche content to thrive alongside mainstream offerings. In a digital ecosystem where distribution costs are minimal, creators can reach audiences that were previously inaccessible, fostering a more varied and inclusive media landscape.

Challenges of User-Generated Content

Despite its advantages, UGC presents several challenges that must be addressed:

- **Quality Control:** The open nature of UGC can lead to a proliferation of low-quality content. Platforms must implement mechanisms to curate and highlight high-quality contributions, ensuring that audiences are not overwhelmed by subpar offerings.

- **Intellectual Property Issues:** As users create and share content, questions surrounding copyright and ownership arise. The ambiguity of intellectual property rights in UGC can lead to legal disputes, necessitating clear guidelines and policies.

- **Misinformation:** The rapid dissemination of information through UGC can facilitate the spread of misinformation. Platforms must develop strategies to combat false narratives while preserving freedom of expression.

- **Digital Divide:** Not all individuals have equal access to the tools and platforms necessary for content creation. This digital divide can exacerbate existing inequalities, limiting the diversity of voices in the UGC landscape.

Examples of User-Generated Content

Several notable examples illustrate the transformative power of UGC:

- **YouTube:** Initially a platform for sharing personal videos, YouTube has evolved into a hub for user-generated content, where creators can monetize their work and build substantial audiences. The platform has given rise to a new class of influencers, reshaping advertising and brand engagement.

- **Wikipedia:** As a collaborative online encyclopedia, Wikipedia exemplifies the power of collective intelligence. Users contribute content, edit entries, and ensure the accuracy of information, creating a valuable resource that is continuously updated and refined.

- **TikTok:** This social media platform has revolutionized short-form video content, empowering users to create and share videos that often go viral. TikTok's algorithm promotes diverse content, allowing users from various backgrounds to gain visibility and engage with global audiences.

- **Reddit:** Known as "the front page of the internet," Reddit allows users to share and discuss content across countless subreddits. This platform fosters community engagement and encourages users to contribute their unique perspectives on a wide range of topics.

Conclusion

The rise of user-generated content represents a paradigm shift in how individuals interact with media and each other. By democratizing content creation, UGC empowers users to become active participants in the cultural conversation, fostering a sense of community and shared experience. However, it also necessitates careful consideration of the challenges it presents, including quality control, intellectual property rights, and the potential for misinformation. As Cultural Connector continues to evolve, addressing these issues will be crucial in harnessing the full potential of user-generated content to foster innovation and social connection.

Disrupting Traditional Media Channels

The emergence of Cultural Connector has significantly disrupted traditional media channels, reshaping how content is produced, distributed, and consumed. This transformation can be understood through several theoretical frameworks, including the Diffusion of Innovations Theory, the Long Tail Theory, and the Participatory Culture model.

Theoretical Foundations

Diffusion of Innovations Theory Everett Rogers' Diffusion of Innovations Theory posits that innovations are communicated through certain channels over time among the members of a social system. In the context of Cultural Connector, the platform serves as a conduit for innovative media practices that spread rapidly among users, leading to a shift away from traditional media consumption towards more participatory forms of engagement. This theory highlights the role of opinion leaders and early adopters in driving the acceptance of new media formats.

Long Tail Theory Chris Anderson's Long Tail Theory suggests that the internet allows for the distribution of niche products that may not be profitable in traditional markets. Cultural Connector exemplifies this by providing a platform where independent creators can share their work with a global audience, thus disrupting the traditional media model that favors mainstream content. This shift allows for a greater diversity of voices and perspectives, as niche content can find its audience without the constraints of traditional gatekeeping mechanisms.

Participatory Culture Henry Jenkins' concept of participatory culture emphasizes the active involvement of audiences in the creation and sharing of media. Cultural Connector embodies this model by enabling users to generate and curate content, fostering a sense of community and collaboration. This participatory approach challenges the traditional media paradigm, where consumers are passive recipients of content produced by a select few.

Problems with Traditional Media Channels

Traditional media channels have faced numerous challenges in the wake of digital innovation. These issues include:

1. **Declining Viewership** As audiences increasingly turn to digital platforms for content consumption, traditional media channels have experienced a decline in viewership. For instance, television networks have seen a significant drop in ratings as streaming services like Netflix and Hulu gain popularity. According to a report by Nielsen, traditional TV viewership among adults aged 18-34 fell by 30% from 2019 to 2021.

2. **Advertising Revenue Loss** The shift to digital media has also led to a decrease in advertising revenue for traditional outlets. Advertisers are reallocating their budgets to online platforms that offer targeted advertising capabilities. A study by eMarketer predicts that digital ad spending will surpass traditional media ad spending by 2024, highlighting the urgency for traditional media channels to adapt.

3. **Gatekeeping and Homogenization** Traditional media channels often operate under strict gatekeeping structures, limiting the diversity of voices and perspectives in the media landscape. This homogenization can lead to a lack of representation and a disconnect between media content and audience interests. Cultural Connector disrupts this model by allowing a wider range of creators to produce and share content, fostering a more inclusive media environment.

Examples of Disruption

Several case studies illustrate how Cultural Connector has disrupted traditional media channels:

1. **User-Generated Content Platforms** Platforms like YouTube and TikTok have revolutionized content creation by allowing users to produce and share their videos. These platforms have become significant competitors to traditional

television networks, with some YouTube creators amassing millions of subscribers and views. For example, the YouTube channel T-Series, which features Bollywood music videos, surpassed traditional media giants like CNN and ESPN in terms of viewership.

2. **Crowdfunding for Media Projects** Cultural Connector has facilitated crowdfunding for independent media projects, enabling creators to bypass traditional funding sources. Platforms like Kickstarter and Indiegogo allow creators to pitch their ideas directly to audiences, who can financially support projects they believe in. This model has led to the successful production of films, documentaries, and web series that may have otherwise struggled to find backing through traditional channels.

3. **Streaming Services and Original Content** Streaming services such as Netflix, Amazon Prime, and Disney+ have disrupted traditional television and film distribution by producing original content that appeals directly to consumer preferences. These platforms leverage data analytics to understand audience behavior and preferences, allowing them to create targeted programming that resonates with viewers. For example, Netflix's original series "Stranger Things" became a cultural phenomenon, drawing in millions of subscribers and redefining how content is consumed.

Conclusion

Cultural Connector's impact on traditional media channels is profound, as it not only disrupts existing structures but also paves the way for new forms of media engagement. By embracing participatory culture, leveraging the Long Tail Theory, and addressing the shortcomings of traditional media, Cultural Connector is reshaping the media landscape into one that is more inclusive, diverse, and responsive to audience needs. As we move forward, it is essential to recognize the ongoing evolution of media channels and the role of innovation in shaping our cultural narratives.

$$\text{Disruption Index} = \frac{\text{New Media Engagement}}{\text{Traditional Media Engagement}} \times 100 \qquad (57)$$

This index can be used to quantify the level of disruption caused by platforms like Cultural Connector in comparison to traditional media channels. A value above 100 indicates a significant shift towards new media engagement, reflecting the transformative power of innovation in the media landscape.

Shifting Power Dynamics in Entertainment

In the evolving landscape of entertainment, the traditional power dynamics that once dictated the industry are undergoing significant transformations. The rise of digital platforms, social media, and user-generated content has democratized access to creation and distribution, leading to a reconfiguration of who holds power in the entertainment ecosystem. This section explores the shifting power dynamics in entertainment, the implications for creators and consumers, and the challenges that arise from this transformation.

Theoretical Framework

To understand the shifting power dynamics in entertainment, we can draw upon the theories of cultural production and media power. According to [?], cultural production is influenced by the interplay of various forms of capital: economic, social, and cultural. In the context of entertainment, this means that traditional gatekeepers—such as studios, record labels, and publishers—have historically controlled access to resources and platforms.

However, the advent of digital technology has altered this landscape. Theories of participatory culture, as articulated by [?], emphasize that audiences are no longer passive consumers but active participants in the creation and dissemination of content. This shift challenges the traditional power structures and allows for more diverse voices to emerge.

Emergence of Independent Creators

One of the most notable changes in the entertainment industry is the rise of independent creators. Platforms such as YouTube, TikTok, and Instagram have enabled individuals to produce and share their content without the need for traditional gatekeepers. For example, YouTube has transformed the landscape of video content, allowing creators like **Lilly Singh** and **Markiplier** to build massive followings and monetize their content independently.

This shift has significant implications for traditional media companies. With audiences gravitating towards content produced by independent creators, established entities must adapt to remain relevant. This phenomenon is evident in the rise of streaming services like **Netflix** and **Amazon Prime**, which have begun to invest heavily in original content, often collaborating with independent creators to attract diverse audiences.

Challenges to Traditional Gatekeepers

The shifting power dynamics also present challenges for traditional gatekeepers. As audiences increasingly seek authenticity and relatability, the polished and often formulaic content produced by major studios may fall out of favor. This shift has led to a crisis for traditional media companies, as they struggle to maintain their relevance in a landscape where independent creators can achieve viral success with minimal resources.

Moreover, the democratization of content creation has raised questions about quality control and the sustainability of independent production. While platforms enable diverse voices to be heard, they also contribute to an oversaturated market, making it difficult for creators to stand out. This phenomenon is often referred to as the "content treadmill," where creators must continuously produce content to maintain visibility in a crowded space.

Examples of Shifting Power Dynamics

Several examples illustrate the shifting power dynamics in entertainment:

- **TikTok and Viral Fame:** TikTok has become a breeding ground for viral content, allowing users to gain fame overnight. Creators like **Charli D'Amelio** rose to prominence through their engaging dance videos, leading to lucrative brand partnerships and even television appearances. This phenomenon exemplifies how power has shifted from traditional media to individual creators.

- **Crowdfunding for Films:** Platforms like **Kickstarter** and **Indiegogo** have enabled filmmakers to bypass traditional funding sources. Projects like **Veronica Mars: The Movie** successfully raised over $5 million from fans, demonstrating that audiences can directly influence production decisions.

- **Social Media Activism:** The #OscarsSoWhite movement highlighted the lack of diversity in Hollywood, leading to increased scrutiny of the industry's practices. This grassroots activism, fueled by social media, empowered audiences to demand change and hold traditional gatekeepers accountable.

Future Implications

As power dynamics continue to shift in the entertainment industry, several implications arise:

1. **Increased Diversity of Voices:** The democratization of content creation allows for a broader range of stories and perspectives to be shared, enriching the cultural tapestry of entertainment.

2. **New Business Models:** Traditional media companies must adapt to new business models that incorporate independent creators. Collaborations, sponsorships, and hybrid models will likely become more prevalent.

3. **Ethical Considerations:** The rise of independent creators raises questions about ethical practices in content creation and distribution. Issues such as copyright infringement, fair compensation, and the impact of algorithm-driven visibility must be addressed to ensure a sustainable ecosystem.

In conclusion, the shifting power dynamics in entertainment represent a fundamental change in how content is created, distributed, and consumed. As traditional gatekeepers lose their grip on the industry, independent creators are emerging as influential voices, reshaping the entertainment landscape. The implications of these changes are profound, offering both opportunities and challenges for creators, consumers, and industry stakeholders alike.

Exploring New Revenue Models

In the rapidly evolving landscape of arts and entertainment, traditional revenue models are being challenged and redefined. The advent of digital platforms and the rise of user-generated content have necessitated the exploration of new revenue streams that align with changing consumer behavior and technological advancements. This subsection delves into innovative revenue models that have emerged, their implications for creators and consumers, and the challenges they present.

The Shift from Ownership to Access

One of the most significant shifts in revenue models is the transition from ownership to access. This paradigm change is epitomized by the subscription-based services such as Netflix, Spotify, and Adobe Creative Cloud. Instead of purchasing individual products or media, consumers now pay for access to a vast library of content.

$$\text{Revenue} = \text{Number of Subscribers} \times \text{Monthly Subscription Fee} \quad (58)$$

This model not only provides a steady revenue stream for companies but also democratizes access to high-quality content for consumers. However, it raises questions about the sustainability of creative industries, as artists may receive a fraction of the revenue generated from their work.

Crowdfunding and Direct Support

Another innovative revenue model is crowdfunding, which allows creators to finance their projects directly through contributions from fans and supporters. Platforms like Kickstarter and Patreon have revolutionized how artists and creators fund their work.

For instance, a musician can launch a campaign on Kickstarter to fund an album, offering backers exclusive rewards such as early access to music or personalized merchandise. This model not only generates revenue but also fosters a sense of community and investment among supporters.

$$\text{Total Funding} = \sum_{i=1}^{n} \text{Pledge}_i \tag{59}$$

where Pledge_i represents the individual contributions from backers.

However, while crowdfunding can provide significant financial support, it also places the burden of marketing and outreach on creators, who must effectively engage their audience to reach funding goals.

Dynamic Pricing Models

Dynamic pricing models, which adjust prices based on demand, have gained traction in the entertainment sector. This approach allows companies to maximize revenue by charging higher prices during peak demand periods and offering discounts during off-peak times. For example, airlines and hotels have long employed this strategy, and it is increasingly being applied to ticket sales for concerts and events.

$$\text{Price}_{dynamic} = \text{Base Price} + k \cdot \text{Demand Factor} \tag{60}$$

where k represents the sensitivity of price to demand, and the demand factor varies based on the time to the event and current ticket sales.

While dynamic pricing can enhance revenue, it risks alienating consumers who may feel exploited by fluctuating prices.

The Role of Data Analytics

Data analytics plays a crucial role in shaping new revenue models. By analyzing consumer behavior, preferences, and trends, companies can tailor their offerings and marketing strategies to maximize engagement and revenue. For example, streaming platforms utilize algorithms to recommend content, enhancing user experience and increasing subscription retention rates.

$$\text{Engagement Rate} = \frac{\text{Total Interactions}}{\text{Total Users}} \times 100 \qquad (61)$$

This formula allows companies to measure the effectiveness of their content and marketing strategies, informing future decisions.

However, reliance on data analytics raises ethical concerns regarding user privacy and the potential for manipulation of consumer choices.

Licensing and Merchandising Opportunities

Licensing and merchandising present additional revenue streams for creators. By licensing their work for use in advertisements, films, or merchandise, artists can generate income while retaining ownership of their intellectual property. For instance, a popular video game franchise may license its characters for use in toys, clothing, and other products.

$$\text{Licensing Revenue} = \text{Royalty Rate} \times \text{Gross Sales} \qquad (62)$$

where the royalty rate is negotiated between the creator and the licensee.

This model not only diversifies income sources but also expands the reach and visibility of the creator's brand. However, it requires careful management to ensure that licensed products align with the creator's vision and values.

Challenges and Considerations

While exploring new revenue models offers exciting opportunities, it also presents challenges. Creators must navigate the complexities of digital rights management, the potential for market saturation, and the need for continuous innovation to stay relevant in a competitive landscape.

Moreover, as revenue models evolve, the relationship between creators and consumers is also changing. Consumers are increasingly seeking authenticity and transparency, prompting creators to engage more directly with their audience and build trust.

In conclusion, the exploration of new revenue models in the arts and entertainment sector reflects the dynamic interplay between technology, consumer behavior, and creative expression. As the landscape continues to evolve, it is imperative for creators to adapt and innovate, ensuring that they can sustain their work while meeting the demands and expectations of their audiences. The future of revenue generation in this space will likely hinge on the ability to balance profitability with artistic integrity and consumer engagement.

The Evolution of Advertising and Branding

The landscape of advertising and branding has undergone a radical transformation in the digital age, driven by advancements in technology and shifts in consumer behavior. The traditional methods of advertising, characterized by one-way communication through print, radio, and television, have given way to a more interactive and dynamic approach. This evolution is closely linked to the rise of social media platforms and the increasing importance of digital marketing strategies.

The Shift to Digital Advertising

The transition from traditional to digital advertising can be encapsulated in the following equation, which illustrates the shift in consumer engagement:

$$E = f(T, I, C)$$

where: - E = Engagement level - T = Type of media (traditional vs. digital) - I = Interactivity of the content - C = Consumer preference for personalized content

As consumers increasingly gravitate towards digital platforms, advertisers have had to adapt their strategies to meet the demands of a more interactive audience. The rise of social media has enabled brands to engage with consumers on a personal level, allowing for two-way communication that fosters brand loyalty and community.

Personalization and Targeting

One of the most significant advancements in advertising is the ability to personalize content. Through data analytics and machine learning, brands can now tailor their advertisements to individual preferences, behaviors, and demographics. This personalization enhances the effectiveness of advertising campaigns, as evidenced by the following findings from a study conducted by the *Digital Marketing Institute*:

- Personalized email campaigns have an average open rate of 29%, compared to 19% for non-personalized emails.
- Targeted ads on social media platforms yield a 50% higher click-through rate than generic ads.

The integration of artificial intelligence (AI) has further revolutionized targeting strategies. Brands can utilize algorithms to analyze consumer data and predict future behaviors, enabling them to deliver the right message at the right time. For example, platforms like Facebook and Google have developed sophisticated targeting options that allow advertisers to reach specific audiences based on interests, location, and online behavior.

The Role of User-Generated Content

In the era of social media, user-generated content (UGC) has become a powerful tool for branding. Brands can leverage UGC to enhance their credibility and authenticity. According to a report by *Nielsen*, 92% of consumers trust organic, user-generated content more than traditional advertising. This shift has led to the emergence of influencer marketing, where brands collaborate with social media influencers to promote their products.

> **Example**
>
> A notable example is the collaboration between Nike and various fitness influencers on Instagram. By showcasing real people using their products in authentic settings, Nike effectively engages a broader audience and builds trust with potential customers.

Challenges in Digital Advertising

Despite the advantages of digital advertising, brands face several challenges. The oversaturation of content on social media platforms has led to consumer fatigue, making it increasingly difficult for advertisements to stand out. Additionally, privacy concerns and regulations, such as the General Data Protection Regulation (GDPR) in Europe, have imposed restrictions on data collection and targeting practices.

The Future of Advertising and Branding

Looking ahead, the evolution of advertising and branding will likely continue to be shaped by emerging technologies such as augmented reality (AR) and virtual reality (VR). These technologies offer new avenues for immersive advertising experiences, allowing consumers to interact with brands in innovative ways. For instance, brands like IKEA have already implemented AR applications that allow customers to visualize furniture in their own homes before making a purchase.

Furthermore, the rise of voice search and smart speakers presents both challenges and opportunities for brands. As consumers increasingly rely on voice-activated devices for information and shopping, advertisers must adapt their strategies to ensure their brands are discoverable in this new landscape.

Conclusion

The evolution of advertising and branding in the digital age underscores the necessity for brands to remain agile and responsive to changing consumer expectations. By embracing personalization, leveraging user-generated content, and exploring new technologies, brands can navigate the complexities of the modern advertising landscape. As we move forward, the ability to connect authentically with consumers will be paramount in building lasting brand loyalty and driving business success.

Navigating the Ethics of Media Consumption

The rapid evolution of media consumption in the digital age presents a complex landscape where ethical considerations play a crucial role. As consumers navigate through a plethora of content, the implications of their choices extend beyond personal preference, impacting society at large. This section delves into the ethical dimensions of media consumption, addressing critical theories, prevalent problems, and illustrative examples.

Theoretical Frameworks

Understanding the ethics of media consumption requires a multi-faceted theoretical approach. Key ethical theories relevant to this discussion include:

- **Utilitarianism:** This theory posits that the best action is the one that maximizes utility, typically defined as that which produces the greatest well-being for the greatest number of people. In media consumption, this raises questions about the societal impact of certain types of content. For instance, sensationalist news may attract viewers but could lead to misinformation and societal harm.

- **Deontological Ethics:** Deontological theories emphasize the importance of duty and adherence to rules. This perspective suggests that consumers have a moral obligation to choose media that upholds truth and integrity. For example, sharing news articles without verifying their authenticity can perpetuate falsehoods, violating ethical duties to fellow consumers.

- **Virtue Ethics:** This approach focuses on the character of the moral agent rather than on rules or consequences. In the context of media consumption, this theory encourages individuals to cultivate virtues such as discernment and responsibility when selecting media. A virtuous consumer would critically evaluate sources and seek out content that promotes positive societal values.

Prevalent Problems in Media Consumption

Several ethical dilemmas arise in the realm of media consumption, including:

- **Misinformation and Disinformation:** The rise of fake news and misleading information poses significant ethical challenges. Misinformation refers to false or misleading information shared without malicious intent, while disinformation involves the deliberate spread of false information to deceive. The consequences can be dire, as seen in the spread of false narratives during elections or public health crises.

- **Privacy Concerns:** The collection and use of personal data by media companies raise ethical questions about consumer privacy. Many platforms track user behavior to tailor content and advertisements, often without explicit consent. This surveillance capitalism model can exploit consumer data, leading to a loss of autonomy and privacy.

- **Representation and Stereotyping:** Media consumption also intersects with issues of representation. The portrayal of marginalized groups can perpetuate harmful stereotypes, leading to societal biases and discrimination. Ethical media consumption involves seeking out diverse and accurate representations, challenging the status quo.

Illustrative Examples

To better understand the ethical landscape of media consumption, consider the following examples:

- **The Role of Social Media in Political Polarization:** Platforms like Facebook and Twitter have been criticized for their role in exacerbating political polarization. Algorithms prioritize content that generates engagement, often leading to echo chambers where users are only exposed to like-minded perspectives. This phenomenon raises ethical questions about the responsibility of platforms to promote balanced discourse and mitigate divisive content.

- **The Impact of Streaming Services on Content Diversity:** Streaming platforms such as Netflix and Hulu have revolutionized media consumption but also face ethical scrutiny regarding their content libraries. While they provide access to diverse programming, they also risk homogenizing culture by prioritizing popular content over niche or culturally significant works. Consumers must navigate these choices, considering the broader implications for cultural representation.

- **The Ethics of Clickbait:** The rise of clickbait headlines exemplifies the tension between attracting views and maintaining ethical standards. While sensational headlines can drive traffic, they often mislead consumers about the content, fostering distrust and diminishing the quality of discourse. Ethical consumption involves recognizing and resisting clickbait tactics.

Navigating Ethical Media Consumption

To navigate the ethics of media consumption effectively, individuals can adopt several strategies:

- **Critical Evaluation:** Consumers should develop critical thinking skills to assess the credibility of sources. This includes verifying information through multiple reputable outlets and being wary of sensationalist claims.

- **Mindful Sharing:** Before sharing content, individuals should consider its accuracy and potential impact. Engaging in responsible sharing practices can help combat the spread of misinformation.

- **Supporting Ethical Media:** Consumers can choose to support media organizations that prioritize ethical journalism, diversity in representation, and transparency in their practices. This can foster a media landscape that values integrity over sensationalism.

- **Engaging in Dialogue:** Encouraging open discussions about media consumption can promote awareness of ethical issues. Engaging with diverse perspectives can enhance understanding and foster a more informed consumer base.

In conclusion, navigating the ethics of media consumption is a vital endeavor in the digital age. By employing theoretical frameworks, recognizing prevalent problems, and adopting responsible practices, consumers can contribute to a media landscape that prioritizes truth, diversity, and ethical integrity. As Riley Dubois's Cultural Connector platform continues to evolve, it stands as a beacon for fostering ethical media consumption in an increasingly complex world.

Media Literacy in the Digital Age

In an era characterized by the rapid proliferation of digital content, media literacy has become a crucial skill for navigating the complexities of the information landscape. Media literacy encompasses the ability to access, analyze, evaluate, and create media in various forms. As Riley Dubois's Cultural Connector platform aims to empower individuals, the importance of fostering media literacy cannot be overstated. This section delves into the theoretical foundations of media literacy, the challenges posed by the digital age, and practical examples that illustrate its significance.

Theoretical Foundations of Media Literacy

Media literacy is grounded in several theoretical frameworks that inform its practice. One such framework is the **Critical Media Literacy** approach, which emphasizes the need for individuals to question and critically assess the media they consume. According to Kellner and Share (2005), critical media literacy involves understanding the socio-political contexts in which media is produced and consumed. This perspective encourages individuals to recognize the power dynamics at play in media representation, which is particularly relevant in a digital landscape where information is often curated and manipulated.

Another important theory is the **Constructivist Learning Theory**, which posits that individuals construct knowledge through interactions with their environment. This theory suggests that media literacy education should be experiential, allowing learners to engage with media content actively rather than passively consuming it. By fostering critical thinking and analytical skills, individuals can become more discerning consumers and creators of media.

Challenges of Media Literacy in the Digital Age

Despite its importance, achieving media literacy in the digital age presents several challenges:

- **Information Overload:** The sheer volume of information available online can overwhelm individuals. According to a study by the Pew Research Center (2016), 62% of Americans feel that the amount of information available makes it difficult to determine what is true. This information overload can lead to cognitive fatigue, making it harder for individuals to engage critically with media content.

- **Misinformation and Disinformation:** The rise of social media has facilitated the spread of misinformation and disinformation. A report by the European Commission (2018) found that 50% of social media users encountered false information regularly. This environment requires individuals to develop skills to discern credible sources from unreliable ones.

- **Echo Chambers and Filter Bubbles:** Algorithms used by social media platforms often create echo chambers, where individuals are exposed primarily to information that aligns with their existing beliefs. Pariser (2011) coined the term "filter bubble" to describe this phenomenon, which can limit exposure to diverse perspectives and hinder critical analysis of media content.

- **Digital Divide:** Access to digital resources is not uniform across demographics. The digital divide exacerbates inequalities in media literacy, as individuals without access to technology or the internet may struggle to develop the necessary skills to navigate the digital landscape.

Practical Examples of Media Literacy Initiatives

To address these challenges, various initiatives have emerged to promote media literacy in the digital age. Here are some notable examples:

- **The News Literacy Project:** This non-profit organization provides educational resources to help students and adults develop critical thinking skills related to news consumption. Their curriculum includes lessons on identifying credible sources, understanding bias, and recognizing misinformation.

- **Common Sense Media:** This organization offers resources for educators and families to promote media literacy among children and teens. Their programs focus on digital citizenship, teaching young people how to navigate online spaces responsibly and critically.
- **MediaSmarts:** A Canadian non-profit organization that focuses on digital and media literacy education, MediaSmarts provides resources for educators and parents to help children understand media messages and develop critical thinking skills. Their initiatives include workshops and online resources that encourage active engagement with media content.
- **Fact-Checking Initiatives:** Organizations such as Snopes and FactCheck.org play a vital role in combating misinformation by providing fact-checking services. These platforms empower individuals to verify the information they encounter online, fostering a culture of accountability and critical evaluation.

Conclusion

In conclusion, media literacy in the digital age is essential for empowering individuals to navigate the complexities of the information landscape. By understanding the theoretical foundations of media literacy, recognizing the challenges posed by the digital environment, and learning from practical initiatives, individuals can become more adept at critically engaging with media. As Riley Dubois's Cultural Connector continues to promote innovation and social connection, fostering media literacy will be a key component in shaping informed, engaged, and responsible digital citizens. The future of media literacy lies in collaborative efforts to equip individuals with the skills needed to thrive in an increasingly complex digital world.

The Future of Journalism

The landscape of journalism is undergoing a seismic shift, driven by technological advancements, changing consumer behaviors, and the evolving role of media in society. As we look to the future, it is essential to explore the implications of these changes, the challenges that lie ahead, and the innovative solutions that may redefine the field.

The Digital Transformation of Journalism

The digital revolution has transformed how news is produced, distributed, and consumed. Traditional print media has seen a significant decline in readership, while digital platforms have emerged as primary sources of information. According to the Pew Research Center, as of 2021, approximately 86% of Americans reported getting their news from digital devices, highlighting a fundamental shift in media consumption habits [2].

This transformation has led to several trends:

- **Rise of Online News Platforms:** Websites and apps dedicated to news delivery, such as BuzzFeed, Vox, and The Huffington Post, have gained popularity, often prioritizing speed and accessibility over in-depth reporting.

- **User-Generated Content:** Social media platforms like Twitter and Facebook have democratized the news landscape, allowing anyone with an internet connection to share information, which can lead to both opportunities and challenges regarding accuracy and credibility.

- **Data Journalism:** The integration of data analysis into reporting has become increasingly important. Journalists now utilize data visualization tools and statistical analysis to provide deeper insights into stories, making complex information more digestible for the audience.

Challenges Facing Journalism

Despite the opportunities presented by digital transformation, journalism faces several significant challenges:

- **Misinformation and Disinformation:** The rapid spread of false information online poses a critical threat to journalism's credibility. The ease of sharing content on social media can lead to the viral spread of misleading narratives, undermining public trust in legitimate news sources.

- **Financial Sustainability:** Many traditional media outlets struggle to generate revenue in a digital-first world. Advertising revenue has shifted online, and subscription models often fail to compensate for lost print income. The decline of local journalism is particularly concerning, as smaller newsrooms are often the first to close, leaving communities without essential reporting.

- **Erosion of Trust:** The perception of bias and sensationalism in news reporting has led to a growing distrust of media institutions. According to a Gallup poll, only 41% of Americans had a great deal or fair amount of trust in the mass media in 2020 [?].

Theoretical Frameworks for Understanding the Future

To navigate the future of journalism, several theoretical frameworks can be applied:

- **Media Ecology:** This theory posits that media is an environment that shapes human experiences and societal structures. Understanding how digital platforms alter the information ecosystem is crucial for journalists aiming to adapt their practices.

- **Constructivist Theory:** This approach emphasizes the role of individuals in constructing their understanding of the world based on their experiences and interactions. Journalists can leverage this theory to engage audiences more effectively, creating content that resonates with diverse perspectives.

- **Networked Journalism:** This model highlights collaboration between journalists and the public, suggesting that news production should be a participatory process. Platforms that facilitate crowd-sourced reporting can enhance transparency and community engagement.

Innovative Solutions for the Future

In response to these challenges, several innovative approaches are emerging:

- **Fact-Checking Initiatives:** Organizations like PolitiFact and FactCheck.org are dedicated to verifying claims made by public figures and media outlets. These initiatives play a crucial role in combating misinformation and restoring trust in journalism.

- **Subscription Models and Crowdfunding:** Some news organizations are successfully implementing subscription models, offering premium content to paying subscribers. Others are exploring crowdfunding as a means to support investigative journalism, allowing readers to invest directly in quality reporting.

- **Enhanced Media Literacy:** Educating the public about media consumption is vital. Initiatives aimed at improving media literacy can empower individuals to critically evaluate news sources, fostering a more informed citizenry.

- **Artificial Intelligence and Automation:** AI technologies are increasingly being used to streamline news production processes. For instance, automated journalism tools can generate reports on routine events, freeing up journalists to focus on more complex stories.

Conclusion

The future of journalism is fraught with challenges, but it also presents opportunities for innovation and growth. As the industry adapts to the digital age, the principles of accuracy, integrity, and accountability must remain at the forefront. By embracing new technologies, fostering collaboration, and prioritizing media literacy, journalism can evolve to meet the needs of a changing society.

In the words of renowned journalist Dan Rather, "The future of journalism is not just about reporting the news; it's about creating a better-informed public." The path forward will require resilience, creativity, and a commitment to the core values that underpin the profession.

Cultivating Independent Media Voices

The digital age has ushered in unprecedented opportunities for the cultivation of independent media voices, allowing diverse perspectives to flourish outside the traditional confines of mainstream media. This section explores the theoretical frameworks, challenges, and real-world examples of how independent media has emerged and thrived in this new landscape.

Theoretical Frameworks

The emergence of independent media can be understood through various theoretical lenses, including *Media Pluralism* and *Participatory Culture*. Media pluralism refers to the diversity of media sources available, which is crucial for a healthy democratic society. According to McQuail (2010), pluralism fosters a marketplace of ideas, enabling citizens to access a variety of viewpoints.

Participatory culture, as described by Jenkins (2006), emphasizes the role of individuals as active participants in the creation and dissemination of content. This shift from passive consumption to active engagement allows independent voices to emerge, challenging the dominance of traditional media narratives.

Challenges Faced by Independent Media

Despite the opportunities presented by the digital landscape, independent media voices encounter several challenges:

- **Funding and Sustainability:** Independent media outlets often struggle to secure funding, leading to questions about their sustainability. Crowdfunding and subscription models have emerged as viable alternatives, but they require a dedicated audience.

- **Visibility and Reach:** With the vast amount of content available online, independent media often faces difficulties in gaining visibility. Algorithms used by social media platforms can favor mainstream content, making it challenging for independent voices to reach their target audiences.

- **Misinformation and Credibility:** In an era where misinformation proliferates, independent media must work diligently to establish credibility. The challenge lies in distinguishing themselves from less reputable sources while maintaining journalistic integrity.

Examples of Cultivating Independent Media Voices

Several platforms and initiatives exemplify the cultivation of independent media voices:

- **Substack:** This newsletter platform has empowered writers to publish independently and monetize their content through subscriptions. Writers like Glenn Greenwald and Anne Helen Petersen have successfully transitioned to this model, allowing for nuanced discussions on topics often overlooked by mainstream media.

- **Patreon:** By enabling creators to receive direct support from their audience, Patreon has fostered a new generation of independent journalists and content creators. This model allows creators to focus on producing quality content without the pressure of traditional advertising.

- **The Correspondent:** This platform, founded by former journalists, focuses on in-depth reporting and analysis rather than breaking news. By emphasizing context and understanding, The Correspondent cultivates a community of engaged readers who value thoughtful journalism.

The Role of Technology in Amplifying Independent Voices

Technology plays a crucial role in amplifying independent media voices. Social media platforms, podcasts, and video-sharing sites provide avenues for content distribution that were previously unavailable. For instance, platforms like YouTube and TikTok allow creators to reach global audiences without the need for traditional gatekeepers.

Moreover, the rise of *Decentralized Media* initiatives, such as *Mastodon* and blockchain-based platforms, offer alternatives to centralized social media, providing users with greater control over their content and data. These technologies promote a more equitable media landscape, where independent voices can thrive.

Conclusion

Cultivating independent media voices is essential for a vibrant and diverse media landscape. By leveraging technology, independent outlets can overcome challenges related to funding, visibility, and credibility. As audiences increasingly seek authentic and diverse perspectives, the role of independent media will continue to grow, shaping the future of journalism and public discourse. In this evolving landscape, fostering independent voices will remain a critical component in the fight for media pluralism and participatory culture.

$$P(M) = \frac{N_I}{N_T} \times 100\% \tag{63}$$

Where:

- $P(M)$ = Percentage of independent media voices
- N_I = Number of independent media outlets
- N_T = Total number of media outlets

This equation highlights the importance of measuring the presence of independent media voices within the broader media ecosystem, emphasizing the need for ongoing support and development of these vital perspectives.

Embracing the Changing Media Landscape

The media landscape is undergoing a seismic shift, driven by technological advancements, evolving consumer behaviors, and the democratization of content creation. In this new paradigm, traditional media outlets are challenged to adapt or risk obsolescence. This section explores the implications of these changes, the theoretical frameworks that inform our understanding, the problems that arise, and notable examples of innovation and adaptation.

Theoretical Frameworks

To understand the changing media landscape, we can draw from several theoretical frameworks:

- **Media Ecology Theory:** This theory posits that media, as environments, shape human experiences and social interactions. As new media technologies emerge, they redefine how information is consumed and produced, leading to shifts in cultural norms and values [?].

- **Uses and Gratifications Theory:** This framework emphasizes the active role of consumers in selecting media that fulfills their needs. As audiences increasingly seek personalized and interactive experiences, traditional media must adapt to cater to these preferences [?].

- **Disruptive Innovation Theory:** Proposed by Clayton Christensen, this theory explains how smaller companies with fewer resources can successfully challenge established businesses. In the media context, digital platforms and independent creators are disrupting traditional media by offering unique and engaging content [?].

Emerging Problems

While the changing media landscape presents opportunities, it also introduces several challenges:

- **Misinformation and Disinformation:** The ease of content creation and distribution has led to the proliferation of fake news and misleading information. This phenomenon undermines trust in media and complicates the public's ability to discern credible sources [?].

- **Monetization Challenges:** Traditional media outlets struggle to adapt to new revenue models. The shift from advertising to subscription-based models has led to financial instability for many organizations [?].

- **Audience Fragmentation:** As audiences consume content across diverse platforms, traditional media faces the challenge of capturing and retaining viewers. The fragmentation leads to decreased advertising revenue and challenges in maintaining a cohesive brand identity [?].

Examples of Adaptation

Despite these challenges, many media organizations are successfully navigating the changing landscape through innovative strategies:

- **The Rise of Podcasts:** Media companies are increasingly investing in podcasting as a means to reach audiences. For example, NPR has embraced this format, creating a range of engaging content that appeals to diverse demographics. Podcasts allow for deeper storytelling and foster a sense of community among listeners [?].

- **User-Generated Content:** Platforms like YouTube and TikTok have empowered individuals to create and share content, challenging traditional media's gatekeeping role. Brands are now collaborating with influencers and content creators to reach younger audiences, exemplified by the partnership between Nike and popular YouTube personalities [?].

- **Interactive Journalism:** News organizations are experimenting with interactive formats to engage readers. The New York Times has implemented interactive graphics and immersive storytelling techniques, allowing audiences to explore complex issues in a more engaging manner [?].

Future Directions

Looking ahead, the media landscape will continue to evolve, influenced by emerging technologies such as artificial intelligence, virtual reality, and augmented reality. These innovations have the potential to transform how content is created, shared, and consumed. For instance, AI-driven algorithms can personalize content recommendations, enhancing user engagement [?].

Moreover, as media literacy becomes increasingly essential, organizations must prioritize educating audiences about navigating the digital landscape. This includes promoting critical thinking skills and fostering an understanding of the implications of media consumption on society.

In conclusion, embracing the changing media landscape requires a proactive approach from traditional media organizations. By leveraging emerging technologies, fostering collaboration with independent creators, and prioritizing audience engagement, the media can not only survive but thrive in this dynamic environment. The future of media lies in its ability to adapt, innovate, and respond to the ever-evolving needs of society.

Conclusion

The Legacy of Riley Dubois

Impact on Education

Riley Dubois's Cultural Connector has significantly transformed the educational landscape by addressing long-standing challenges and embracing innovative solutions. This section explores the multifaceted impact of Cultural Connector on education, highlighting key theories, problems, and practical examples.

Revolutionizing Learning

At the heart of Cultural Connector's impact on education lies the philosophy of constructivism, which posits that learners construct knowledge through experiences and interactions. This approach emphasizes active engagement, collaboration, and critical thinking. According to Piaget's theory of cognitive development, learners progress through stages of understanding, and Cultural Connector harnesses technology to cater to diverse learning needs.

$$\text{Learning Outcome} = f(\text{Engagement, Collaboration, Critical Thinking}) \quad (64)$$

This equation illustrates that the learning outcome is a function of engagement, collaboration, and critical thinking, all of which Cultural Connector fosters.

Creating Interactive Learning Experiences

Cultural Connector has pioneered interactive learning experiences that captivate students' attention and enhance retention. For instance, the platform utilizes gamification techniques to create a sense of achievement and motivation. Research by Deterding et al. (2011) indicates that game-based learning can lead to higher engagement and improved educational outcomes.

$$\text{Engagement} \propto \text{Game Elements} \times \text{Learning Goals} \qquad (65)$$

Where engagement is proportional to the product of game elements and learning goals, demonstrating how gamification can effectively bridge the gap between fun and education.

Breaking Down Barriers to Education Access

One of the most pressing issues in education is the lack of access to quality learning resources, particularly in underserved communities. Cultural Connector addresses this challenge by providing free or low-cost educational materials and resources online. This democratization of education aligns with the theory of equitable access, which asserts that all students, regardless of their socioeconomic background, should have access to quality education.

$$\text{Access} = \frac{\text{Quality Resources}}{\text{Cost}} \qquad (66)$$

This equation highlights that access to education improves as the quality of resources increases and the cost decreases.

Bridging the Gap Between Traditional and Digital Education

Cultural Connector serves as a bridge between traditional and digital education, allowing educators to integrate technology seamlessly into their classrooms. This hybrid model is supported by the TPACK framework (Technological Pedagogical Content Knowledge), which emphasizes the interplay between technology, pedagogy, and content knowledge.

$$\text{TPACK} = \text{Content Knowledge} + \text{Pedagogical Knowledge} + \text{Technological Knowledge} \qquad (67)$$

This framework illustrates that effective teaching requires a balance of all three components, which Cultural Connector promotes through its resources and training.

Empowering Educators with New Tools

Cultural Connector equips educators with innovative tools that enhance their teaching practices. For example, the platform offers data analytics capabilities that allow teachers to track student progress and tailor instruction to meet individual needs. This aligns with the theory of differentiated instruction, which advocates for adapting teaching methods to accommodate diverse learning styles.

$$\text{Differentiated Instruction} = \text{Assessment} + \text{Adaptation} + \text{Engagement} \quad (68)$$

This equation emphasizes the importance of assessment and adaptation in creating an engaging learning environment.

Improving Educational Outcomes for All

The ultimate goal of Cultural Connector is to improve educational outcomes for all students. By fostering collaboration, critical thinking, and creativity, the platform prepares students for future challenges. Research by Hattie (2009) indicates that collaborative learning strategies can lead to significant gains in student achievement.

$$\text{Student Achievement} = \text{Collaboration} \times \text{Engagement} \quad (69)$$

This equation underscores the importance of collaboration and engagement in driving student achievement.

Making Learning Fun and Interactive

Cultural Connector emphasizes the importance of making learning enjoyable. This approach is supported by theories of intrinsic motivation, which suggest that students are more likely to engage in learning when they find it enjoyable. Techniques such as interactive storytelling and immersive simulations create a dynamic learning environment.

$$\text{Intrinsic Motivation} = \text{Enjoyment} + \text{Challenge} + \text{Autonomy} \quad (70)$$

This equation illustrates that intrinsic motivation is influenced by enjoyment, challenge, and autonomy, all of which Cultural Connector fosters.

Fostering Collaboration and Critical Thinking

Cultural Connector promotes a culture of collaboration and critical thinking among students. By providing platforms for group work and discussions, students learn to value diverse perspectives and develop essential problem-solving skills. The Socratic method, which encourages dialogue and inquiry, is a foundational element of this approach.

$$\text{Critical Thinking} = \frac{\text{Dialogue} \times \text{Inquiry}}{\text{Assumptions}} \qquad (71)$$

This equation shows that critical thinking is enhanced through dialogue and inquiry while challenging assumptions.

Adapting to Different Learning Styles

Recognizing that students have varied learning styles, Cultural Connector offers customizable learning paths that cater to individual preferences. The VARK model (Visual, Auditory, Reading/Writing, Kinesthetic) serves as a framework for understanding these differences.

$$\text{Learning Style} = \text{Visual} + \text{Auditory} + \text{Reading/Writing} + \text{Kinesthetic} \qquad (72)$$

This equation illustrates that effective education considers all learning styles, allowing for a more inclusive approach.

Expanding Cultural Awareness through Education

Finally, Cultural Connector plays a crucial role in expanding cultural awareness among students. By integrating global perspectives into the curriculum, students learn to appreciate diversity and understand the interconnectedness of cultures. This aligns with the intercultural competence framework, which emphasizes the ability to communicate effectively across cultures.

$$\text{Cultural Awareness} = \text{Knowledge} + \text{Skills} + \text{Attitudes} \qquad (73)$$

In conclusion, the impact of Riley Dubois's Cultural Connector on education is profound and multifaceted. By addressing key challenges and leveraging innovative solutions, the platform not only enhances learning experiences but also prepares students for a rapidly changing world. The legacy of Cultural Connector in education will continue to shape future generations of learners, fostering a culture of collaboration, creativity, and cultural awareness.

Impact on Social Connection

The rise of Riley Dubois and her innovative platform, Cultural Connector, has fundamentally transformed the landscape of social connection. By leveraging technology to bridge cultural divides, Riley has created a space where individuals can engage meaningfully across geographical, linguistic, and cultural boundaries. This section explores the multifaceted impact of Cultural Connector on social connection, emphasizing its role in fostering understanding, empathy, and community engagement.

Fostering Understanding and Empathy

At the core of Cultural Connector's mission is the promotion of understanding and empathy among diverse populations. The platform utilizes various tools and features designed to encourage users to share their stories and experiences, thus humanizing individuals from different backgrounds. According to social psychologist [?], empathy is crucial for reducing prejudice and fostering social cohesion. Cultural Connector facilitates this by allowing users to participate in virtual dialogues, where they can discuss their cultural heritage, traditions, and personal narratives.

For example, a user from Japan can share their experience of the Cherry Blossom Festival, while another from Brazil can discuss the significance of Carnival. This exchange not only educates participants about different cultures but also cultivates a sense of shared humanity, which is essential in our increasingly polarized world.

Connecting Individuals from Different Backgrounds

Cultural Connector has effectively dismantled barriers that traditionally hinder social interaction among individuals from different backgrounds. By providing a user-friendly interface that supports multiple languages, the platform allows users to connect without the constraints of language barriers. This is particularly significant in a globalized world where migration and multiculturalism are prevalent.

The implementation of real-time translation features enables users to communicate seamlessly, fostering connections that would otherwise be impossible. As noted by sociologist [?], the ability to communicate across cultures enhances social networks and promotes inclusivity. Cultural Connector exemplifies this by encouraging users to engage in collaborative projects, such as art initiatives or community service, that require teamwork and cooperation among diverse participants.

Breaking Down Language Barriers

Language is often a significant barrier to social connection. Cultural Connector addresses this challenge by integrating advanced language processing technologies, allowing users to engage in conversations in their preferred languages. This initiative aligns with the theory of linguistic relativity, which posits that language influences thought and social interaction [?].

By enabling users to express themselves in their native languages, Cultural Connector not only preserves linguistic diversity but also enhances the richness of interactions. For instance, a user from Spain can share a traditional story in Spanish, while others can read it in their own languages through translation features. This process not only promotes linguistic appreciation but also enriches the cultural tapestry of the platform.

Promoting Cultural Exchange and Appreciation

Cultural Connector serves as a catalyst for cultural exchange and appreciation. By organizing events such as virtual cultural fairs and art exhibitions, the platform allows users to showcase their heritage and artistic expressions. These initiatives encourage participants to engage with and appreciate cultures different from their own, fostering a spirit of collaboration and mutual respect.

The concept of cultural exchange is supported by [?], who argues that such interactions can lead to increased intercultural competence. For example, a virtual cooking class where users learn to prepare traditional dishes from various cultures not only educates participants about culinary practices but also creates a shared experience that strengthens social bonds.

Encouraging Meaningful Dialogue

Cultural Connector emphasizes the importance of meaningful dialogue in building social connections. The platform provides users with tools to engage in discussions that address pressing social issues, such as racism, gender equality, and climate change. By facilitating conversations around these topics, Cultural Connector empowers users to share their perspectives and advocate for social change.

This aligns with the principles of deliberative democracy, which emphasizes the role of dialogue in fostering civic engagement and collective decision-making [?]. For instance, users can participate in moderated discussions where they can express their views on social justice initiatives, share resources, and mobilize support for various causes. This not only enhances social awareness but also cultivates a sense of agency among users.

Challenging Stereotypes and Bias

Cultural Connector actively works to challenge stereotypes and biases that often hinder social connection. By promoting diverse narratives and amplifying marginalized voices, the platform encourages users to confront their preconceived notions and engage with perspectives that differ from their own.

The theory of social identity suggests that individuals categorize themselves and others based on group affiliations, which can lead to in-group favoritism and out-group discrimination [?]. Cultural Connector counters this by fostering interactions that highlight commonalities among users, thereby reducing the likelihood of bias. For example, collaborative storytelling projects that bring together individuals from various backgrounds can help dismantle stereotypes and promote understanding.

Nurturing Global Citizens

In an era of globalization, Cultural Connector nurtures global citizens who are aware of and engaged in global issues. The platform encourages users to participate in initiatives that promote social responsibility and environmental sustainability. By connecting individuals who share a commitment to making a positive impact, Cultural Connector cultivates a sense of global community.

The concept of global citizenship is rooted in the idea that individuals have responsibilities that extend beyond their local contexts [?]. Cultural Connector embodies this by facilitating collaborations on projects that address global challenges, such as climate change advocacy or humanitarian efforts. This not only empowers users to take action but also reinforces the interconnectedness of global communities.

Celebrating Diversity

Cultural Connector celebrates diversity by highlighting the unique contributions of various cultures to the global community. The platform showcases cultural events, festivals, and artistic expressions, encouraging users to engage with and appreciate the richness of human experience.

This celebration of diversity aligns with the multiculturalism theory, which posits that diversity should be acknowledged and valued in society [?]. By fostering an environment that honors different cultural identities, Cultural Connector promotes inclusivity and social harmony. For instance, users can participate in cultural appreciation events that allow them to learn about and celebrate the traditions of others, thereby reinforcing social connections.

Building Bridges in a Divided World

In a world increasingly characterized by division and polarization, Cultural Connector serves as a bridge that connects individuals across cultural and ideological divides. The platform encourages users to engage in constructive dialogues that promote understanding and collaboration, essential for addressing societal challenges.

Research by [?] indicates that social networks can enhance community engagement and cohesion. Cultural Connector exemplifies this by fostering connections that transcend differences, allowing users to collaborate on initiatives that promote social good. For example, community-based projects that bring together individuals from diverse backgrounds can strengthen social ties and create a sense of belonging.

Empowering Individuals to Share Their Stories

Finally, Cultural Connector empowers individuals to share their stories, fostering a culture of openness and vulnerability. By providing a platform for users to express their experiences and perspectives, Cultural Connector encourages authentic connections that transcend superficial interactions.

The narrative paradigm theory suggests that humans are inherently storytellers, and sharing personal narratives can foster empathy and understanding [?]. Cultural Connector harnesses this power by encouraging users to share their journeys, struggles, and triumphs. This not only enriches the community but also reinforces the idea that every voice matters in the tapestry of human experience.

In conclusion, Cultural Connector's impact on social connection is profound and far-reaching. By fostering understanding, breaking down barriers, promoting cultural exchange, and nurturing global citizens, Riley Dubois has created a platform that not only connects individuals but also empowers them to create a more inclusive and empathetic world. The legacy of Cultural Connector lies in its ability to transform social interactions, encouraging individuals to engage meaningfully and embrace the richness of diversity.

Impact on Arts and Entertainment

The impact of Riley Dubois's Cultural Connector on the arts and entertainment sector has been profound and multifaceted, redefining how creators, audiences, and industries interact in the digital age. This section explores the various dimensions of this impact, including the transformation of creative industries, the evolution of entertainment experiences, and the shifting dynamics of media.

Transforming Creative Industries

The advent of Cultural Connector has redefined the landscape of creative industries by fostering a more inclusive and interactive environment. One of the core principles of Cultural Connector is the democratization of access to arts and entertainment. This has allowed artists from diverse backgrounds to showcase their work without the traditional barriers imposed by gatekeepers in the industry.

Redefining Audience Engagement   Through innovative platforms, Riley Dubois has enabled artists to engage with their audiences in real-time, creating a more participatory experience. For instance, the integration of live streaming and interactive features allows audiences to influence the creative process, blurring the lines between creators and consumers. This phenomenon is supported by the theory of *participatory culture*, which emphasizes the role of audiences as active contributors rather than passive consumers [?].

Creating Interactive Art Experiences   The Cultural Connector has also facilitated the emergence of interactive art experiences, where technology plays a crucial role. For example, virtual and augmented reality installations have become increasingly popular, allowing audiences to immerse themselves in the artwork. This shift aligns with the concept of *immersive storytelling*, where narrative experiences are enhanced through audience participation and interaction [?].

Redefining Entertainment Experiences

As Cultural Connector continues to evolve, it has redefined entertainment experiences by integrating technology into the fabric of storytelling. The use of augmented reality (AR) and virtual reality (VR) has transformed how stories are told and experienced.

Immersive Storytelling   Immersive storytelling has gained traction, with creators leveraging technology to engage audiences on a deeper emotional level. For instance, the use of VR in film has allowed viewers to step into the narrative, experiencing the story from a first-person perspective. This approach not only enhances emotional engagement but also creates a sense of presence, as outlined in the *transportation theory* [?].

Creating Unique Audience Experiences   Additionally, platforms driven by Cultural Connector have enabled the creation of unique audience experiences through personalized recommendations and curation. Algorithms analyze user preferences to deliver tailored content, enhancing viewer satisfaction and engagement. This shift towards personalized experiences reflects the growing importance of user-centric design in the entertainment industry [?].

The Impact of Cultural Connector on Media

Cultural Connector's influence extends to the media landscape, disrupting traditional channels and empowering independent voices. The rise of user-generated content has transformed how media is consumed and produced.

Disrupting Traditional Media Channels The traditional media model, characterized by top-down communication, has been challenged by the rise of social media and digital platforms. Independent creators now have the tools to produce and distribute their content, circumventing traditional gatekeepers. This shift is exemplified by platforms like YouTube and TikTok, where creators can reach global audiences without the need for traditional media outlets.

Shifting Power Dynamics in Entertainment The power dynamics in entertainment have shifted, with audiences wielding greater influence over content creation and distribution. This is evident in the success of crowd-funded projects and the popularity of platforms that allow fans to support their favorite creators directly. The concept of *crowdsourcing* has become a vital part of the creative process, enabling artists to gather resources and feedback from their communities [?].

Conclusion

In conclusion, Riley Dubois's Cultural Connector has had a transformative impact on the arts and entertainment sector. By redefining audience engagement, fostering interactive experiences, and disrupting traditional media channels, Cultural Connector has paved the way for a more inclusive and dynamic creative landscape. As we look to the future, the continued evolution of technology and audience participation will shape the trajectory of arts and entertainment, ensuring that creativity remains at the forefront of cultural expression.

Reflections on Cultural Connector's Future

The Power of Technology in Shaping Society

The evolution of technology has been a significant catalyst for societal transformation, influencing how individuals interact, learn, and engage with the world around them. The advent of the digital age has not only revolutionized communication but has also introduced complex dynamics that shape cultural norms, economic structures, and educational methodologies. In this section, we will explore the multifaceted power of technology in shaping society, focusing on its theoretical underpinnings, inherent challenges, and practical examples.

Theoretical Frameworks

To understand the role of technology in societal change, we can draw upon several theoretical frameworks. One prominent theory is the **Social Construction of Technology (SCOT)**, which posits that technology is not merely a tool but is shaped by social processes and cultural contexts. According to SCOT, the development and use of technology are influenced by various social groups, each with its interests and power dynamics. This perspective highlights that technology can reinforce existing social structures or challenge them, depending on how it is utilized.

Another relevant theory is **Technological Determinism**, which suggests that technology is the primary driver of societal change. This theory argues that technological advancements dictate the direction of social evolution, often leading to profound shifts in cultural practices and economic frameworks. While this view emphasizes the influence of technology, it can sometimes overlook the reciprocal relationship between society and technology, where societal needs and values also shape technological development.

Challenges and Ethical Considerations

Despite the potential benefits of technology in shaping society, several challenges and ethical considerations arise. One major concern is the **Digital Divide**, which refers to the gap between individuals who have access to technology and those who do not. This divide can exacerbate existing inequalities, particularly in education and economic opportunities. For instance, students in underprivileged areas may lack access to the internet or digital learning tools, hindering their educational outcomes compared to their more affluent peers.

Moreover, the rapid pace of technological advancement raises concerns about **data privacy** and **surveillance.** As individuals increasingly share personal information online, the risk of misuse and exploitation of this data becomes a pressing issue. The Cambridge Analytica scandal serves as a stark reminder of how personal data can be weaponized for political gain, highlighting the need for robust regulations to protect individual privacy rights.

Examples of Technological Impact

One of the most significant examples of technology's impact on society is the rise of social media platforms. These platforms have transformed how individuals communicate, share information, and engage with social issues. For instance, movements such as #BlackLivesMatter and #MeToo have gained momentum through social media, mobilizing millions to advocate for social justice and equality. These platforms have empowered marginalized voices, fostering a sense of community and collective action.

In education, technology has revolutionized learning environments through the integration of digital tools. The use of **Learning Management Systems (LMS)** such as Moodle and Canvas has facilitated online learning, enabling educators to reach students across geographical boundaries. Furthermore, the incorporation of **Artificial Intelligence (AI)** in education provides personalized learning experiences, adapting to individual student needs and promoting engagement.

However, the reliance on technology in education also presents challenges, particularly in terms of equity. The COVID-19 pandemic underscored the importance of digital access, as many students were left behind due to insufficient resources for remote learning. This situation highlights the need for policies that ensure equitable access to technology for all students, regardless of socioeconomic status.

Conclusion

In conclusion, the power of technology in shaping society is profound and multifaceted. While it offers opportunities for innovation, connectivity, and empowerment, it also presents significant challenges that must be addressed. The interplay between technology and society is complex, necessitating a critical examination of how technological advancements can be harnessed to promote equity, inclusivity, and ethical practices. As we move forward, it is essential to embrace the potential of technology while remaining vigilant about its implications for the future of society.

Embracing the Challenges and Opportunities Ahead

As Riley Dubois and Cultural Connector continue to evolve, they face a landscape that is both fraught with challenges and ripe with opportunities. The rapid pace of technological advancement, shifting societal norms, and the complex interplay of global cultures present unique hurdles that must be navigated. However, these challenges also offer the potential for transformative innovation and growth.

The Challenge of Technological Advancement

One of the most significant challenges facing Cultural Connector is the relentless march of technology. As new tools and platforms emerge, there is a constant need to adapt and integrate these innovations into existing frameworks. This includes not only the development of new features but also the ongoing education of users—both educators and students—on how to leverage these technologies effectively.

For instance, the integration of artificial intelligence (AI) in educational platforms has the potential to personalize learning experiences. However, it also raises questions about data privacy and the ethical use of AI. According to a study by [?], 70% of educators express concerns over student data security when using AI-driven tools. This apprehension must be addressed through transparent policies and robust security measures.

The Digital Divide

Another pressing challenge is the digital divide, which exacerbates inequalities in education and social connection. While Cultural Connector aims to democratize access to resources, disparities in technology access persist. According to the *Pew Research Center*, approximately 15% of U.S. households with school-aged children do not have a reliable internet connection. This gap limits the effectiveness of digital platforms and hinders the potential for widespread educational reform.

To combat this issue, Cultural Connector must explore partnerships with organizations that provide technology access to underserved communities. For example, initiatives like *EveryoneOn* work to connect low-income families with affordable internet and devices, which could be a model for collaboration.

Opportunities for Global Collaboration

Despite these challenges, the global nature of Cultural Connector presents unprecedented opportunities for collaboration. The platform can serve as a bridge between diverse cultures, fostering understanding and empathy. By facilitating cross-cultural exchanges, Cultural Connector can empower users to share their stories and experiences, enriching the educational landscape.

The potential for online cultural exchange programs is vast. For instance, virtual pen pal initiatives can connect students from different countries, allowing them to engage in meaningful dialogue. A study by [?] found that students participating in such programs reported a 30% increase in cultural awareness and empathy towards others.

Leveraging Data for Continuous Improvement

Another opportunity lies in the use of big data to inform decision-making and enhance user experiences. By analyzing user interactions and feedback, Cultural Connector can identify trends and areas for improvement. For example, machine learning algorithms can be employed to tailor content recommendations based on individual user preferences, thereby increasing engagement and satisfaction.

The equation for user engagement can be represented as:

$$E = \frac{I \times C}{T} \qquad (74)$$

where E is engagement, I is the interaction rate, C is the content relevance score, and T is the time spent on the platform. By maximizing I and C, Cultural Connector can enhance overall engagement.

Navigating Ethical Considerations

As Cultural Connector embraces these opportunities, it must also navigate the ethical considerations that arise from its technological integration. Issues such as misinformation, online harassment, and the impact of social media on mental health require careful attention. Developing a robust framework for ethical guidelines will be crucial in maintaining user trust and promoting positive online interactions.

For instance, implementing features that promote digital literacy can empower users to critically evaluate the information they encounter. Programs that educate users about identifying misinformation can significantly enhance the platform's credibility and user experience.

Conclusion: A Vision for the Future

In conclusion, embracing the challenges and opportunities ahead will require a multifaceted approach. By prioritizing technological adaptation, addressing the digital divide, fostering global collaboration, leveraging data, and navigating ethical considerations, Cultural Connector can continue to innovate and impact society positively. The future holds immense potential for Riley Dubois and Cultural Connector to redefine the landscape of education, social connection, and cultural appreciation.

Through a commitment to these principles, Cultural Connector can not only overcome the challenges it faces but also seize the opportunities that lie ahead, paving the way for a more inclusive and connected future.

Cultural Connector's Continued Impact on Innovation

The Cultural Connector, spearheaded by Riley Dubois, has not only transformed the landscapes of education, social connection, and the arts but has also laid a robust foundation for ongoing innovation across various sectors. By leveraging technology to foster collaboration, creativity, and cultural exchange, the platform has become a catalyst for new ideas and solutions to pressing global challenges.

The Role of Technology in Innovation

At the heart of Cultural Connector's impact on innovation is its integration of cutting-edge technology. Tools such as artificial intelligence (AI), big data analytics, and immersive technologies have been harnessed to enhance user experience and drive engagement. For example, AI algorithms analyze user interactions to tailor educational content, making learning more personalized and effective. This adaptability is crucial in a rapidly changing world where knowledge and skills must evolve continuously.

$$E = mc^2 \qquad (75)$$

This equation, famously attributed to Albert Einstein, underscores the principle of energy-mass equivalence, illustrating how foundational theories can lead to groundbreaking innovations. Similarly, Cultural Connector embodies the idea that foundational cultural understanding can lead to innovative solutions. By fostering an environment where diverse perspectives intersect, the platform encourages the cross-pollination of ideas, which is essential for innovation.

Addressing Global Challenges

Cultural Connector's innovative approach also addresses pressing global challenges, such as climate change, social inequality, and health crises. The platform facilitates collaborative projects that bring together experts from various fields to develop sustainable solutions. For instance, a recent initiative connected environmental scientists with community leaders to create educational programs that promote sustainable practices in local communities. This collaborative effort not only raised awareness but also empowered individuals to take action, demonstrating the power of collective innovation.

Fostering a Culture of Innovation

The Cultural Connector promotes a culture of innovation by encouraging experimentation and risk-taking. This is evident in its support for startups and entrepreneurs who leverage the platform to test new ideas. By providing resources such as mentorship, funding opportunities, and access to a global network, Cultural Connector nurtures the next generation of innovators.

One notable example is the partnership with a tech startup that developed an app aimed at reducing food waste. By utilizing big data to analyze consumption patterns, the app connects consumers with local food banks, ensuring surplus food is redistributed to those in need. This innovative solution not only addresses food insecurity but also contributes to sustainability efforts.

Challenges and Ethical Considerations

Despite its successes, Cultural Connector must navigate several challenges and ethical considerations in its mission to drive innovation. Issues such as data privacy, algorithmic bias, and the digital divide require careful attention. As the platform collects vast amounts of user data to enhance personalization, it is imperative to implement robust data protection measures to safeguard user privacy.

Moreover, the potential for algorithmic bias in AI systems can perpetuate existing inequalities. Cultural Connector is committed to addressing these concerns by fostering transparency and inclusivity in its technological developments. By actively involving diverse stakeholders in the design and implementation of its technologies, the platform aims to mitigate bias and ensure equitable access to its resources.

The Future of Cultural Connector and Innovation

Looking ahead, the Cultural Connector is poised to continue its trajectory of innovation. The emergence of new technologies, such as blockchain and augmented reality, presents exciting opportunities for further enhancing user engagement and collaboration. For instance, blockchain technology could be utilized to create decentralized platforms for creative professionals, enabling them to share and monetize their work more effectively.

Furthermore, as global challenges become increasingly complex, the need for innovative solutions will only grow. Cultural Connector's commitment to fostering interdisciplinary collaboration will be crucial in addressing these challenges. By bringing together diverse perspectives and expertise, the platform can facilitate the development of holistic solutions that consider the multifaceted nature of contemporary issues.

In conclusion, Cultural Connector's continued impact on innovation is a testament to the power of cultural exchange and technological integration. By fostering a collaborative environment that encourages creativity and experimentation, the platform not only drives innovation but also empowers individuals to become agents of change in their communities. As we navigate an ever-evolving landscape, the principles of inclusivity, adaptability, and ethical responsibility will remain central to Cultural Connector's mission, ensuring its relevance and effectiveness in shaping the future of innovation.

Acknowledgments

Inspirations and Influences

Riley Dubois, the visionary behind Cultural Connector, drew inspiration from a myriad of sources, each shaping her innovative approach to bridging cultural divides through technology. Her journey reflects a synthesis of ideas from various fields, influential figures, and pressing societal challenges.

One of the primary influences on Riley's work was the theory of **Social Constructivism**, which posits that knowledge is constructed through social interactions and cultural contexts. This theory, championed by educational theorists such as *Lev Vygotsky*, emphasizes the importance of collaborative learning and the role of cultural tools in shaping understanding. Riley recognized that in a globalized world, learning must transcend geographical boundaries, and she sought to create platforms that fostered collaboration among students from diverse backgrounds.

Riley's early exposure to the challenges of educational inequity profoundly impacted her vision. Growing up in a community where access to quality education was limited, she witnessed firsthand the barriers that marginalized groups faced. This experience ignited her passion for educational reform and inspired her to develop solutions that would empower learners everywhere. The **Digital Divide**—the gap between those who have access to digital technologies and those who do not—became a focal point of her mission. According to the *Pew Research Center*, as of 2021, approximately 15% of Americans still lacked access to high-speed internet, highlighting the urgency of addressing this issue.

Furthermore, Riley's admiration for influential figures in technology and social activism, such as *Sheryl Sandberg* and *Malala Yousafzai*, fueled her determination to leverage technology for social good. Sandberg's work at Facebook emphasized the power of social media in connecting people, while Yousafzai's advocacy for girls' education underscored the importance of empowering marginalized voices. These leaders exemplified how one can harness their platform to effect change, and Riley aimed to emulate their impact through Cultural Connector.

The concept of **Cultural Intelligence** also played a significant role in shaping Riley's approach. Cultural intelligence refers to the ability to relate to and communicate effectively across cultures. As defined by *Christopher Earley* and *Soon Ang*, it encompasses cognitive, emotional, and behavioral aspects that enable individuals to navigate diverse cultural contexts. Riley understood that fostering cultural awareness was essential for meaningful connections, and she integrated this principle into the design of her platforms, ensuring they promoted understanding and empathy among users.

Riley's commitment to inclusivity was further inspired by the **Universal Design for Learning (UDL)** framework, which advocates for creating educational environments that accommodate diverse learners. UDL emphasizes the importance of providing multiple means of engagement, representation, and action/expression. By incorporating these principles, Riley aimed to design Cultural Connector in a way that catered to various learning styles and backgrounds, making education accessible to all.

In addressing the challenges of online communication, Riley also drew insights from the field of **Communication Theory**. The *Uses and Gratifications Theory* posits that individuals actively seek out media to satisfy specific needs, such as information, personal identity, integration, and social interaction. Understanding this theory helped Riley tailor Cultural Connector's features to meet the diverse needs of its users, ensuring that the platform provided value and relevance in their educational and social interactions.

Moreover, Riley's vision was influenced by the ongoing discourse around **Digital Citizenship**. As technology becomes increasingly integrated into daily life, the importance of responsible and ethical online behavior has come to the forefront. Riley recognized that fostering digital citizenship was crucial for creating a safe and respectful online community. She incorporated educational resources on

ACKNOWLEDGMENTS

digital ethics, online safety, and responsible use of technology into Cultural Connector, empowering users to navigate the digital landscape with confidence and integrity.

Riley's journey was not without its challenges. She faced skepticism from those who doubted the feasibility of her vision, as well as the complexities of navigating the tech industry. However, she drew strength from the concept of **Resilience**, which refers to the capacity to recover from difficulties and adapt to change. Embracing a growth mindset, she viewed obstacles as opportunities for learning and innovation. This resilience allowed her to pivot her strategies, refine her ideas, and ultimately launch Cultural Connector as a transformative platform.

In conclusion, the inspirations and influences that shaped Riley Dubois's journey are multifaceted, stemming from educational theories, personal experiences, influential figures, and pressing societal challenges. By synthesizing these diverse influences, Riley crafted a vision for Cultural Connector that not only addresses the needs of learners but also fosters meaningful connections across cultures. Her commitment to inclusivity, cultural awareness, and ethical digital practices continues to inspire the next generation of innovators, leaving a lasting legacy in the realm of education and social connection.

Gratitude to the Team

In the journey of creating Cultural Connector, it is imperative to acknowledge the remarkable contributions of the diverse team that made this vision a reality. Each member brought unique talents, perspectives, and unwavering dedication, which were instrumental in overcoming the myriad challenges we faced.

The Importance of Collaboration

Collaboration is not merely a buzzword; it is the foundation of innovation. According to [?], effective teamwork can lead to enhanced creativity and problem-solving capabilities. The synergy generated by diverse minds coming together allows for a richer exploration of ideas, resulting in solutions that a single individual may not conceive.

In the context of Cultural Connector, our team comprised educators, technologists, artists, and social scientists. This multidisciplinary approach enabled us to address the multifaceted issues surrounding education, social connection, and the arts.

Acknowledging Individual Contributions

- **Jane Smith, Chief Technology Officer:** Jane's expertise in software development and her visionary approach to digital solutions were crucial in designing the platform's infrastructure. Her ability to foresee technological trends ensured that we remained ahead of the curve.

- **Mark Johnson, Head of Educational Outreach:** Mark's extensive experience in education allowed us to tailor our offerings to meet the needs of students and educators alike. His insights into pedagogical strategies helped shape our interactive learning experiences.

- **Emily Chen, Creative Director:** Emily's artistic vision transformed our content into engaging and immersive experiences. Her understanding of user engagement principles ensured that our platform resonated with a diverse audience.

- **Raj Patel, Social Media Strategist:** Raj's expertise in digital marketing and social media dynamics was invaluable. He crafted campaigns that not only promoted Cultural Connector but also fostered meaningful conversations within our community.

- **Dr. Lisa Gomez, Cultural Consultant:** Dr. Gomez's research on cultural dynamics provided a framework for our initiatives. Her work in fostering understanding and empathy among diverse groups was essential in shaping our mission.

Each team member's contributions were vital, yet they also faced their own challenges. For instance, Jane often navigated the complexities of integrating cutting-edge technology while ensuring user-friendliness. This balancing act is encapsulated in the equation for user experience (UX):

$$UX = \frac{(Usability + Usefulness)}{UserEffort}$$

This equation illustrates that a successful user experience is contingent upon both the usability and usefulness of a product, balanced against the effort required by the user. Jane's relentless pursuit of this balance was instrumental in our platform's success.

Overcoming Challenges Together

As a team, we encountered numerous obstacles, from technical glitches to differing opinions on project direction. However, our commitment to open communication and mutual respect allowed us to navigate these challenges effectively. The theory of *constructive conflict* [?] posits that disagreements, when managed properly, can enhance team performance.

For example, during the development phase, a debate arose regarding the integration of gamification elements. While some team members advocated for a robust gaming approach, others expressed concern about potential distractions. Through structured discussions, we were able to synthesize these viewpoints, resulting in a balanced implementation that enhanced engagement without compromising educational integrity.

Celebrating Team Achievements

Our collective efforts culminated in the successful launch of Cultural Connector, which has since impacted thousands of users globally. This achievement is a testament to what can be accomplished when talented individuals unite toward a common goal.

Moreover, we have established a culture of continuous learning and improvement. Regular feedback loops and team retrospectives have allowed us to refine our strategies and celebrate our successes. As we look to the future, we remain committed to fostering an environment where creativity thrives and innovation flourishes.

Looking Ahead

As we move forward, the lessons learned from our collaborative efforts will continue to guide us. The importance of teamwork, resilience, and adaptability cannot be overstated. We are excited about the future of Cultural Connector and the potential it holds for further innovation.

In conclusion, I extend my heartfelt gratitude to each member of the Cultural Connector team. Your passion, creativity, and hard work have not only brought this project to life but have also laid the groundwork for a brighter, more connected future. Together, we have demonstrated that when we unite our strengths, we can transcend barriers and create meaningful change in the world.

Thank You to the Readers

In the journey of creating *Cultural Connector: Riley Dubois's Social Platforms*, it is essential to pause and express heartfelt gratitude to you, the readers. Your engagement with this work not only enriches the narrative but also fosters a community of like-minded individuals who are passionate about innovation, education, and social connectivity.

The Role of Readers in Shaping Ideas

Readers are not merely passive consumers of content; they are active participants in the dialogue surrounding the themes explored in this biography. Each page reflects a collaborative effort, informed by the diverse perspectives and experiences you bring. As Riley Dubois's story unfolds, it becomes clear that the impact of *Cultural Connector* extends beyond its digital platforms and into the hearts and minds of those who engage with it.

Feedback and Interaction

Your feedback is invaluable. It informs future iterations of the work, helping to refine ideas and broaden the scope of discussion. In the realm of innovation, constructive criticism is a catalyst for growth. It encourages us to explore new avenues, challenge existing paradigms, and ultimately enhance the relevance of our contributions to society.

Consider the example of educational technology. The rapid evolution of digital tools in classrooms has been largely driven by user feedback. Platforms like *Cultural Connector* thrive on the insights of educators, students, and parents alike. By sharing your experiences, you help shape the tools that empower learning and foster collaboration.

Building a Community of Innovators

The essence of *Cultural Connector* lies in its ability to bring people together. As readers, you form a vital part of this community. Your engagement creates a network of innovators, educators, and advocates for social change. This collective effort is essential in addressing the challenges we face today, from educational inequities to the digital divide.

For instance, initiatives that promote cultural exchange and understanding are strengthened by the active involvement of readers who share their stories and insights. By participating in discussions, attending events, and utilizing the tools

ACKNOWLEDGMENTS

offered by *Cultural Connector*, you contribute to a larger movement aimed at fostering empathy and collaboration across diverse backgrounds.

The Future of Our Journey Together

As we reflect on the journey of *Cultural Connector*, it is important to acknowledge that this is just the beginning. The future holds immense potential for growth and innovation, and your continued support will be crucial in navigating this landscape. Together, we can explore new frontiers in education, social connection, and the arts.

The challenges ahead are significant, but they also present opportunities for transformative change. By embracing technology and fostering a spirit of collaboration, we can redefine the way we learn, connect, and create. Your role as a reader is pivotal in this process, as you help to amplify the voices of those who are often unheard and champion the causes that matter most.

Conclusion: A Shared Vision

In closing, thank you for being an integral part of this journey. Your passion for innovation and commitment to social change inspire us all. As we move forward, let us continue to build a brighter future together—one that is inclusive, equitable, and enriched by the diverse perspectives of our community.

Let us remember that the impact of *Cultural Connector* is not confined to the pages of this biography; it lives on in the actions we take and the connections we forge. Together, we can create a legacy of innovation that resonates for generations to come.

$$\text{Impact} = \text{Engagement} \times \text{Collaboration} \tag{76}$$

This equation encapsulates the essence of our shared mission. The more we engage with one another and collaborate on ideas, the greater the impact we can achieve. Thank you for your commitment to this vision. Together, we will continue to innovate and inspire.

Index

a, 1–12, 15–23, 25, 27, 29–32, 34, 35, 38, 40–44, 46–51, 53–56, 58–63, 65–68, 70, 71, 75–78, 80, 83, 85, 88, 90, 91, 93, 96, 98–100, 103, 104, 106–108, 113, 116–119, 121, 123–132, 134–137, 139–142, 144, 145, 147, 148, 150–152, 154, 156, 157, 159, 160, 162–164, 167, 169, 171, 172, 175–177, 179–198, 203–205, 207, 208, 210–212, 214–219, 221–226, 228, 229, 233, 235–238, 241–243, 246–256, 259, 261, 264–266, 268–285, 287–291

ability, 1, 3–5, 7, 21, 29, 47, 51, 60, 122, 132, 134, 163, 175, 179, 198, 238, 254, 256, 259, 268, 272, 276

abuse, 163

acceptance, 246

access, 2, 11, 13, 31, 33–35, 43, 58, 68, 80, 83, 98, 99, 137, 149, 160, 163, 164, 175, 181, 184, 190, 196–198, 212, 216, 217, 231, 233, 237, 239, 243, 249, 251, 252, 259, 270, 277, 280, 284

accessibility, 6, 11, 43, 58, 75, 116, 119, 187, 195, 196, 243

accolade, 2

accountability, 164, 264

accuracy, 118, 187, 264

achievement, 271, 289

acquisition, 117

act, 180

action, 12, 128, 129, 165, 167, 179, 180, 186, 193, 222, 284

activism, 2, 130, 159, 164–167, 172, 175–180, 183–185, 187, 188, 193

activist, 179, 184

actualization, 5

ad, 247

adaptability, 58, 93, 285, 289

adaptation, 93, 130, 144, 171, 266, 271, 282

addition, 12

address, 3, 5–7, 12, 13, 16, 22, 31, 42, 56, 68, 70, 88, 95, 97, 99, 100, 116–118, 121,

123, 129, 140, 143, 157,
159, 167, 180, 187, 189,
195, 198, 200, 216, 241,
260, 274, 287
adoption, 3, 57
adult, 108
advance, 177, 183, 214, 221
advancement, 55, 91, 99, 108, 205,
221, 281
advent, 38, 56, 60, 66, 73, 83, 119,
151, 175, 188, 196, 198,
223, 231, 251, 277, 279
adversity, 18
advertising, 237, 247, 254, 256
advocacy, 165, 185–188
advocate, 2, 100, 136, 159, 165, 169,
184, 186, 210, 274
age, 1, 3, 9, 71, 98, 139, 142, 145,
150, 154, 156, 162, 164,
167, 177, 182, 185, 188,
190, 191, 198, 199, 201,
205, 207, 210, 221, 238,
240, 243, 254, 256,
259–261, 264, 276, 279
agency, 77, 100, 180–182
aggression, 140
Albert Einstein, 283
album, 212, 252
Alex, 212
Alex Rivera, 212
algorithm, 99
alignment, 58
ally, 159
alternative, 237
Amartya Sen, 180
amount, 99
amplification, 162, 164, 187, 209,
210
analysis, 48, 85

anonymity, 140
anxiety, 216
app, 284
appeal, 11
application, 44, 199, 217, 220, 221
appreciation, 6, 30, 53, 119, 121,
131, 135, 136, 274, 283
approach, 4–6, 10–12, 15, 16, 19,
21, 29, 34, 41, 43, 57, 59,
63, 66, 70, 75, 77, 80, 88,
91, 98, 106, 118, 123, 125,
135, 136, 140, 148–150,
154, 178, 180, 184, 188,
192–195, 217, 218, 229,
242, 247, 252, 254, 256,
268, 269, 271, 272, 282,
283, 285, 287, 289
appropriation, 121
area, 116, 119
art, 2, 32, 131, 134, 191, 193–196,
204, 206, 207, 210, 211,
214, 227, 228, 230,
241–243, 274
artist, 198, 242
artistry, 233
artwork, 194, 242
aspect, 21, 130, 136, 162, 175, 185,
223
assault, 164, 179
assessment, 87–91, 100, 271
atmosphere, 51
attention, 25, 176, 204, 227, 229,
282, 284
audience, 11, 19, 32, 191–194, 198,
207, 224, 227–229, 233,
236, 246–248, 252–255,
268, 278
audits, 79
authenticity, 142, 243, 250, 253

Index

authority, 123
authorship, 243
autonomy, 152, 231, 271
availability, 39, 197
avenue, 65
awareness, 10, 31, 51–54, 77, 126, 136, 164, 169, 172, 184, 186, 242, 272, 284, 287

background, 12, 31, 41, 96, 270
backing, 248
backlash, 163, 186
balance, 80, 152, 184, 223, 239, 254, 270, 288
balancing, 66, 150, 151
barrier, 4, 98, 195
basis, 12
beacon, 124, 259
beginning, 25
behavior, 140, 141, 151, 162, 184, 222, 228, 251, 253, 254
being, 1, 75, 87, 100, 147, 156, 160, 190, 216, 223, 251, 252
belief, 1, 12
belonging, 2, 5, 17, 118, 128, 131
benefit, 32, 49, 60, 237
bias, 96, 100, 118, 119, 126, 127, 151, 152, 177, 284
biography, 7
birth, 6, 9
Bishop, 194
blend, 2
blending, 219
blockchain, 211, 284, 285
brainstorm, 47
brand, 253, 254, 256
branding, 254, 256
Brazil, 32, 117, 273

bridge, 1, 6, 12, 22, 31, 36, 43, 93, 98, 117, 270, 273, 276, 281
bridging, 35, 116, 132, 133, 285
brother, 1
building, 17, 18, 21, 134, 150, 152–154, 256, 274
burden, 252
burnout, 216
business, 10–12, 21, 116, 217, 256

California, 1
call, 12
campaign, 118, 126, 131, 132, 179, 186, 252
campus, 2
canvas, 235
capability, 183
capacity, 177, 180
capital, 2, 132, 147
career, 1
Carol Ann Tomlinson, 66
case, 34, 40, 43, 77, 92, 113, 118, 178, 187, 188, 193, 209, 212, 237, 242, 247
cast, 222
catalyst, 134, 157, 214, 274, 279, 283, 290
cater, 11, 38, 43, 49, 67, 89, 90, 269
cause, 186
celebration, 130
censorship, 151
center, 46
century, 5, 47, 60
challenge, 4, 16, 32, 35, 47, 66, 98, 124–126, 139, 150, 162, 163, 169, 195, 198, 214, 215, 230, 242, 270, 271, 275, 290
champion, 207, 291

change, 2, 4, 6, 16, 31, 35, 54, 77, 80, 93, 118, 124, 128, 136, 157–160, 163, 164, 166, 167, 173, 175, 177–180, 182, 185–188, 210, 214, 242, 243, 251, 274, 283, 285, 289, 291
channel, 248
character, 186
characteristic, 183
charge, 77, 243
child, 1, 3
China, 176
choice, 18
Chris Anderson's, 246
citizenry, 68
citizenship, 15, 30, 127, 128, 165
Claire Bishop, 194
classroom, 50, 58–61, 79, 87
climate, 31, 77, 124, 179, 180, 184, 186, 242, 274, 283
clothing, 253
co, 2, 47, 193, 194, 229, 242
coalition, 11
cohesion, 12, 14, 135
collaboration, 8, 17, 18, 32, 38, 46–48, 60, 80, 106, 116, 119, 130, 132, 134, 152, 154, 188, 190, 193–196, 198–201, 217, 241, 242, 247, 255, 264, 268, 269, 271, 272, 274, 276, 281, 283, 285, 291
collective, 147, 152, 159, 163, 165, 179, 180, 190, 193, 210, 229, 243, 284, 289
college, 1, 2
color, 242
combat, 45, 139, 140, 159, 170, 209

combating, 176
combination, 137, 223, 224
commentary, 194
commerce, 214
commercialization, 214, 243
commitment, 2, 4, 18, 21, 25, 31, 38, 75, 93, 96, 101, 121, 124, 126, 127, 129, 134, 137, 139, 164, 171, 190, 196, 212, 275, 283, 285, 287, 291
commodification, 243
communication, 1, 2, 6, 8, 20, 31, 36, 77, 116, 118, 119, 123, 147, 175, 176, 180, 254, 278, 279
community, 1–3, 17, 18, 23, 25, 32, 43, 96, 117, 119, 121, 128, 134, 136, 137, 141, 151–155, 163, 193, 194, 196, 211, 212, 229–231, 238, 242, 246, 247, 252, 254, 273, 275, 284
comparison, 248
compensation, 211, 216
competence, 272
competition, 198
compliance, 12
component, 51, 53, 90, 141, 150, 261, 266
comprehension, 27, 43
computer, 1
concept, 2, 3, 16, 27, 49, 63, 66, 96, 127, 132, 142, 144, 162, 165, 241, 246
concern, 148, 184, 186, 289
concert, 226
conclusion, 5, 7, 9, 18, 25, 55, 75, 85, 87, 93, 100, 116, 121, 150,

Index

152, 154, 162, 177, 185, 190, 196, 201, 212, 214, 223, 235, 241, 251, 254, 259, 261, 268, 272, 276, 278, 280, 282, 285, 287, 289
conduit, 246
conference, 117
conflict, 123, 133
confluence, 7
confusion, 176, 186, 204
connection, 2, 5, 7, 9, 15, 18, 21, 23, 25, 71, 116, 124, 127, 130, 136, 137, 142, 154–156, 160, 162, 175, 212, 228, 243, 246, 261, 273, 275, 276, 283, 287
connectivity, 35, 280
connector, 1
consent, 100, 164, 186
conservation, 77
consideration, 195, 246
conspiracy, 176
constraint, 16
constructivism, 66, 128, 194, 269
consumer, 203–205, 251, 253, 254, 256, 261, 266
consumption, 192, 246, 256–259, 268, 284
content, 6, 24, 31, 43, 58, 59, 61, 117, 121, 126, 131, 151, 186, 192–198, 203–205, 211, 212, 221–224, 227–229, 235, 236, 246, 247, 249–253, 256, 259, 265, 266, 278, 282
context, 30, 59, 61, 93, 117, 119, 140, 186, 193, 194, 199, 231, 238, 241, 246, 287
contrast, 36, 132
control, 75, 150, 231, 246, 250
convenience, 31
convergence, 203, 214
conversation, 150, 204, 241, 246
cooking, 131
copyright, 204, 205, 238–241
core, 19, 54, 58, 277
cornerstone, 27, 71, 124, 175
cosmopolitanism, 128
cost, 270
council, 2
count, 91
craft, 5, 211
creation, 117, 139, 172, 194, 195, 203, 204, 236, 246, 247, 249, 250, 266
creativity, 5, 15, 19, 47, 89, 100, 196, 205, 207, 214, 235, 243, 272, 278, 283, 285, 289
creator, 203, 205, 239, 253
credibility, 48, 176, 186, 266, 282
crisis, 250
criticism, 290
cross, 2, 4, 130, 282, 283
crowdfunding, 211, 248, 252
cultivation, 182, 264, 265
Cultural Connector, 17
culture, 2, 20, 21, 48, 119, 121, 151, 194, 203, 214, 223, 246, 248, 266, 272, 276, 284, 289
curation, 221, 223
curiosity, 1, 5
currency, 148
curricula, 35, 50, 55, 65, 91
curriculum, 16, 54, 58, 272
cutting, 11, 93, 243
cyberbullying, 6, 139–142, 151

cycle, 27

dance, 204
data, 12, 43, 79, 83, 85, 89, 99, 100, 118, 148–150, 177, 183, 184, 221, 223, 228, 242, 253, 271, 282–284
day, 23, 126
debate, 2, 289
decision, 19, 83, 282
decrease, 247
dedication, 287
delivery, 228
demand, 104, 252
democratization, 196–198, 204, 236, 238, 250, 266, 270, 277
design, 24, 63, 188, 195, 284
desire, 1, 5, 243
determination, 15
devaluation, 204
development, 7, 27, 30, 38, 47, 85, 100, 108, 118, 192, 266, 269, 285, 289
dialogue, 6, 9, 27, 47, 114, 116, 117, 122–125, 127, 130, 131, 134, 144, 147, 152, 163, 169, 171, 207, 272, 274
digitization, 58–60
dignity, 101
dilemma, 204
direction, 193, 229
director, 222
disadvantage, 99
disconnect, 7, 247
disconnection, 142
discourse, 196, 266
discovery, 207, 223
discrimination, 169

discussion, 48, 124, 187, 229, 256, 290
disinformation, 186
disparity, 99, 216
disruption, 248
dissemination, 175, 177, 186, 203
dissent, 176
distance, 73
distinction, 203
distribution, 235–237, 246, 249, 265
diversity, 1, 15, 19, 21, 32, 49, 53, 54, 124, 130–132, 136, 210, 246, 247, 259, 272, 274–276
divide, 2, 75, 96–99, 118, 121, 159, 163, 167, 177, 190, 214, 283, 284
division, 124, 132, 176, 186, 276
document, 48, 136
documentation, 195
dot, 242
down, 1, 33–35, 71, 87, 118, 119, 276, 278
dream, 35
drive, 77, 160, 173, 180, 185, 186, 226, 284
dynamic, 18, 21, 29, 38, 56, 60, 63, 66, 91, 142, 160, 185, 214, 226, 235, 242, 252, 254, 268, 271, 278

ease, 185
echo, 134, 180
economy, 214–217, 233
ecosystem, 13, 42, 61, 237, 241, 249, 266
edge, 11, 93, 243
editing, 48

Index

educating, 31, 268
education, 1, 2, 6, 7, 12–16, 18, 21, 27, 32–38, 40, 43, 44, 46, 47, 49, 51–54, 56, 58, 60, 61, 63, 65, 66, 68, 71, 73, 75, 77, 78, 80–83, 85, 87, 90, 91, 93, 94, 96, 98–100, 103, 106–108, 116, 123, 126, 128, 132, 136, 141, 149–152, 269, 270, 272, 280, 283, 287
effect, 9, 175, 184, 194
effectiveness, 16, 29, 38, 85, 113, 115, 121, 141, 165, 174, 178, 193, 229, 253, 285
efficacy, 180
effort, 163, 171, 210, 284, 288
element, 272
emergence, 175, 191, 235, 246, 284
emotion, 243
empathy, 1, 5, 6, 30, 107, 112–114, 116, 119, 122, 124–127, 129, 130, 135, 136, 147, 273, 281
empowering, 2, 75, 77, 96, 119, 136, 175, 177, 182, 190, 233, 261, 278
empowerment, 1, 19, 75, 77, 137, 150, 169, 177, 180, 190, 231, 233, 280
endeavor, 5, 18, 21, 35, 63, 127, 164, 196, 243, 259
energy, 77, 283
enforcement, 151
engagement, 10, 17, 24, 27, 29, 31, 32, 36, 38, 43, 46, 50, 51, 54, 58, 60, 63, 65, 66, 75, 77, 80, 87, 89, 96, 116, 118, 119, 128, 130, 146, 152, 154, 160, 163, 172, 179, 182, 190–194, 196–198, 205, 207, 214, 221, 223, 224, 226–230, 233, 238, 246, 248, 253, 254, 268–271, 273, 278, 282, 285, 289
enhancement, 53
enjoyment, 45, 271
entertainment, 191, 194, 196–198, 203, 205, 220, 221, 223, 226, 227, 230, 231, 238, 241, 243, 249–252, 254, 276–278
enthusiasm, 9, 16
entry, 215, 236
environment, 1, 2, 16, 19, 20, 31, 32, 35, 38, 40, 49, 51, 53, 58, 61, 63, 66, 75, 77, 80, 100, 106, 117, 119, 123, 132, 137, 141, 145, 147, 152, 176, 188, 189, 194, 205, 212, 243, 247, 261, 268, 271, 277, 283, 285, 289
envision, 96
equality, 162, 169, 171, 185, 274
equalizer, 96
equation, 3, 11, 54, 61, 66, 77, 91, 98–100, 137, 140, 147, 160, 172, 180, 185, 190, 197, 198, 205, 207, 218, 224, 233, 239, 254, 266, 269–272, 282, 283, 288, 291
equity, 38, 60, 80, 93, 96, 100, 164, 185, 198, 280
equivalence, 283
era, 25, 75, 132, 148, 169, 180, 227, 259, 275

erosion, 6
essence, 5, 77, 207, 212, 291
establishment, 10, 138
esteem, 5
evaluation, 48, 90
event, 2, 23, 176
Everett Rogers', 246
evolution, 29, 106, 108, 142, 183, 194, 201, 219, 223, 225, 233, 235, 238, 248, 254, 256, 276, 278, 279
examination, 280
example, 21, 43, 49, 76, 77, 80, 89, 99, 107, 117, 124, 131, 133, 136, 151, 176, 183, 184, 186, 187, 189, 197, 204, 211, 222, 228, 248, 252, 253, 255, 271, 273, 282, 284, 289
exception, 83
exchange, 10, 32, 107, 116, 117, 119–121, 124, 132, 172, 273, 274, 276, 283, 285
excitement, 23
exercise, 182
exhibit, 228
exhibition, 193
experience, 1, 2, 10, 16, 27, 30, 32, 46, 51, 53, 61, 77, 80, 89, 136, 180, 194, 196, 210, 217, 223, 226, 228–230, 238, 246, 253, 273, 275, 282, 288
experimentation, 20, 284, 285
expertise, 8, 17, 195, 285
exploitation, 150, 211
exploration, 16, 82, 87, 205–207, 226, 251, 254
explosion, 242

exposure, 1, 3, 211
expression, 142, 143, 150–152, 184, 194, 198, 207, 212, 214, 231, 235, 241–243, 254, 278

fabric, 212, 235
face, 18, 35, 39, 40, 50, 56, 80, 91, 93, 98, 114, 136, 159, 163, 176, 195, 198, 210, 231, 281
facilitator, 123
fact, 152
failure, 4, 20, 47
fair, 2, 211, 216, 217
fairness, 100
family, 43
fan, 204, 211
fashion, 204
father, 1
favor, 250
favoritism, 169
fear, 4, 47, 163
feature, 211
fee, 11
feedback, 66, 88, 90, 150, 193, 282, 289, 290
fiction, 204
field, 261
fight, 142, 185, 266
figure, 123
film, 222, 235–238
filter, 3, 223
filtering, 222, 223
finding, 226
firm, 11
fitness, 255
flexibility, 11, 31, 48
flourish, 122, 124, 233, 264

Index

fluidity, 142
focus, 25, 31, 88, 118, 160, 177, 183, 211
following, 6, 13, 19, 24, 118, 212, 239, 254, 257
font, 43
food, 2, 284
footage, 212
force, 15, 177, 212, 236
forefront, 75, 144, 179, 185, 187, 205, 214, 238, 264, 278
foresight, 12
form, 194, 219
formation, 19, 152
formula, 24, 48, 253
foster, 9, 12, 14, 22, 46, 47, 51, 58, 60, 63, 66, 71, 91, 96, 98, 116, 126, 128, 133, 139, 147, 149, 151, 152, 154, 156, 157, 169, 181, 187, 188, 201, 223, 238, 241, 246, 283
fostering, 5, 6, 8, 12, 17, 19, 20, 25, 30–32, 38, 46–49, 51, 61, 80, 93, 100, 107, 112, 113, 116, 117, 119, 122, 124, 125, 127, 130–132, 134–137, 139, 143–145, 150, 159, 162–164, 175, 180, 182, 184, 185, 189, 190, 196, 207, 210, 212, 216, 226, 229, 242, 246, 247, 259, 261, 264, 266, 268, 272–274, 276–278, 281, 283–285, 289, 291
foundation, 1, 12, 19, 131, 283
fraction, 252
fragmentation, 180
framework, 5, 12, 33, 56, 66, 127, 130, 186, 222, 239, 270, 272, 282
franchise, 253
freedom, 150–152, 184
fruition, 8
fun, 44, 46, 270
function, 98, 205, 218, 269
functionality, 11
fund, 252
funding, 4, 11, 16, 237, 248, 252, 266, 284
fundraise, 159
fundraising, 177, 187
fusion, 1, 235
future, 1–3, 5, 12, 15, 21, 25, 32, 35, 46, 56, 58, 68, 71, 80, 83, 85, 87, 91, 93, 96, 98, 101, 103–106, 108, 130, 132, 142, 150, 152, 160, 162, 175, 183–185, 190, 194–196, 201, 205, 207, 212, 214, 216, 221, 223, 226, 235, 238, 243, 253, 254, 261, 263, 264, 266, 268, 272, 278, 280, 283, 285, 289, 290

gain, 186, 198, 211, 231
gallery, 228
game, 63, 253, 270
gamification, 46, 56, 63–66, 270, 289
gaming, 289
gap, 5, 35–38, 93, 123, 163, 270
garden, 3
Gardner, 58
gatekeeping, 197, 246, 247
gender, 136, 274

generation, 29, 130, 185, 214, 254, 284, 287
genre, 222
gig, 216
globalization, 9, 275
globe, 6, 9, 30, 32, 134, 175
goal, 8, 44, 96, 188, 208, 289
good, 15
government, 176, 184
grading, 100
graduation, 85
gratitude, 289
Greta Thunberg, 179
grip, 251
ground, 233
groundwork, 2, 3, 7, 10, 12, 289
group, 49, 132, 136, 169, 272
growth, 12, 25, 51, 91, 93, 106, 215, 264, 281, 290
guest, 23
guidance, 140
guide, 123, 289
guideline, 148

hand, 1, 59, 187, 222
happiness, 186
harassment, 139–141, 151, 163, 164, 176, 179, 187, 282
harm, 150, 151, 186, 187
hate, 150, 151
head, 7, 236
health, 151, 155, 156, 216, 282, 283
healthcare, 87, 187
heart, 228, 269
help, 92, 148, 149, 152, 183, 184, 291
Henry Jenkins, 194
Henry Jenkins', 246
heritage, 131, 274

hierarchy, 5
hindrance, 117
hiring, 19, 126
home, 1, 43
homogenization, 247
honesty, 186
Hong Kong, 184
hope, 124
Howard Gardner's, 49, 90
human, 5, 7, 121, 124, 136, 162, 210, 238, 243, 275
humanity, 134, 273
hybrid, 11, 38, 184, 242

idea, 203, 283
identification, 5, 6, 10, 44
identifying, 4, 5, 7, 130, 282
identity, 2, 142–144, 154, 169
imagination, 241–243
imitation, 140
immersion, 218, 228
impact, 2, 3, 5, 7, 9, 12, 18, 25, 34, 40, 44, 63, 70, 116, 118, 130, 133, 136, 137, 156, 160, 171, 172, 177, 180, 185, 188, 190, 204, 212, 223, 233, 237, 248, 269, 272, 273, 275, 276, 278, 282, 283, 285, 291
imperative, 54, 77, 82, 93, 96, 98, 100, 106, 132, 152, 162, 164, 210, 254, 284, 287
implementation, 10, 44, 50, 58, 63, 64, 67, 195, 221, 284, 289
importance, 1, 7–9, 19, 20, 23, 27, 30, 47, 49, 52, 66, 69, 89, 90, 93, 99, 106, 108, 113, 124, 127, 132, 134, 135, 139, 140, 162, 180,

Index

182–184, 186, 187, 193, 194, 207, 208, 254, 259, 260, 266, 271, 274, 280, 289
imposter, 2
improvement, 24, 282, 289
inception, 7
inclusion, 98, 154
inclusivity, 11, 19, 41, 50, 93, 96, 116, 129, 132, 136, 139, 164, 184, 185, 195, 198, 280, 284, 285, 287
income, 43, 99, 211, 212, 253
increase, 85
India, 136
Indiegogo, 248
individual, 2, 66, 67, 89, 137, 140, 182, 186, 204, 228, 251, 271, 282
individualism, 165
industry, 220, 221, 223, 226, 235–238, 249–251, 264, 277
inequality, 136, 169, 189, 215, 283
influence, 2, 140, 156, 163, 193, 194, 204, 229, 278
information, 48, 49, 66, 149–152, 175–177, 184–186, 189, 221, 256, 259, 261, 282
infringement, 151
initiative, 11, 12, 31, 118, 124, 130, 131, 180, 189, 212, 284
injustice, 186
innovation, 3, 5, 7, 18–21, 29, 38, 75, 87, 91, 96, 101, 196, 207, 213, 226, 233, 235, 246–248, 253, 261, 264, 266, 280, 281, 283–285, 289, 290

innovator, 2, 3, 5, 15
inquiry, 47, 48, 272
insecurity, 284
insight, 5, 126
inspiration, 285
instability, 233
instance, 11, 32, 43, 47, 48, 88, 117, 124, 126, 136, 151, 159, 176, 186, 204, 211, 222, 229, 237, 243, 252, 253, 265, 274, 282, 284, 285
institution, 2
instruction, 50, 66, 271
instructor, 36
integration, 27, 35, 36, 38, 44, 52–54, 58, 63, 78, 81, 83, 88, 89, 93, 98, 100, 103, 106, 183, 220, 234, 241, 243, 282, 285, 289
integrity, 176, 184, 186, 254, 259, 264, 289
intelligence, 43, 49, 85, 89, 183
intent, 117
interaction, 7, 9, 10, 21, 25, 27, 30, 36, 47, 61, 87, 180, 191, 194, 195, 221, 273
interactivity, 27, 29, 45, 194, 230
interconnectedness, 130, 272
interdependence, 172
interest, 1
interface, 273
intermediality, 214
internet, 1, 2, 31, 73, 99, 142, 163, 198, 223, 246
interpersonal, 49, 58, 90
interplay, 162, 185, 216, 218, 254, 280, 281
intersection, 5, 160, 233, 235, 242
introduction, 23

intuition, 243
investment, 193, 252
involvement, 2, 43, 141, 194, 246
Iran, 176
isolation, 1, 132
issue, 6, 99, 150, 204, 243
it, 3, 5–7, 9–12, 15, 18, 21, 29, 35, 38, 40, 42, 46, 53, 54, 60, 63, 68, 77, 82, 85, 90, 91, 96, 98–100, 103, 106, 108, 116, 121, 130, 131, 139, 140, 142, 152, 156, 159, 160, 162, 164, 167, 171, 177, 180, 184, 186, 187, 190, 198, 201, 203–206, 210, 214, 217, 222, 223, 226, 229, 233, 238, 242, 243, 246, 248, 250, 252–254, 259, 261, 264, 267, 271, 274, 280, 282–284, 287, 289

Jamie, 77
Jane, 288
Japan, 32, 117, 273
jargon, 100
Jean Piaget, 66
job, 103, 108
journalism, 261–264, 266
journey, 2, 4, 5, 10, 15, 18, 21, 25, 56, 58, 75, 93, 100, 130, 171, 207, 210, 285, 287
judgment, 47
justice, 1, 2, 118, 124, 126, 159, 162, 164, 167, 169–172, 185, 193

kindness, 147

knowledge, 2, 27, 35, 38, 47, 58, 59, 66, 73, 90, 100, 103, 106, 128, 163, 194, 231, 269
Kolb, 27

lack, 4, 6, 99, 163, 184, 247, 270
landscape, 7, 10, 12–14, 17, 21, 27, 35, 38, 40, 44, 46, 54, 60, 68, 83, 87, 90, 91, 93, 98, 100, 106, 108, 139, 144, 147, 152, 156, 157, 160, 164, 175–177, 182, 184, 185, 187–191, 194, 196–198, 203, 205, 207, 208, 210, 212, 214, 216, 221, 223, 226, 231, 233, 235, 238, 239, 241, 243, 247–251, 253, 254, 256, 257, 259, 261, 264, 266–269, 273, 277, 278, 281–283, 285
language, 31, 43, 114, 116–119, 223, 273
launch, 2, 4, 9, 12, 21–23, 25, 252, 289
law, 238, 241
leader, 7, 12
leadership, 21, 144
learner, 42, 51, 68, 101
learning, 1, 13, 15, 20, 27–32, 35, 36, 38, 42–47, 49–51, 53, 55–61, 63, 65–68, 73–75, 77, 80, 83, 85, 87–91, 93, 98–100, 106–108, 117, 131, 140, 154, 164, 219, 223, 228, 261, 269–272, 280, 282, 289
legacy, 272, 276, 287
lens, 5, 185

lesson, 131
Lev Vygotsky, 66
level, 185, 195, 205, 218, 228, 248, 254
leverage, 14, 32, 56, 87, 189, 221, 238, 284
leveraging, 12, 29, 43, 46, 56, 60, 63, 67, 68, 75, 77, 85, 106, 108, 116, 121, 132, 141, 154, 156, 158, 160, 162, 167, 171, 175, 180, 188, 201, 210, 212, 223, 229, 232, 248, 256, 266, 268, 272, 273, 283
library, 251
licensee, 253
licensing, 211, 253
lie, 15, 261, 283
life, 2, 7, 126, 127, 207, 289
like, 5, 48, 66, 68, 75, 77, 103, 106, 108, 132, 133, 148, 149, 152, 159, 163, 175–177, 179, 180, 194, 242, 247, 248, 252, 265, 278
likelihood, 140
Lil Nas X, 204
listening, 6, 123, 223
literacy, 47, 69–71, 80, 151, 163, 183–185, 189, 190, 198, 259–261, 264, 268, 282
literature, 1
live, 23, 212, 223–226, 229
location, 196
love, 1
loyalty, 254, 256

machine, 85, 117, 228, 282
mainstream, 204, 246, 264
maintenance, 138

make, 5, 100, 149, 151, 180
makeshift, 3
making, 19, 35, 44, 73, 83, 88, 90, 116, 119, 141, 201, 204, 229, 250, 271, 275, 282
management, 77, 253
manipulation, 253
manner, 124
Maria Gonzalez, 2
market, 4, 103, 198, 204, 205, 233, 250, 253
marketing, 252–254
Maslow, 5
mass, 283
material, 27, 44, 205
matter, 10, 30, 77, 210, 291
mean, 186
meaning, 194
means, 2, 6, 142, 197
measure, 253
media, 1, 4, 9, 77, 139, 142, 148, 150–152, 155, 156, 165, 169, 175, 176, 179, 183–185, 193, 197, 203, 204, 214, 217, 238, 246–251, 254, 256–261, 264–268, 276, 278, 282
medium, 194
member, 19, 287, 289
memorization, 47, 88
mentorship, 237, 284
merchandise, 252, 253
merchandising, 253
message, 77, 176
messaging, 184
method, 272
microchip, 91
migration, 273
mindset, 93

miscommunication, 117
misinformation, 6, 134, 150, 151, 159, 167, 176, 177, 184–186, 189, 190, 246, 282
misrepresentation, 163
mission, 2, 11, 12, 15, 19, 20, 71, 75, 127, 141, 175, 284, 285, 291
mitigation, 100
mobile, 175
mobility, 2
mobilization, 172, 176, 177
model, 10–12, 47, 49, 66, 117, 193, 212, 237, 246–248, 252, 253, 278
modeling, 140
moment, 7, 195, 223
momentum, 179
monetization, 211, 212, 237
Moore, 91
morality, 128, 186
mother, 1
motivation, 44, 46, 65, 77, 271
mouth, 175
movement, 7, 21, 164, 165, 176, 179, 185, 186
multiculturalism, 273
multimedia, 48, 58, 131
multiplicity, 142
music, 2, 204, 223, 248, 252
musician, 212, 252
myriad, 78, 207, 238, 285, 287

narrative, 134, 217, 219, 238
nationality, 128
nature, 9, 145, 185, 195, 196, 207, 214, 216, 240, 281, 285

necessity, 29, 38, 46, 47, 132, 148, 256
need, 5–7, 9, 22, 27, 40, 98–100, 138, 139, 169, 181, 184, 186, 217, 227, 241, 253, 265, 266, 278, 280, 284, 285
negativity, 147
negotiation, 239
neighborhood, 1, 43
Neil Fleming's, 49
network, 59, 183, 284
niche, 246
non, 2, 11, 31, 63, 98, 189
notion, 30, 44, 66
number, 91
nurture, 129

objective, 44
obligation, 150
observation, 140
observer, 7
obsolescence, 266
obstacle, 17
offering, 11, 31, 55, 76, 98, 185, 189, 196, 221, 251, 252
oligopoly, 236
on, 2, 5, 7, 11, 19, 20, 27, 31, 32, 36, 40, 43, 44, 48–50, 59, 77, 79, 88, 91, 99–101, 107, 117–119, 123, 124, 126, 128, 130, 134, 136, 137, 139, 140, 147, 151, 155, 156, 160, 175, 176, 180, 183–186, 188, 192, 193, 199, 205, 211, 212, 216, 222, 223, 226, 229, 233, 236, 237, 248, 251–256,

268, 269, 272, 273, 276, 278–280, 282, 285, 291
one, 15, 16, 66, 88, 106, 124, 127, 142, 152, 186, 248, 254, 291
online, 1, 2, 9, 124, 137–143, 145–147, 152–154, 162–167, 176–180, 183–189, 198, 229, 247, 270, 282
openness, 276
opinion, 152, 246
opportunity, 20, 63, 77, 91, 96, 98, 137, 198, 282
oppression, 177
option, 38
organization, 2, 19, 184
originality, 243
other, 59, 165, 221, 222, 246, 253
outcome, 194, 269
outlook, 215
outreach, 183, 184, 252
outsider, 1
overload, 221
overwhelm, 243
ownership, 193, 204, 242, 251, 253

pace, 43, 91–93, 108, 214, 243, 281
pandemic, 176, 184, 280
paradigm, 58, 246, 247, 251, 266
part, 152
participation, 43, 47, 56, 127, 159, 194, 196, 198, 224, 229, 278
partnership, 11, 284
passion, 1, 2, 5, 21, 77, 289
past, 175, 185, 222
Paulo Freire, 128
peace, 134

peak, 252
pedagogy, 27, 41, 53, 128
peer, 36, 117, 140
people, 1, 5, 6, 9, 173, 179, 255
perception, 126, 142
performance, 43, 48, 91, 229, 233–235
perpetuation, 163
perseverance, 5
persistence, 97
person, 184
personalization, 194, 223, 230, 256, 284
perspective, 119, 128, 186
petition, 159
phase, 22, 289
phenomenon, 165, 203, 204, 223, 250
philosophy, 269
piece, 204
Pierre Lévy, 188
pilot, 15, 43
place, 2, 176, 242
planning, 10, 12, 18, 22
platform, 4, 6, 7, 9–13, 15, 17, 18, 22, 24, 25, 28, 29, 31, 32, 41, 43, 46–48, 53, 75–77, 93, 95, 96, 106–108, 113, 116–119, 121–124, 127, 130, 131, 134–137, 141, 143, 148, 162–164, 169, 172, 177, 188–191, 193, 204, 210–212, 228, 236–238, 241, 246, 259, 271–276, 281–285, 288
play, 5, 100, 119, 217, 223, 256
player, 190
plethora, 256
plot, 229

pluralism, 266
point, 241
polarization, 6, 14, 124, 132, 276
policy, 35, 151
pollination, 283
pollution, 77
popularity, 204
portmanteau, 203
positivity, 145–147
post, 175
potential, 1, 2, 4–6, 15, 16, 19, 21, 25, 27, 36, 40, 46, 56–59, 61, 66, 75, 78, 80–83, 85, 87, 99, 100, 114, 118, 121, 126, 128, 133, 142, 146, 153, 158–160, 163, 165, 167, 169, 173, 175, 177, 178, 180, 181, 183–186, 188, 193, 195, 196, 198, 201, 204, 207, 214–216, 218–221, 223, 225, 228, 235, 238, 243, 246, 253, 255, 280, 281, 283, 284, 289
power, 3, 10, 15, 18, 32, 63, 85, 91, 132, 160, 164, 166, 167, 169, 179, 180, 185, 215, 218, 231, 233, 239, 245, 248–251, 279, 280, 284, 285
practice, 29, 58, 117, 122, 205, 207
preference, 256
premium, 11
preparation, 103
preparedness, 54
presence, 36, 147, 266
preservation, 195
pressure, 31, 216
prevalence, 164, 179

pricing, 252
principle, 75, 100, 283
print, 175, 254
priority, 142
privacy, 12, 85, 99, 100, 118, 148–150, 177, 184, 186, 223, 253, 284
privilege, 35, 41
problem, 3, 6, 18, 47, 106, 134, 188, 272
process, 5, 7, 19, 47, 48, 77, 88, 90, 127, 144, 182, 194, 221, 236, 242, 243, 274, 291
processing, 49, 223
producer, 203
product, 88, 140, 270, 288
production, 236, 248, 250
professional, 19, 38, 142
professor, 1
profit, 11, 98
profitability, 254
program, 43, 131
progress, 5, 43, 172, 238, 269, 271
project, 3, 16, 31, 46–48, 77, 126, 133, 242, 289
proliferation, 185, 259
promise, 43, 160, 162
promotion, 71, 119, 122, 145, 169
property, 12, 204, 246, 253
prosumer, 203, 205
prosumerism, 204
protection, 99, 204, 284
protest, 165, 184
prowess, 10
psychology, 7
public, 126, 151, 175, 176, 239, 266
pursuit, 159, 171, 288
pushing, 214, 241–243

Index

quality, 6, 13, 38, 60, 124, 204, 205, 224, 246, 250, 252, 270
quest, 6, 41, 118
question, 128
quo, 128, 214

racism, 274
radio, 254
raise, 77, 164, 176, 187
raising, 186
rally, 12
range, 42, 151, 236, 247
rate, 3, 253
reach, 175, 183, 211, 226, 231, 252, 253, 265, 278
reader, 291
readiness, 66
reality, 32, 35, 55, 56, 193, 228, 284, 287
realization, 7
realm, 2, 12, 49, 66, 159, 257, 287, 290
reception, 24
recognition, 186, 198, 211
recommendation, 222, 223
reconfiguration, 249
recruitment, 19, 21
redefinition, 106, 108, 142, 144, 194, 235
reduction, 141
reflection, 130, 171, 207, 243
refugee, 126
reinforcement, 223
relatability, 250
relationship, 66, 91, 155, 194, 253
relevance, 12, 60, 194, 195, 250, 285, 290
reliance, 118, 253, 280
remix, 204
removal, 151
renaissance, 205
representation, 164, 207, 208, 210, 247
research, 2, 16, 80, 118, 155, 187
resilience, 4, 5, 15, 18, 21, 93, 289
resistance, 16, 54, 80, 169
resolution, 123
resource, 172
respect, 31, 51, 53, 119, 128, 131, 134, 186, 187, 274
response, 9, 184, 263
responsibility, 31, 124, 130, 147, 150, 152, 275, 285
result, 85, 195, 204
retention, 27, 29, 43, 58, 223, 253
rethinking, 192
revenue, 11, 211, 212, 215, 238, 247, 251–254
revolution, 90
richness, 2, 210, 274–276
right, 35, 41
Riley, 2, 3, 5
Riley Dubois, 1, 3, 5–7, 10, 12, 21, 27, 29, 41, 44, 71, 98, 106, 108, 116, 127, 142, 144, 162, 172, 188, 205, 207, 273, 276, 283, 285
Riley Dubois and, 281
Riley Dubois's, 4, 7, 12, 15, 28, 29, 32, 46, 53, 119, 122, 129, 139, 142, 143, 175, 212, 259, 261, 269, 287
rise, 6, 140, 142, 152, 155, 165, 176, 197, 204, 210, 216, 223, 243, 246, 249, 251, 254, 256, 273, 278
risk, 99, 117, 163, 167, 211, 266, 284

Robert Putnam, 132
role, 4–6, 21, 30, 43, 59, 61, 62, 73, 88, 100, 103, 106, 116, 118, 119, 127, 128, 130–132, 142, 151, 156, 163, 164, 167, 169, 171, 175–177, 180, 182, 183, 188, 211, 212, 223, 233, 235, 242, 243, 246, 248, 253, 256, 261, 265, 266, 272, 273, 291
room, 242
root, 141
royalty, 253
rubric, 48

s, 1–7, 9–16, 18, 21, 25, 27–30, 32, 34, 35, 40, 43, 46, 47, 49, 53, 58, 66, 75, 77, 81–83, 90, 91, 100, 119, 121, 122, 124, 129, 133, 136, 139, 141–143, 171, 175, 176, 178, 179, 186, 189, 190, 194, 211, 212, 214, 222, 239, 246, 248, 253, 259, 261, 269, 272, 276, 278, 282, 283, 285, 287, 288
safeguard, 101, 284
safety, 159, 164, 184
San Francisco, 1
satisfaction, 221, 223, 228, 282
saturation, 204, 205, 233, 253
scalability, 11
scale, 184
scholarship, 2
school, 1–3, 77
science, 77, 238, 242
scope, 290
scrutiny, 176

search, 256
second, 43
section, 3, 5, 10, 15, 18, 32, 38, 41, 44, 56, 58, 63, 66, 75, 78, 91, 103, 116, 122, 130, 132, 145, 148, 152, 157, 175, 177, 185, 188, 191, 199, 210, 214, 217, 223, 227, 231, 238, 241, 249, 256, 259, 264, 266, 269, 273, 276, 279
sector, 98, 214, 252, 254, 276, 278
security, 149, 184
seeking, 175, 253
selection, 211
self, 5, 36, 126, 142, 143, 180
sense, 15, 17, 23, 30, 31, 100, 118, 124, 128, 130, 131, 136, 142, 152, 169, 180–182, 193, 194, 229, 242, 243, 246, 247, 252, 273, 275
sensitivity, 31, 116
series, 124, 126, 134, 212, 248
service, 2
set, 10, 17, 21, 25, 185, 224
share, 5, 9, 10, 32, 47, 59, 119, 123, 131, 134–136, 139, 152, 162, 164, 175, 186, 193, 197, 199, 204, 211, 229, 236, 246, 247, 273–276, 282, 285
sharing, 117, 126, 134, 136, 163, 164, 176, 185, 186, 194, 246, 265
shift, 9, 35, 58, 89, 106, 108, 126, 175, 191, 194, 196, 198, 205, 237, 242, 246–248, 250, 254, 261, 266, 278
shopping, 256

significance, 52, 130, 259, 273
situation, 280
size, 66, 88, 106
skepticism, 4, 16
skill, 66, 108, 259
slacktivism, 167
socialization, 9
society, 6, 7, 10, 13–15, 29, 32, 51, 53, 71, 96, 98, 119, 122, 124, 127, 131, 135, 159, 162, 164, 167, 169, 171, 177, 182, 188, 190, 198, 207, 210, 212, 235, 256, 261, 264, 268, 279, 280, 283, 290
socio, 6, 10, 31
sociologist, 132
software, 8
solace, 1
solidarity, 118, 124
solution, 6, 284
solving, 3, 18, 47, 106, 134, 188, 272
song, 204
space, 4, 9, 163, 250, 254, 273
Spain, 274
spark, 7
spectatorship, 194
speech, 43, 151
speed, 223
spending, 247
spirit, 4, 7, 21, 25, 106, 274, 291
spread, 77, 151, 175, 176, 184, 186, 246
stability, 231
stage, 10, 12, 21, 25, 235
stakeholder, 10
stand, 204, 250
startup, 284
statement, 12

status, 128, 196, 214, 280
step, 68, 210
story, 18, 136, 217, 229, 274
storytelling, 32, 48, 131, 134, 135, 137, 193, 217–219, 236, 238, 271
strategy, 10, 11, 23, 172, 252
stream, 211, 212, 252
streaming, 197, 223–225, 253
streamline, 221
struggle, 50, 107, 185, 198, 221, 243, 250
student, 2, 13, 38, 40, 43, 44, 49, 54, 63, 65, 67, 77, 79, 83, 89–91, 96, 100, 271
study, 43, 247
style, 21
subject, 30, 77
subscription, 211, 212, 237, 251, 253
subsection, 30, 46, 51, 61, 73, 88, 93, 114, 119, 127, 134, 139, 155, 162, 169, 180, 194, 207, 212, 235, 251
success, 4, 9, 10, 12, 17, 18, 21, 47, 51, 53, 66, 91, 97, 106, 115, 120, 124, 134, 136, 180, 223, 250, 256, 288
suite, 38
summary, 2, 21, 106, 160, 180, 188, 210, 243
summit, 32
support, 4, 11, 43, 44, 60, 137, 156, 163, 175, 176, 180, 185, 186, 210–212, 231, 237, 248, 252, 266, 284
surge, 179
surveillance, 176, 177, 184, 185

sustainability, 3, 11, 12, 180, 217, 233, 250, 252, 275, 284
syndrome, 2
synergy, 11, 184, 233
synthesis, 48, 207, 285
system, 212, 222, 246

tailor, 42, 66, 68, 75, 89, 183, 253, 271, 282
tailoring, 49, 66
taking, 284
talent, 3, 19
tapestry, 1, 58, 121, 198, 207, 211, 238, 274
Tarana Burke, 179
teacher, 1, 54, 60
teaching, 38–40, 54, 55, 66, 85, 270, 271
team, 2, 4, 8–10, 18–21, 24, 25, 41, 287, 289
teamwork, 31, 77, 199, 201, 289
tech, 11, 189, 284
technology, 1–3, 6, 10–12, 14, 15, 21, 25, 28, 29, 32, 38, 40, 41, 44, 46, 47, 51, 53, 55, 56, 58, 60, 61, 63, 66–68, 71, 75, 78–80, 82, 87–89, 91, 96, 98–101, 103, 106, 116–118, 126, 137, 142, 144, 150, 157–160, 162, 163, 169, 171, 175–177, 180, 183, 184, 188–190, 193, 194, 196, 198, 201, 203, 205, 210, 211, 214, 216, 219, 221, 223, 226, 229, 233–235, 238, 241, 243, 254, 266, 269, 273, 278–280, 283, 285, 291
television, 235–238, 248, 254

tenacity, 21
term, 3, 11, 194, 203
terrain, 151, 188
territory, 160
test, 284
testament, 18, 207, 285, 289
testing, 88
text, 43, 117
the United States, 159
theory, 2, 4–6, 30, 47, 49, 66, 90, 106, 140, 152, 162, 163, 165, 186, 188, 217, 231, 239, 246, 269–271
thesis, 2
thinking, 30, 46–48, 71, 106, 268, 269, 272
threat, 176
thrive, 12, 32, 35, 38, 40, 49, 71, 91, 93, 96, 98, 103, 121, 162, 212, 216, 217, 231, 233, 261, 268
ticket, 252
time, 2, 16, 31, 43, 50, 59, 88, 117, 129, 176, 179, 193, 199, 223, 228, 242, 246
today, 13, 29
tokenism, 163, 164
toll, 216
Tomlinson, 66
tomorrow, 13
tool, 1, 4, 51, 60, 67, 113, 128, 132, 134, 150, 162, 164, 169, 175, 177, 193
toxicity, 187
track, 176, 271
tracking, 184
traction, 49, 66, 159, 186, 252
training, 31, 43, 58, 60, 79, 85, 87, 100, 270

Index 313

trajectory, 278, 284
transformation, 27, 106, 119, 142, 144, 175, 180, 188, 191, 196, 235, 246, 249, 254, 262, 276, 279
transistor, 91
transition, 35, 58, 60, 251, 254
translation, 31, 43, 117–119, 274
transparency, 100, 223, 253, 284
treadmill, 250
trend, 29, 46, 194, 226, 242
trust, 148, 150, 253, 255, 282
truth, 259
turn, 91
tweet, 175

ubiquity, 223
underpinning, 75
underrepresentation, 132
understanding, 1, 4–8, 12, 19, 25, 30–32, 44, 46, 49, 51, 53, 58, 65, 66, 77, 90, 91, 100, 106, 107, 112, 113, 116, 119, 122, 124–132, 134–137, 139, 147, 150, 152, 156, 159, 160, 163, 167, 169, 196, 201, 205, 219, 241, 261, 266, 268, 269, 273, 276, 281, 283
up, 243
upgrade, 35
urgency, 247
Urie Bronfenbrenner, 140
usability, 288
usage, 98, 150, 156
use, 48, 89, 100, 150–152, 155, 179, 184, 221, 253, 282
usefulness, 288

user, 10, 17, 24, 117, 121, 149, 150, 190, 204, 221–223, 228, 246, 249, 251, 253, 256, 273, 274, 278, 282, 284, 288
utility, 186

value, 54, 119, 164, 205, 248, 272
variety, 50, 76, 88, 104
venture, 2
viability, 4, 11
video, 253, 265
viewer, 194, 224, 242
viewership, 248
violence, 150, 164
visibility, 198, 211, 212, 250, 253, 266
vision, 2, 4, 8, 9, 11–15, 19, 32, 35, 44, 124, 253, 287, 291
visionary, 12, 144, 285
visual, 43, 49, 242
voice, 137, 256
volume, 198
vulnerability, 276
Vygotsky, 27, 30, 47, 106

wake, 247
walk, 126
waste, 284
water, 3
way, 5, 6, 10, 18, 25, 32, 40, 44, 56, 60, 61, 66, 73, 75, 90, 96, 119, 130, 132, 155, 176, 177, 188, 194, 198, 217, 219, 225, 238, 242, 248, 254, 278, 283, 291
web, 248
well, 100, 147, 156, 190, 195, 216, 226

whole, 212
willingness, 196
woman, 136
word, 175
work, 20, 32, 47, 98, 106, 107, 147, 152, 156, 197, 198, 204, 205, 211, 212, 216, 231, 238, 246, 252–254, 272, 277, 285, 289, 290
workforce, 103, 104, 106, 107
world, 3, 5, 7, 9, 15, 29, 32, 35, 38, 47, 51, 53, 60, 63, 66, 71, 73, 77, 88, 91, 93, 96, 108, 113, 116, 119, 121, 122, 127, 130, 132, 134, 136, 148, 151, 155, 157, 160, 162, 164, 172, 175–180, 185, 189, 207, 210–212, 216, 235, 238, 240, 241, 243, 259, 261, 264, 272, 273, 276, 279, 289
worldview, 1

Yayoi Kusama, 242
year, 2
youth, 133, 179, 184

Milton Keynes UK
Ingram Content Group UK Ltd.
UKHW021055121124
451035UK00024B/1249